Flamboyant Lawyer in a Maverick Western Town

FLAMBOYANT LAWYER in a Maverick Western Town

LAS VEGAS THROUGH THE EYES OF
HARRY CLAIBORNE

Enjoy the Past

Bruce Alverson

by
J. Bruce Alverson

Printed in the United States of America

First Edition

Editor: Becky Linford
Cover Design: Glen Scott
Author Photo: Bryan Hainer
Cover Photo: Getty Images

Prior publications by J. Bruce Alverson:
The Camp Without A Failure: Searchlight, 1903-1907
The Limits of Power: Comstock Litigation, 1859-1864
Brain Mapping: Should This Controversial Evidence Be Excluded?
Hedonic Damages - Methodology and Admissibility
Nevada Law Summary
Nevada Business Law Summary

Alverson, J. Bruce
Flamboyant Lawyer in a Maverick Western Town: Las Vegas Through the Eyes of Harry Claiborne
266p

Published by:
J. Bruce Alverson
Alverson Taylor Mortensen & Sanders
7401 West Charleston Blvd, Las Vegas, NV 89117
702-384-7000 Fax 702-385-7000
www.alversontaylor.com

This book is dedicated to the members of the Nevada legal community, particularly those of the post-war era who paved the way for the rest of us.

CONTENTS

FOREWARD

Before we were law partners, Bruce Alverson and I were battery mates. I first met him on our high school's baseball diamond, where he hurled fire from atop the pitcher's mound and I crouched down behind home plate to catch his heat.

He was good. Really good. If I had known then how much of himself he puts into everything he does, I wouldn't have been so surprised. But my hand would probably still have stung just the same.

Decades later, I'm still impressed by Bruce - by his interest in Nevada's history and his mastery of the people who sculpt it. Years ago and without each other's knowledge, we simultaneously started researching the story of Searchlight, Nev., the small mining town where I was born. He wrote a paper on it for a graduate history course he was taking at UNLV, and I used his resarch as a resource when I wrote a book on my hometown.

Many histories take a broad view of its subject, telling an expansive narrative or tracing an extensive evolution. But Bruce knows that the cast makes the story, and that to know Las Vegas, you have to know its people: how they think, how they interact, whom they befriend and whom they betray.

Bruce and I grew up in the Nevada legal system. We had a law practice, Reid and Alverson, and together we witnessed Las Vegas's remarkable twentieth-century transformation. We know well the community, the contributors and Harry Claiborne himself.

The story he tells in these pages is appropriately political, legal and historical - but at it's heart, it is personal. In Claiborne - Nevada's most celebrated criminal-defense attorney and one of his city's most colorful, controversial and accomplished players - Bruce has picked a fitting main character.

Claiborne's journey wasn't always a scenic one. But this story is a realistic window into his life and legacy. As a lawyer, a judge, a politician, a father and a public official, Claiborne was one of the many who moved Nevada - and he evolved right along with it.

I've followed my friend Bruce's career closely and with great pride. He's soundly represented the alumni of Basic High School in Henderson, Nev., from his successes on the baseball field to the courtroom to the bookshelves. This insightful and incisive collection of recollections is only the latest in a long line of achievements.

This time, I'm not so surprised. Claiborne always advised, "Work on the facts; the law doesn't matter much." Bruce took his subject's advice, and hasn't sugarcoated a single grain of this story. It's all recounted just as it happened, for better or worse. True to form, Bruce has approached and accomplished this task the same way he faced down batters from the mound - he's delivered yet another strike down the middle.

Harry Reid
United States Senator
Searchlight, Nevada
February 2011

ACKNOWLEDGEMENT

When Brad Williams, Director of the Ninth Judicial Circuit Historical Society, asked me to conduct the oral history of Harry Claiborne, I jumped at the chance. Although I was aware of his stature as a trial lawyer and reputation in the community, I had no idea as to the power of his personality, his ability to recall events and people, his perception of events as they evolved over time - and particularly his story telling talents. Claiborne was a storyteller. His Arkansas accent, his infectious laugh, his timing (honed by years of practice), could turn an ordinary story into one that people would laugh about for years. It was a gift that he put to good use in front of a jury.

The oral history itself almost never happened. When Williams called, he said Cliff Young, retired Nevada Supreme Court Justice, had talked to Claiborne and he was awaiting my call. I called Claiborne several times, but got no response. I assumed he had second thoughts and did not want to re-hash his legal problems. Six months elapsed when Williams called to say that he understood the oral history was on schedule. When I told him otherwise, he promised to call Young again. Based on that, I began calling Claiborne again, but with the same lack of success. One day, out of the blue, Claiborne called and wanted to know when we could get started. I said tomorrow.

On our first meeting, I stressed that I was not interested in talking about his legal problems. Rather, I was interested in his recall and perception of the legal and political community in Las Vegas from the post-war years to about 1980, shortly after he went on the federal bench. It was on this basis that our interviews began, but over time it was apparent he was getting more comfortable and wanted to tell "his side of the story" - which he did.

I want first to acknowledge my appreciation to Claiborne himself. He knew little about me other than I was a Las Vegas lawyer. I appreciated the courtesy he extended to me in this project. We spent over 40 hours together, with a microphone and a tape recorder between us, and it was a once in a life time experience for me. Armed with newspaper clippings and court decisions dating back to April 1946, I began the interviews. I was shocked at the depth of his recall, reciting names of parties, lawyers, judges, legal issues involved, and even quoting verbatim a phrase in a Nevada Supreme Court decision. Seemingly, each case spawned a related, or sometimes a not so related, story which he told with great relish. He enjoyed it immensely, as did I. One thing he said has always stuck in my mind: He once read that the most enjoyable part of life is your old age because you can engage in reminiscing about the events of your life - he now agreed. Maybe that gives us all something to look forward to.

Because he was such a gifted storyteller, I quoted as much of his actual interview as was practical, rather than try to paraphrase him. This allows his personality to come through to the reader in a more vivid fashion. When he spoke his thought process was so well organized that very little editing was necessary. Many of his contemporaries called his legal arguments and jury summations "spell-binding," and I can see why based on many hours of listening to him. On the other hand, he was 85 years old when we began these interviews, and not in good health. Occasionally he would say something that was in conflict with other information I had available to me and I have made some appropriate corrections to the book. But it was not my intention to verify everything he told me. If a reader comes upon something which does not seem right, please just accept the fact that this is the way Claiborne remembered it so many years afterwards, right or wrong. The book will be much more enjoyable if you give him, and yourself, that flexibility.

This oral history and book have been a great joy to me on several different levels. I returned home to practice law in Las Vegas after law school in 1974, just at the end of the "Claiborne era" as I have described the time period in this book. Many of the people Claiborne talked about were still active lawyers, businessmen and politicians. They frequently met at the coffee shop across the street from the court house and regaled the younger lawyers with stories of "the good old days," many of which were the same as Claiborne later recounted to me. Louie Wiener, Cliff Jones, Judge Roger D. Foley, George Foley, David Goldwater, Rex Jemison, and so many others provided me with a wonderful background and appreciation of the history of our legal community. My wife worked for U.S. Senator Howard Cannon from 1974 until 1982, and through that connection we met many members of the political scene, including former governor Grant Sawyer, Ralph Denton, Jon Collins, future governor and United States Senator Richard Bryan, and basically all the politically "elite" in Nevada.

Harry Reid, currently Nevada's Senior United States Senator and Senate Majority Leader, and an excellent trial lawyer in his own right, and I not only attended high school together, but also practiced law together from 1974 until he was elected to Congress in 1982. Mike O'Callaghan, our high school history teacher and later Nevada's Governor, appointed Reid as Chairman of the Nevada Gaming Commission during the difficult times of the late 1970s, which were graphically depicted in the movie Casino, based upon Nicholas Pileggi's book of the same name. These experiences gave me a front row seat to Nevada politics and the world of gaming, both then and in the past. With this background, and as a lawyer and historian, I recognized the tremendous opportunity that Claiborne's oral history would provide in creating a vehicle to write about Las Vegas history.

I am grateful to many other people as well. The transformation from an interview to a 360 page transcript, to a dissertation, to a book, requires a lot of effort by skilled and enthusiastic supporters. Eugene P. Moehring, Ph.D., history professor at the University of Nevada, Las Vegas, spent countless hours reviewing my work and giving it direction both in his capacity as Chairman of my Dissertation Examination Committee and as a friend. David S. Tanenhaus, Ph.D., also a history professor at the University of Nevada, Las Vegas, gave much needed direction in putting Nevada's legal development within a national historical perspective. Michael Green, Ph.D., history professor at the College of Southern Nevada, was invaluable in helping to make the transition from a dissertation to a book. I owe them all a debt of gratitude.

As to the nuts and bolts, I want to acknowledge and thank three of my co-workers. Becky Linford made everything work by attending to every detail from footnotes to publication requirements. No one has greater patience. Rhonda Powell and Sabrina Mansanas performed yeoman, yet enjoyable, work by transcribing the often raucous and laugh filled tape recordings, giving them a front row seat at Claiborne's storing telling and memories.

Thank you again, one and all.

INTRODUCTION

Eighty-five people killed, hundreds injured, and property destruc-
tion in the millions of dollars resulted when the MGM Grand Hotel and
Casino burned on November 21, 1980. It was the second most deadly
hotel fire in the United States and greatest catastrophe in Nevada history.
Attorneys from all over the country descended upon Southern Nevada
to represent the injured parties and the 118 companies that were sued,
bringing with them tactics and technologies never before seen in the
Nevada legal community. Overnight, the legal environment transformed
from a congenial, "your word is your bond" relationship among lawyers
who had long-standing relationships with one another, to one involving
the "Rambo" style litigation tactics commonplace among non-Nevada
lawyers. In short, the signed stipulation replaced the handshake as a
way of doing business. The ultimate payout of $223 million to claim-
ants and millions in legal fees testifies to the enormous consequences of
the fire. Never again would the legal community return to the pre-fire
atmosphere, thereby ending a unique and colorful 30-plus year era in Las
Vegas dating from the post-war years. One lawyer's career epitomizes
this bygone era: Harry Eugene Claiborne.[1]

"My greatest joy in my whole life was walking into the courtroom. I felt
so good when I walked into that courtroom. That was my home. I loved
every bit of it.[2] I had more fun practicing law than any man living. It
was really wonderful.[3] Even if I lost, it was a tremendously good feeling,"
Claiborne recalled.[4] But, for him, the law was a jealous mistress. He

---

1 In Re MGM Fire Litigation 570 F Supp. 913 (1983).
2 Harry E. Claiborne, interview by J. Bruce Alverson, 2002-2003, 136.
3 Ibid., 233.
4 Ibid., 136.

once admitted, "I had a love affair with the courtroom. I couldn't wait to get into the courtroom to try a case. I was happier in that courtroom than I was any other place in the whole world. Bar none. I love the atmosphere. I love the system. It was my whole life. Cost me four marriages. I couldn't help it. So, I really can't say that it was worth it. But, I think it was."[5] He enjoyed re-living it, as well, observing, "I read somewhere that the most enjoyable part of life is your old age. You can engage in reminiscing about the events of your life. I think that's about true."[6]

Claiborne died as he lived - on his own terms. On January 20, 2004, at age 86, he killed himself rather than succumb to debilitating, cancer-related health problems. This closed a colorful chapter in Nevada legal history. Spanning nearly sixty years, Claiborne's legal career reflected both the spirit of a young Las Vegas and the no-holds-barred attitude of frontier lawyers. Moving to Las Vegas initially in 1943 while in the military, he began practicing law in 1947. Claiborne participated in, and many said led, the development of the legal community during the mid-century growth period of Southern Nevada. Possibly the state's most active trial lawyer, he argued his first jury trial in 1947 and his last in 1993, a span of 46 years. Yet, more than longevity, his colorful and engaging style made him one of the most high-profile attorneys in Nevada history.

This is not simply a biography of Claiborne. This is a study of mid-century Las Vegas as seen through Claiborne's eyes. His ascent to the federal bench in 1978 climaxed his career as a trial lawyer. His conviction on federal income tax charges, impeachment, imprisonment, and fight to keep his Nevada law license fascinated, if not stunned, the community. Although Claiborne returned to private practice in 1988, he was 71 years old and his best trial years were certainly behind him. He practiced at his own pace for the next 15 years until his death. But the practice of law had changed since 1978 and his age and circumstances meant that he was no longer at the forefront of the profession. Consequently, the Claiborne "era," as I define it, runs from the post-war years until his elevation to the bench, just two years before the MGM fire.

5 Ibid., 325.
6 Ibid., 42.

Claiborne's career bridged two eras of federal scrutiny - the Kefauver Crime Committee investigations of the early 1950s and the "sting" operations of the 1980s, with only brief threats by United States Attorney General Bobby Kennedy in the 1960s. Otherwise, Las Vegas did what it wanted without much federal intervention. Crime and corruption soared. By the late 1970s, organized crime headed by the likes of Frank "Lefty" Rosenthal and Anthony "Tony the Ant" Spilotro dominated the local scene more than Benjamin "Bugsy" Siegel and his mob ever dreamed. Local law enforcement was unable to effectively control them. Political corruption was rampant. Bribes were apparently a way of life in some of the highest echelons of politics. The "good ole boy" system was unable, or unwilling, to control the runaway forces acting in the county. Indeed, maybe even looked the other way in some instances.

In some respects, Claiborne's fall from his status as a nationally recognized trial lawyer and federal judge to impeachment and prison was almost predictable. The business and social community evolved from a small town environment where Claiborne's flamboyance and maverick attitude made him a favorite within the small town. He had a colorful reputation, some deserved, some not. Claiborne recalled, "There's more stories going around about me than you can shake a stick at. Some of them are kind of based on fact, but most of them are not. It's like a story that was floating around for years. I'm in a bar and a guy knocked a woman off of a bar stool. I jumped up and went over to the guy and he said, 'Who in the hell are you.' I hit him and knocked him out and put my professional card on his chest and told the bartender, 'Tell the son-of-a-bitch who I am when he comes to.' I bet I've heard that story 200 times through the years. It never happened. Never happened." But, he certainly was "good copy" on a slow news day as will be seen. As the community grew and attracted more national attention, these same personality traits, and reputation based on and/or enhanced by such stories, especially when showcased from the federal bench, acted as a lightening rod for criticism and even change. He was elevated by the old and fading system of the 1950s and 1960s, and brought down by a new era dominated by large corporations and federal scrutiny.[7]

How - why - did this happen? Why was Claiborne criminally prosecuted for not reporting a relatively small amount of income - $19,000 and $88,000 for the years 1979 and 1980 - particularly when Claiborne did not deny he received the money. He claimed he told his accountant about the money and the accountant failed to properly report it. Gerald Swanson, then District Director of the Internal Revenue Service in Nevada, said the IRS would have normally resolved these tax issues through routine civil proceedings. "It was one of those things that typically would have been a civil tax issue." So why was it a criminal matter? One man, Joseph Yablonsky, Special Agent in Charge of the Las Vegas office of the Federal Bureau of Investigation.[8]

Yablonsky, the self proclaimed "King of Sting," came to Las Vegas with the attitude that everyone was a crook. Within a couple short years, he broke organized crime's grip on the city. Rosenthal and Spilotro, as well as their associates and influence, vanished. Yablonsky had similar success in the political arena. His sting operations exposed corruption at the highest levels of state and local government. He ferreted out corruption where he believed it existed, sometimes overstepping his bounds in pursuing it. To Yablonsky, the end justified the means, according to Swanson. But, was the end justified simply because Yablonksy thought it was? Was this the classic, self appointed, one-man "judge and jury" mentality frequently seen in overzealous cops? Proof aside, was he determined to punish someone just because he thought the person was guilty? Even after Claiborne's death, a bitter Yablonsky commented that he "was a crook, and there are other cases besides Conforte" in which the judge was suspected of taking bribes. He offered no evidence to support that opinion either. During his tenure, the FBI had the reputation of leaking to the press unfavorable items, i.e., "dirt", on people they investigated but did not have the evidence to prosecute, thereby punishing people in the press and smearing community reputations.[9]

---

7 Claiborne interview, 79.

8 *Sun*, March 30, 2001.

9 *Las Vegas Mercury*, January 29, 2004: Also, retired FBI Agent Gary Magneses writes about an attempted placement of a wire tap and a seizure of evidence that were thwarted and opines that,

Certainly, Claiborne was part of the old network that included many of the crooked politicians Yablonsky later prosecuted. Because of Claiborne's long and close ties with these "corrupt" community leaders, his flamboyant lifestyle, his outspoken nature, his background as a criminal defense lawyer, and his sometimes harsh treatment of federal prosecutors, he must be guilty of something. Yablonsky was convinced of that even before he arrived in town.

Or was it revenge. Claiborne was outraged at what he believed was bullying of the community by federal agents. As was his nature, he publicly said so in his typical colorful fashion and without regard to personal repercussions. As one newspaper reported, "The Justice Department and the FBI were so incensed at Judge Claiborne that the need for revenge blinded them to everything but one burning desire. The federal government could not rest after Claiborne denounced its Strike Force lawyers as 'rotten bastards' and 'crooks and liars.' It could not bear Claiborne's other insinuations without retaliating. So it dug and dug, and when (Joe) Conforte put out his bait, the government swallowed it right up to the fishing pole."[10]

Yablonsky convened four grand juries before getting an indictment against Claiborne. He succeeded only by making an unconscionable deal with Joe Conforte (a convicted felon who had skipped bail and federal sentencing to seek a safe haven from prosecutors in Brazil) to testify that Claiborne solicited bribes from him. Despite the "bought" testimony of Conforte, the jury refused to convict Claiborne on bribery charges and the trial ended in a hung jury. Recognizing the unreliability of Conforte's testimony, the federal prosecutors dropped the bribery charges and went with their old standby - criminal tax evasion. "Why did Harry Claiborne, unlike most other citizens, not have the opportunity to face an IRS audit in the civil division before criminal prosecution charges occurred?" asked

---

"(M)y guess is that Claiborne, or someone else, perhaps a double agent informant" tipped the mobsters off in advance. He offers no evidence to support his "guess" and concedes that "I can't prove my theory." Yet, consistent with Yablonsky's custom, he does not hesitate to publish such a condemning allegation in the absence of proof. See Gary Magnesen, Strawmen: A Former Agent Recounts How the FBI Crushed the Mob in Las Vegas (Minneapolis: Mill City Press, 2010), 214-217.

10 Gazette-Journal, Conforte Reels in Some Mighty Big Suckers, June 29,1984.

Senator David H. Pryor, D-Ark., during the impeachment hearings.[11] If Yablonsky had not brought in Conforte to "dirty up" Claiborne, the tax matter would have been a routine civil proceeding was the explanation, according to Swanson.[12] It was a criminal prosecution simply because that is what Yablonsky wanted, regardless of long standing custom and precedent to the contrary.

By 1980, Las Vegas was no longer the sleepy, yet growing, frontier town Claiborne encountered in 1943 on his first army visit, or even the post-war city of 1947 when he was admitted to the Bar. Clark County's population increased nearly ten fold from the 1940s to the late 1970s, reaching approximately 460,000 in 1978. By then, the dominant economic force was the resort industry. The county boasted more than 30 resort casinos, employing 43,700 workers in 1975, compared with two resorts and 719 employees when Claiborne moved to Las Vegas. In 1978, it claimed one of the largest hotels in the world, The International, built in 1969 by Kirk Kerkorian. In the 1960s, and with Howard Hughes as a role model, Kerkorian, William Harrah and Conrad Hilton led the industry in Nevada toward corporate ownership and away from individual ownership and partnerships, a change that greatly increased the resorts' access to large pools of capital that could finance construction of large new facilities. By 1977, annual gaming revenue topped $1 billion, as the Strip and city continued to boom. Government expanded also. Indeed, the county budget increased from less than $2.3 million in 1945 to more than $91.6 million in 1970. Few American metropolitan cities grew as quickly as Las Vegas in such a relatively short period of time.[13]

By the 1970s, Clark County was unquestionably the state's political center. The sheer increase in population, fueled by the booming economy, was a major factor, and with the United States Supreme Court's Baker v. Carr and Reynolds v. Sims decisions mandating the "one man, one vote" principle, political influence based on geographical location was turned on its ear.[14] These reapportionment rulings forced the

11 State Bar of Nevada, at 155-156.
12 Sun, March 30,2001.
13 Eugene P. Moehring, Resort City in the Sunbelt: Las Vegas, 1930-1970 (Reno and Las Vegas: University of Nevada Press, 1989), 111, 269.
14 Baker v. Carr, 369 U. S. 189 (1962); Reynolds v. Sims, 377 U. S. 533 (1964).

shift of political power from a land-based ideology to one predicated
on population centers. Reapportionment of each state's legislature was
mandatory to comply with the court's ruling. Nevada Governor Grant
Sawyer called a special legislative session in October 1965 for the sole
purpose of reapportioning the state's legislative districts. Clark County
gained an immediate majority in both legislative houses, awarding it a
dominant position in state politics – at least from a statistical standpoint.
For example, when Claiborne served in the 1949 legislature, Clark County
had only one of 17 state senators and 6 of 43 assemblymen. Under this
system, Clark County had only 6% and 14% of the state's representation
in the senate and assembly, respectively, even though it contained over
30% of the state's population. At the end of the Claiborne "era" in 1978,
Clark County claimed 11 (55%) of the state's 20 s enators and 22 (55%) of
the 40 assemblymen, which resembled its 58% share of the state's population. The population explosion in Southern Nevada also qualified the
state for a second U.S. congressional district by 1982, which lay mostly in
Clark County.[15]

The change in the judiciary during that time period was just as dramatic. By 1978, the Nevada Supreme Court had expanded from 3 to 5
justices. The federal District Court judges increased from one to three
(after the addition of Judge Edward Reed in 1979), plus one senior judge
for a total of four. State court judges in Clark County jumped to 12, a
startling increase over the lone judge in 1943.[16] In many states, including
Nevada, the governor appointed judges to the bench when an old judge
died or retired. The power of incumbency was never stronger than in the
judiciary. When judges ran for re-election, they rarely faced real opposition. Few judges were ever defeated. From a practical standpoint, a state
court appointment was tantamount to a federal court judge's lifetime
tenure. In 1940, Missouri challenged the tradition of the governor being
solely responsible for appointments. By the 1960s, other states followed
Missouri's example and established selection committees.[17] In response

15 Political History of Nevada, 1996 (10th Edition), issued by Dean Heller, Nevada Secretary of State
    (1996), 191, 200, 207.
16 Political History, 238, 221-222.
17 Lawrence M. Friedman, A History of American Law (New York: Simon and Schuster, 1973) 592-593.

to the growing need for a sophisticated judiciary capable of meeting the
new challenges, Nevada changed the state court judicial selection process
in 1978 and created the Commission on Judicial Selection.[18] Comprised
of a Supreme Court justice, three members of the Bar, and three non-
lawyers, the Commission recommends three nominees to the governor
who then must select one of them. This reform improved the quality of
the process by screening applicants and removing the arbitrariness and
some of the politics from the appointment process.

The Nevada State Bar Association membership also reflected this
growth during the course of Claiborne's era. The post-war population
shift was well underway by 1950 as lawyers abandoned the ranching and
mining communities for the major growth areas of Las Vegas and Reno.
The shift from 1950 to 1977 was even more pronounced. While 65 lawyers practiced in Las Vegas in 1950, representing 23% of the total Bar, the
membership increased to 544 in 1977, accounting for 48% of the total.
Although Washoe County added 241 lawyers during that same period, its
percentage of Bar membership dropped from 57% to 36%.[19] The rapid
growth of the mid-1940s demanded that the Bar better protect the public
from unqualified lawyers by imposing formal and objective standards for
admitting its members, including strict educational requirements and
an objective measure upon which to examine an applicant's knowledge
of the law. Claiborne was one of the first applicants to come within the
revised admission requirements.

The nature of the practice of law also changed. No longer did sole
practitioners with a general law practice dominate the Bar.[20] Rather, law
firms consisting of numerous attorneys specializing in various areas of
the law were common. A survey of lawyers in Clark County in October
1976 revealed that three firms had five, four firms had six, and four other
firms each had seven, nine, eleven and sixteen lawyers, respectively. So,
82 lawyers worked for only eleven firms. That was a significant departure from the 1940s pattern, and drastically changed the manner in

18 Constitution of the State of Nevada, Article 6, Section 20.
19 Nevada State Bar Journal (Reno and Las Vegas: State Bar of Nevada), April 1950, Vol 15, No 2;
    January 1977, Vol 42, No. 1
20 Claiborne interview, 37.

which law was practiced. By 2009, Nevada had several firms with over 40 lawyers each and out-of-state firms with Nevada offices employ hundreds of lawyers.[21] The reasons are obvious: technology has made the world smaller and more accessible. Businesses can provide services from halfway around the world now, with the same efficiency and timeliness as local establishments can perform. So it is with law services. A legal contract can be drafted in New York City and electronically mailed to Clark County as quickly as a Las Vegas firm can do it. Further, as litigation and business become more complex, specialization in the law becomes more necessary. Larger firms with many specialists and multiple offices throughout the country or world are immediately available by technology and have changed the practice of law in Las Vegas, as elsewhere, dramatically since Claiborne's time.

Nationwide, technology and expensive office space combined to significantly alter the geographical location of law firms. Before the computer age, virtually all law offices were located near the courthouse. Although convenient access to the courtroom was desirable, the main reason was proximity to the county law library, which was usually in the courthouse. Law libraries are expensive to establish, maintain, and house; that is, firms not only purchase the books but pay high rental rates for space to store them. The solution for most firms was to maintain a small library and rely primarily upon the county library. Out of necessity, all law offices were clustered within walking distance of the courthouse, which drove up the cost of office space. By the late 1970s, computers allowed lawyers to access data bases containing more case law and legal treatises than even the county law library maintained - and they could do it from their offices. Suddenly, the main reason for having offices near the courthouse vanished, as did the law firms from downtown. They moved offices to the less expensive suburbs. Clark County was no exception. Although the cost of rent went down, so did the collegiality among Bar members because they had much less personal contact with each other. This, coupled with the influx of both new lawyers and out-of-state firms, made

---

21 Legal Directory for Southern Nevada: Revised to October 1, 1976 (Las Vegas: Nevada Legal News), 1976.

the Clark County Bar much less personal than in Claiborne's era.

The United States Supreme Court, under the leadership of Chief Justice Earl Warren (1953-1969), provided tremendous opportunities for lawyers practicing criminal law. The Warren Court dramatically changed the laws applicable to state court criminal actions. As late as 1947, the Supreme Court decided that the Bill of Rights was solely for the protection of the individual against the federal government and its provisions were inapplicable to similar actions by the states, and specifically rejected the argument that the Fourteenth Amendment incorporated those rights into state courts.[22] The Bill of Rights, however, as legal scholar Lawrence M. Friedman later argued, "was a kind of mini-code of criminal procedure, rules to guarantee trials against unfairness, against the tyranny and power of the state."[23] Warren agreed. Through a series of legal opinions within a span of seven years, the Warren Court "incorporated" the Bill of Rights into state criminal proceedings through the application of the Fourteenth Amendment's Due Process Clause.[24] The concept of the government paying for the representation of indigent persons charged with a crime, as required under the Sixth Amendment's "right to counsel," created a whole new sector of criminal law practitioners.[25] Governments established Public Defender's offices in both the federal and state court systems. In 1966, District Court Judge John C. Mowbray secured a Ford Foundation grant to establish Nevada's first public defender program - the Clark County Public Defender's Office with Richard Bryan, future state attorney general, governor, and U. S. senator, as the first public defender- and later secured state legislation to establish a statewide public defender program.[26] Governments also created panels of paid outside lawyers for those whom these offices could not represent due to conflicts of interest. Rather than Bar members donating time to represent indigents, as Claiborne's generation did, a whole new area of specializa-

22 Adamson v. California 332 U.S. 46 (1947).
23 Lawrence M. Friedman, Crime and Punishment in American History (New York: Basic Books, 1993) 296.
24 Duncan v. Louisiana 391 U.S. 145 (1968).
25 Gideon v. Wainwright 372 U.S. 335 (1963).
26 Nevada Reporter, In Memoriam: John Cody Mowbray, 117 Nev. 105 (2003); A. D. Hopkins and K. J. Evans, eds., The First 100: Portraits of the Men and Women Who Shaped Las Vegas (Las Vegas: Huntington Press, 1999), 187.

tion emerged for attorneys who focused on criminal law and were now assured of getting paid for their time. Criminal defense lawyers realized broadened benefits for their clients (and their law practices) when the Supreme Court restructured the rules of the admission of evidence at trial when it made the "exclusionary rule" binding on all states, thereby rejecting evidence obtained from unreasonable searches and seizures as a violation of the Fourth Amendment.[27] The Warren Court dramatically changed criminal law rules when it held that confessions given before the administration of the "Miranda warnings" would be excluded from evidence, confirming that defendants have the Fifth Amendment right to stand mute in the face of accusations.[28] For the first time, not only could attorneys use the defenses of the Bill of Rights in state courts to exclude constitutionally tainted evidence from trial, but they also could get paid for their efforts. A criminal defense lawyer's practice in a city like Las Vegas - Claiborne's, for example - greatly benefitted from these decisions.[29]

The dramatic changes that occurred during the Claiborne era's 30-plus years - economically and in the legal community - beg the question: Did the law simply respond to the economic growth or did the law establish conditions necessary for such growth? During this era, several factors fueled this phenomenal growth. Federally backed projects such as Nellis Air Force Base, the Henderson industrial park, and the Nevada Test Site, just to name a few, infused millions of dollars into the economy, as did general business endeavors such as transportation, retirement living and, to a lesser degree, ranching, mining, and agriculture. The legal community generally followed economic growth from these industries. Nevada also pro-actively stimulated business in 1931 by enacting laws pertaining to divorce and gambling, eventually creating unique and profitable opportunities for the legal community. For example, by shortening the residency requirements for divorce actions from three months to six weeks, the legislature intended to attract divorce business from states requiring a longer residency - that is, provide "quickie divorces." Although the divorce trade was significant between 1931 and 1945, the war had a major

27 Mapp v. Ohio 367 U.S. 643 (1961).
28 Miranda v. Arizona 384 U.S. 436 (1966).
29 Friedman, Crime and Punishment, 300-304.

impact upon marriages. Reunited couples frequently realized that time had extinguished their pre-war relationship, and the national divorce rate soared. The divorce business boomed throughout Nevada. Reno was known as the "divorce capital of the world," and Las Vegas eventually followed in its wake. It also brought a certain star quality to the state when celebrities "resided" in Nevada for the required six weeks. This book shares much of this through Claiborne.[30]

The gaming industry was slower to embrace the new opportunities the legislature provided in 1931. Initially uncertain as to the federal government's reaction, and the impact of national opinion, the gaming industry maintained a low profile for fear of retribution by moralists who considered gambling repugnant to national mores. By the end of the war, however, the industry brazenly advertised on a national basis, even initiating live entertainment as a means of attracting more players. The resulting boom in the casino business created the need for the state to enact regulatory safeguards to protect the integrity of the growing gaming industry, providing a unique and profitable opportunity for the legal community. Casino growth provided an economic stimulus to personal injury lawyers as well. The combination of 24-hour gambling, eating, and drinking (frequently provided complimentary to patrons) created greater opportunities for slip and falls, security issues, and other legal torts. Finally, the unique combination of legalized gambling, a perpetual party atmosphere, and legalized (or at least tolerated) prostitution provided an "anything goes" atmosphere that contributed to a maverick attitude by visitors and businesses alike, all providing legal issues not seen in other communities. Fortunately, we witness them through Claiborne.

The experiences of Claiborne and his contemporaries provide a useful lens for viewing Las Vegas and its legal community at this time. These experiences, along with the backgrounds of judges, lawyers, and local businessmen, contribute to our overall understanding of why Las Vegas

30 James Willard Hurst, Law and Economic Growth (Cambridge: Harvard University Press, 1950); Hurst, The Legitimacy of the Business Corporation in the Law of the United States, 1780-1970 (Charlottesville: University of Virginia Press, 1970); Hurst, Law and Markets in the United States (Madison: University of Wisconsin Press, 1982); Gordon Morris Bakken, The Development of Law on the Rocky Mountain Frontier, 1850-1912 (Westport, CT: Greenwood Press, 1983); Glenda Riley, Divorce: An American Tradition (New York: Oxford University Press, 1991).

developed as it did during that time. For example, today's judges and lawyers all graduated from four year universities and American Bar Association accredited law schools. Most had no meaningful employment until after law school grazduation. This contrasts sharply with judges and lawyers practicing in Las Vegas in the 1940s when Claiborne first arrived. Many did not attend law school, or even college. Instead, they worked and studied in the office of a practicing attorney and learned the law on the job. When ready, they took a Bar examination, which was not uniform across the country, but prepared by local attorneys who were not trained, or even knowledgeable, about how to construct comprehensive examinations. These tests often included oral examination as well as written. For many, their character was hardened by the times; the depression and military service in one of the two world wars, or both. Yet, in many ways, theirs was a simpler and less hectic community than the local legal profession today.[31]

This book seeks to capture these changes through the prism of Harry Claiborne. That does not make this solely a biography nor a re-examination of his troubles with the FBI, his 1984 conviction for federal income tax evasion, or his 1986 impeachment by Congress and removal from the federal bench. Although these are interesting and historic, this book will neither re-try Claiborne's criminal case nor question the veracity of the evidence against him. Simply put, the jury has spoken. But it will discuss the background of these matters to put them in perspective as to prevailing attitudes.

Much was written about Claiborne's case at the time, including extensive articles in the state's leading newspapers. Investigative reporters combed the files, examined the evidence, interviewed witnesses, and argued endlessly about the propriety of the government's role in prosecuting his case. The Las Vegas Sun documented the various allegations in a seven-part series in 1982, while the Review-Journal countered with information reportedly leaked by the FBI and Justice Department. It was the subject of law review articles published by law schools and studies presented in historical journals. Finally, the Nevada Supreme

---

31 For a national perspective, see Friedman, A History of American Law, 592-593.

Court issued a 131-page opinion in 1988 that analyzed every aspect of the investigation, trial, and impeachment proceedings and refused to revoke Claiborne's license to practice law in Nevada.[32]

Claiborne observed the legal community for nearly 60 years, and was in its forefront for much of the time. Colorful, forceful, and hardworking, he quickly established a reputation as the lawyer of choice for many prominent companies and individuals in Las Vegas. Through Claiborne's career and observations, we can look "behind the scenes" of landmark legal decisions such as the Thunderbird Hotel case in which the resort challenged the state's authority to regulate holders of gaming licences, the licensing of the Sands Hotel and Frank Sinatra by Nevada gaming authorities (along with the subsequent revocation proceedings against Sinatra), as well as the criminal prosecution of many high profile individuals in Nevada's courts. Viewing legal history through the prism of Claiborne's political career will shed light on the backroom deals and other episodes that anecdotally help describe and increase our understanding of mid-century Nevada politics. So, this is the story of a dynamic legal community that developed in a rogue town dominated by casino operators, often with mob connections—a legal community that came of age during Claiborne's career. What better way to see that unfold than through the eyes and ears of its most forceful and outspoken participant, Harry Claiborne.

---

32 State Bar of Nevada v. Claiborne, 104 Nev. 115 (1988); for more on the impeachment, see Eleanore Bushnell, "Judge Harry E. Claiborne and the Federal Impeachment Process," Nevada Historical Society Quarterly, XXXII, No. 4 (1989), 235-260; More recently, see Mike Vernetti's excellent book entitled Lies Within Lies

CHAPTER ONE

YOUTH AND WAR

Born in McRae, White County, Arkansas on July 2, 1917 and reared
on his father's farm, young Claiborne developed not only a down-home
personal and courtroom style, but also the strong work ethic often found
in farm communities. An ancestor obtained a French land grant of 3,000
acres that established the Claiborne family in present-day Arkansas. His
great grandfather, a colonel in the 7th cavalry in Robert E. Lee's Army of
Northern Virginia during the Civil War, died during the battle of Chan-
cellorsville.[33] When his grandfather's children began to marry, he gave
them 40 to 60 acres in an attempt to keep his family around him.[34]

Created by the Territory of Arkansas in 1840, White County was named
after Hugh Lawson White, a judge and senator from Tennessee, who
was a candidate for the United States Presidency near the end of Andrew
Jackson's term. Searcy, the county seat, is located one hundred miles
west of the Mississippi River, near the foothills of the Ozarks, and fifty
miles northeast of Little Rock. Although the first settler arrived in 1789,
there were no permanent white settlers between him and the Rocky
Mountains for the next 25 years. A 1817 treaty gave the Cherokees a
tract of land west of Searcy, but by 1828, continual problems with white
settlers caused them to cede their claims to Arkansas and move to the
Indian Territory of Oklahoma. Claiborne's birthplace received its name
from Confederate General Dandridge McRae, a graduate from the University of South Carolina who moved to Searcy in 1853, "read " the law
and was admitted to the Arkansas bar in1854. After the war, he returned

33 Claiborne interview, 177.
34 Ibid., 1-2.

to practice law in Searcy and was later appointed Deputy Secretary of State in Arkansas.[35]

Claiborne's father, Arthur, raised cotton on his 120 acre farm and was one of the first farmers in the county to rotate crops. Although a big strawberry producer, the county relied principally on cotton. In those days, farmer's children usually worked on the farm, and Claiborne and his siblings were no exception. Harry confessed that he had no pleasant memories about farm life.[36]

Arthur Claiborne instilled a sense of independence and fairness in his son at an early age. At 13 years of age, Harry watched his father stand up to the grand wizard of the Klu Klux Klan, who criticized him for being the only white farmer in the valley who was not a Klan member. The Klan of the 1920s targeted not only African-Americans, but also immigrants and certain religious groups. Arthur responded, "I won't join any organization whose members need to wear hoods over their faces." Only days later, his father saved an immigrant farmer from a lynching when he sheltered the man and his family in the Claiborne home. Armed with a shotgun, Arthur went to the man's farm and waited. When the Klansmen rode in that night, Claiborne stopped them at gunpoint. When one of the intruders rode toward the barn with a flaming torch in his hand, Arthur knocked him off his horse with a round of buckshot. Never again was a man lynched by the Klan in his community, because the night riders knew they would have to answer to Arthur Claiborne, his proud son later boasted. To young Harry, this was a life altering event. Not to be outdone, his mother Minnie, a school teacher, was a proponent of racial integration in the 1920s when such activism was dangerous in the Deep South. Clearly, his parents taught him to stand up for his beliefs, even when they were unpopular, and even when there may be personal consequences. He did.[37]

Even at an early age, Claiborne found the court system fascinating. At that time, jurors in Arkansas were not selected at random. The judge

---

35 Raymond Lee Muncy, *Searcy, Arkansas: A Frontier Town Grows Up With America* (Searcy: Harding Press, 1976), 1-10, 31.

36 Claiborne interview, 5.

37 Ibid., 1; *Las Vegas Sun*, January 21, 2004; *Las Vegas Review-Journal*, January 21, 2004.

selected the jury panel himself. He selected the grand jury and the petit jury from prominent people in the community. Usually it was the same people every year. Because Claiborne's grandfather was a local patriarch, he always served on the grand or petit jury. He took his grandson with him. The courthouse, set on a classic court square at the county seat in Searcy, was a magnificent old building, Claiborne recalled. He loved to watch the old lawyers. Some were great orators, at least to a young observer. They all dressed alike - blue serge-sayer suits with watch chains coming out of their vests. He wondered if some of them even had watches attached because he never saw them pull out a watch. Nonetheless, a chain was anchored to each side of the vest.[38]

Claiborne never lost his interest in the law. After he graduated from high school in 1932, the woman who ran McRae's only general store called to discuss his future. When he told her that he wanted to be a lawyer but had no money for college, she arranged for him to attend Ouachipa Baptist College. Once there, Claiborne worked in the kitchen and dining room in the dormitory to finance his education. Because a college degree was not yet required for admission to law school, he left after three years for law school.[39]

Claiborne's selection of a law school was unusual. He initially applied to Louisiana State University in Baton Rouge. During the interview, the assistant dean informed him that admissions for out of state students were closed for several years. As he hitchhiked home to Arkansas, a drunken tobacco salesman named Schneider gave him a ride. The back seat of the car was filled with hand fans with a big red rooster on the back, and underneath it said "Rooster Snuff." Schneider drove around small towns, located churches, grabbed a bunch of fans, and put them in the pews. Because no air conditioning existed in the churches, the fans were put to good use. This Depression era marketing gimmick apparently worked. During the trip home, Schneider proceeded to get so drunk that young Claiborne had to take over the wheel. They "marketed" all the way to Memphis. After learning of Claiborne's problem with law school

38 Claiborne interview, 8.
39 Ibid., 12.

admission, Schneider wrote a letter, addressed and sealed it, and told Claiborne to take it to A. B. Neil, who was judge of the Davidson County Circuit Court in Nashville, Dean of the Cumberland University School of Law, a law professor since 1930, and future Tennessee Supreme Court justice. Claiborne went home and showed the letter to his father, who encouraged him to go to Nashville and deliver it.[40]

Following his father's advice and motivated by his own desire to attend law school, Claiborne traveled to Tennessee, handed Schneider's letter to the judge's secretary and waited. Neil soon came out and introduced himself. As it turned out, the snuff salesman was a boyhood friend of the judge. Claiborne believed the two had had a lot of fun together because the judge "sat and chuckled, and chuckled, and chuckled." Judge Neil wrote a letter that secured Claiborne's admission to Cumberland, as well as a job. Benefitting from this "connection", or "juice" in Las Vegas parlance, was a harbinger of the world which Claiborne would experience in Southern Nevada. He graduated in June 1941. Cumberland later sold its law school to Samford University in Birmingham, Alabama. Claiborne later recalled, "To this day, whenever a case looks bleak, I recall that story. I wouldn't even be a lawyer if I hadn't been hitchhiking and was picked up by a drunken snuff salesman."[41]

Following graduation, Claiborne moved to Little Rock and started working for a small law firm. Within two months, however, he received his military draft notice. Earlier that year, Congress had authorized a peacetime draft as war raged in Europe. After telling his senior partner that he had to report for a physical exam, Claiborne's boss offered some sound advice: "You're very articulate. You, I'm sure, would make a helluva trial lawyer, but you'd make a better politician. Don't get drafted. Go down to Camp Robinson and volunteer. Come back after the war. You volunteered to serve your nation in this time of great trouble. Run for public office. You'll get elected. You'll be governor of this state some day." Claiborne recalled going home that night, thinking about it, and

---

40 Ibid., 14; Review-Journal, January 21, 2004.
41 Review-Journal, January 21, 2004; David J. Langum and Howard P. Walthall, From Maverick to Mainstream: Cumberland School of Law, 1847-1997 (Athens University of Georgia Press, 1997) Claiborne interview, 14.

concluding, "By God, I'll make a good governor." He volunteered three days later.[42]

Claiborne reported to the Santa Ana Army Air Base in 1942. His primary duty was to locate Japanese families and remove them to a holding area at the Santa Anita Race Track. President Franklin D. Roosevelt's Executive Order 9066 authorized the internment of approximately 110,000 people of Japanese heritage to housing facilities called "War Relocation Camps" in the wake of Japan's attack on Pearl Harbor. The Order allowed military commanders to designate "exclusion zones" and was used, in part, to declare that all people of Japanese ancestry were excluded from all of California and most of Oregon and Washington, except for those in internment camps. Implementing Special Order 9066 was disagreeable for someone reared to oppose racial repression, but Claiborne followed orders. He recalled the Japanese were "stoic, unexpressive, like they understood, but disapproved," never argued, and never had an altercation. The MPs were constantly reminded that they were to be understanding and gentle. None of the officers he knew approved of what they were ordered to do.[43]

Still, this experience illustrates Claiborne's early willingness to expose himself to personal risk to do what he believed was right. The general "round up" missed one Japanese farmer and Claiborne's squad was ordered to get him. They found him hiding in a thicket. He was crippled. He worked less than one acre of land where he grew melons and raised pigs. Although he probably slept in his house at night, the farmer left before daylight and camped in the thicket. Claiborne's squad found him and loaded him in the truck. He was crying. He asked what would happen to his animals, but Claiborne did not know. In an act of compassion, Claiborne decided to free the man but told the interpreter to explain to the farmer that he would be arrested if he ever came out of the thicket during daylight. Although the squad nodded their approval, the interpreter said he would have to report Claiborne. "You do and you are going to live about one hour after you tell somebody," Claiborne threatened.

42 Claiborne interview, 15-17.
43 Ibid., 20-22.

The interpreter never reported him.[44]

Claiborne first visited Las Vegas in May 1943 with other soldiers to respond to a security problem at the Cotton Club. General George Patton's
armored division trained at the Desert Warfare Center near Needles, California. Some of his troops came to Las Vegas on weekend leave. According to Claiborne, a few of the soldiers got rowdy one night and barricaded
themselves inside the Club. They stabbed Woody Pierce, a Las Vegas
captain of detectives, in the stomach and held him captive. When Claiborne's unit arrived, Major Donald L. Barnell met them and, armed with
six hand grenades, they drove to the Cotton Club. Barnell got a bullhorn
and announced to the occupants that he was unarmed and going into the
Club. He told Claiborne, "Give me 20 minutes. If I'm not out of there in
20 minutes, blow the Goddamn building down." Claiborne responded,
"You've got to be kidding. You'll be in there." Barnell replied, "No. Every
building has a back door. I'll be out of there, don't you worry." He was a
very "gutsy bastard," Claiborne thought. Barnell brought the 8 or 9 men
out in about 10 minutes. Barnell, like Claiborne later demonstrated, put
integrity and duty above personal risk. Claiborne and his group then
"did the town for three days. Wasn't much either. It was all downtown."
Later that year he was transferred to Las Vegas. Little did he know how
Las Vegas would eventually shape his life and the influence he would
exert on the town's and state's legal community over the next 60 years.[45]

44 Ibid., 21-22.
45 Ibid., 29-30; Louis Wiener, Harry Claiborne, and George Foley, interview by Cliff Young,
    1995-1997, 1.

Photo Courtesy of the Claiborne Family

Photo Courtesy of the Claiborne Family

CHAPTER TWO

WARTIME NEVADA AND LAS VEGAS

Wartime Nevada and Las Vegas and early twenty-first century Nevada and Las Vegas were very different. In 1940, the state's population was roughly 110,000. The largest city was Reno, and political power was concentrated in the northern part of the state. Clark County was still relatively new, having been formed from the southern portion of Lincoln County in July 1909. In 1941, Las Vegas exerted little political influence beyond Clark County. Only the year before, for the first time, a Clark County resident had been part of the state's congressional delegation when Berkeley Bunker was appointed to fill the U. S. Senate seat of Key Pittman, who had been re-elected on November 5, 1940, but died before the term began.

Southern Nevada was a constellation of diverse communities, ranging from the semi-ghost mining town of Searchlight in the far south to small, mostly Mormon, farming hamlets in the north. Large government construction projects created two cities in Clark County. The Boulder Canyon Project spawned Boulder City in 1931, and the defense industry's need for magnesium resulted in the creation of Henderson in 1941. Wartime Las Vegas was still relatively small. Claiborne recalled that Rancho Road and Charleston Boulevard formed the western and southern boundaries of Las Vegas, while 10th Street and Owens Avenue, the boundary of North Las Vegas defined the eastern and northern limits.[46]

Despite its small population, Clark County enjoyed a relatively broad-based economy during the war. The Army Gunnery School (located at

46 Claiborne interview, 31.

today's Nellis Air Force Base) provided an economic stimulant as did
the construction and operation of the massive Basic Magnesium plant
in Henderson. Maintaining and safeguarding Hoover Dam provided
a steady economy for Boulder City, while the railroad connected these
operations with the rest of the country. While Las Vegas' resort industry
was still in its infancy during the war, change was evident. Indeed, the
gaming corridor along Fremont Street demonstrated its growth potential with several casinos, led by the El Cortez in 1941. At the same time,
cabins and motels sprouted along Fifth Street and, across the city line,
two resorts, the El Rancho Vegas and the Hotel Last Frontier, opened in
1941 and 1942, respectively. Although gaming eventually overwhelmed
the war industries' impact on the state, the war and subsequent defense
spending "really transformed the sleepy little desert town." The town
Claiborne encountered would not be the same town he came to know.[47]

Block 16 in Las Vegas provided an economy of a different type: prostitution. Although closed down in 1942 at the army's request, next to gambling, Block 16's prostitution was the town's main attraction, according to
one time City Attorney Paul Ralli. By day, Block 16 was an inconspicuous
row of eight or nine clubs fronted by a common porch just above street
level. But at night, the Block assumed a more forbidding guise where
mystery, sin, and taboo all mingled. Considered legal by many, prostitution was a local industry and the Block was a must-see for visitors. Many
residents acted as guides to visiting friends, and no trip to Las Vegas was
complete without a tour of the bars in the Block, or at least a ride down
the middle of the street. On one occasion, while entertaining a well-
known Hollywood director and his wife, Ralli arranged for one of the
prostitutes to come out and greet the director by his first name as they
drove slowly by in an open car. The director blushed and, to his wife's
amazement, quickly offered this explanation, "She must have worked for
me in the past as an extra in the movies." This prank was used time and
again without any unpleasant consequences, Ralli observed.[48]

47 Robert V. Nickel, "Dollars, Defense, and the Desert: Southern Nevada's Military Economy and
    Word War II", Nevada Historical Society Quarterly, Volume 47, No. 4 (Winter, 2004), 303.
48 Paul Ralli, Nevada Lawyer: A Story of Life and Love in Las Vegas, 1930-1970 (Culver City: Murray
    and Gee, Inc., 1949), 38-39.

If Las Vegas society reflected the state's last frontier atmosphere, so did the legal community. In 1943, this community was small (particularly with a number of its members in the military), geographically diverse, general law practices rather than specialization, informally educated for the most part, and struggling to maintain meaningful qualifying standards for its members. In short, the Bar exuded an "Old West" appearance and attitude, just like the state. The Nevada State Bar Association in 1943 consisted of 234 attorneys statewide. Washoe County had 122 attorneys and still represented the state's legal and commercial center. Clark County counted 37 attorneys, while Carson City and Elko had 16 and 13, respectively. No other county had even ten attorneys.[49]

Political power was concentrated in the north, which also controlled the State Bar. Lawyers from throughout the state met at the Washoe County Courthouse in Reno on September 23, 1911 to permanently organize the Nevada Bar Association. With the adoption of a constitution and by-laws, they elected Hugh H. Brown of Reno as the first president. The first annual meeting was held in 1929 in Reno, as were the next 19. Not until 1943 was a Las Vegan, Artemus W. Ham, chosen as Bar president, and not until 1948 did a meeting take place in Las Vegas. Harvey Dickerson became president in 1953, but that is deceptive, because Dickerson's father, Denver, was acting Governor from 1908 until 1911. Although originally from Ely, the family remained in Carson City after the governor's term expired. The second Las Vegan with no northern Nevada ties to become Bar president was V. Gray Gubler in 1958-1959, the 32nd man to hold that position. So, only two of the first thirty-two Bar presidents were from Southern Nevada. Moreover, the Bar exam was administered only in Reno until 1971, forcing Las Vegas area applicants to endure the inconvenience of the long travel.[50]

For years, admission standards were lax. During the 1940s, the Bar Association re-examined its rules for admission. There was no uniformity in either the bar examinations of the various states or uniformity for admission to practice law. Some states had standards with little or

49 Nevada Bar Journal, April 1943, vol 8, No. 2, 50.
50 Nevada Lawyer (Reno and Las Vegas: State Bar of Nevada,) January 2003, 11-15; Diamond Jubilee Celebration: 75 Years of Service, 1928-2003 (Las Vegas: State Bar of Nevada, 2003), 57, 62, 20-21.

no value in determining the legal ability of an applicant, while others provided highly selective testing standards to correlate the law school records of the applicants. A national standard bar examination was overwhelmingly opposed by the various state bars, until the 1970s when states began accepting a uniform multiple choice test for a portion of the examination. Because no nationwide "standards" existed to serve as guidelines for bar examinations and admission systems, Nevada attempted to devise a system patterned after parts of the systems of other states. The Nevada admission system contained three parts: the qualifications for taking the examination, the successful completion of a written examination, and the recommendation as to character and fitness. The admission process always required the applicant to be a day over the age of 21 years, an American citizen, and a Nevada resident for six months. Population shifts during and after the war prompted the state to institute new rules to provide more objective and standardized examination and educational requirements. Gradually, the Bar tightened its standards. In 1943, the association abolished the reciprocity system and required all applicants, including lawyers in other states, to pass a written examination. The Bar acknowledged that in some cases examining lawyers from other states appeared unnecessary, but members argued that it helped maintain high standards by keeping marginally qualified lawyers out of Nevada. This reform would ultimately force Claiborne to take and pass the Bar examination.[51]

A second important change occurred in 1945 when the Nevada Supreme Court abolished the rule permitting an applicant to take the Bar examination if he possessed the "equivalent" of a high school, college and law school formal education. The new rule required not only at least two years of college, but more importantly, a degree from a law school approved by the American Bar Association. Correspondence school and law office training no longer met the educational qualification for admission. The former rule imposed upon the Board of Bar Examiners the duty to assess the informal education of applicants to determine its "equiva-

---

51 Gordon Morris Bakken, Practicing Law in Frontier California (Lincoln: University of Nebraska Press, 1991), 19-25; Nevada State Bar Journal, October 1954, vol. 19, No. 4, 162-167.

lency" to the formal training of a law school. However, it provided no standards or basis to make that determination and a certain degree of arbitrariness was inevitable. The new procedure provided an objective basis for at least a minimum of formalized training for all applicants. An interim rule permitted admission of war veterans under certain conditions, providing relief for some caught just short of a law degree when the war began. After it provided relief for those members, the Bar repealed that provision.[52]

In 1943, the Nevada Supreme Court justices reflected the diverse backgrounds of the Bar members themselves. All westerners, their legal education ranged from a prestigious eastern law school to no college at all, but their legal experiences were similar - all were elected to the non-partisan positions of District Attorney and later District Court judge before ascending to the Supreme Court. The Supreme Court consisted - as it had since statehood in 1864 and would remain until 1967- of three elected justices. William Edwin Orr was the sole justice from Southern Nevada. His background was representative of many lawyers and judges during that age. Orr attended grammar school in Pioche and, with no high school in Lincoln County at that time, enrolled in a prep course at the University of Nevada. That was the extent of his formal education. He never had the benefit of college or law training, yet he served on the Nevada Supreme Court until 1945, then he resigned to accept an appointment to the U.S. Court of Appeals for the Ninth Circuit based in San Francisco. In a circuit dominated by California, Washington, and Oregon, Orr was the first Nevadan to serve on that court. This reflects favorably not only on Orr's character and reputation, but also upon the political influence of Nevada's senior U. S. Senator Pat McCarran, who secured his nomination.[53] Although Claiborne dealt with Orr only in his capacity as a judge, he knew of Orr's reputation as a "helluva trial lawyer" in Pioche, an important quality in the standing and reputation of a mining town lawyer.[54] Florence Boyer, clerk of the Clark County Court remembered Orr as one of the few "absolutely incorruptible" people she

52 Nevada State Bar Journal, October 1954, vol. 19, No. 4, 162-167.
53 Nevada State Bar Journal, October 1966, vol. 31, No. 4, 8; Diamond Jubilee Celebration, 35-36.
54 Claiborne interview, 250-251.

knew. Nothing could persuade Orr to do anything he considered wrong. She further recalled that he was "very dignified." [55]

Attorney George Foley believed Orr would have liked to have been a teacher, and he would have made a good one. He remembered that each Saturday morning Judge Orr held court to set the court calendar for the following week. The attorneys frequently sent office boys, now called runners, to the calendar call to make notes of the times of scheduled hearings. Many runners were the sons of practicing lawyers. After the session, Orr regularly called the young men into his chambers and delivered a lecture on the law. Frequently, he would take a legal issue on that morning's calendar and use it as a topic for a short lecture so they would understand what had occurred and why. Nearly all the young men became lawyers, in part due to Orr's inspiration, Foley believed. When Foley attended Hastings Law School in San Francisco from 1954 to 1956, Orr was sitting on the Circuit Court. Frequently, Foley and Orr would meet in a nearby coffee shop and Orr would ask how he was getting along in school. They would get out Foley's case book, read the cases together, and if there was a question Orr could not answer, he would ask Foley to call him in an hour. That gave Orr time to have one of his law clerks research the issue. On one occasion, the dean of Hastings Law School and two of Foley's professors walked into the coffee shop and saw them. As Foley laughingly recalled, the professors treated him with much greater respect after seeing him studying law with a Ninth Circuit Court judge. Foley also remembered Las Vegas residents treating Orr with great respect. When they passed him on the street, everyone said hello and spoke to him, and he would always tip his hat and respond, "And how are you?" Orr was a "most gracious man," according to Foley.[56]

Nevada's sole United States District Court judge when Claiborne started in Las Vegas was Frank Norcross. He was one of four members of the University of Nevada's first four-year graduating class. After serving on the Nevada Supreme Court, he joined former Nevada Attorney General George Thatcher and retired Washoe County District Attorney William

---

55 Florence M. Boyer, Las Vegas, Nevada: My Home for Sixty Years, interview by Mary Ellen Glass (Reno: University of Nevada Oral History Program, 1967), 154.

56 Wiener interview, 89.

Woodburn to form the state's most influential firm, and it would remain
so for years, eventually representing the state's political powerhouses,
including Nevada kingpin George Wingfield. Woodburn's father started
practicing law in Virginia City in 1866, giving the firm deep roots in the
Nevada legal community. [57] Claiborne would encounter this firm on
several of his high profile cases. Norcross first came to the attention of
the federal judiciary as a candidate to fill a vacancy on the Ninth Circuit
in 1925, but a United States Attorney General's memorandum noted that
"Judge Norcross is so persistently and actively against the 18th Amendment (prohibition) that it would strongly influence his action against the
enforcement of the law if he were put on the bench." As a result, the
Coolidge Administration did not appoint him, although the President
later named him to the U. S. District Court in Nevada in 1928, where he
remained for 17 years. [58]

According to one assessment of his judicial skills, Norcross was a
good and fair judge, but not considered "brilliant." Despite his 17 years
presiding over trials in Federal Court, lawyers generally viewed him as
a better appellate judge. Norcross tended to be "slow and deliberate" in
his decision making process, characteristics more suitable to the appellate process than the quicker paced trial court room. However, he had
the reputation for being both "profound and proficient" while serving on
either bench.[59]

The majority of the lawsuits and trials in a community occur within the
state courts. They are the backbone of the local judicial system, and the
venue where new lawyers, such as Claiborne, would begin and spend the
bulk of their trial careers. Due to Las Vegas' relatively small population
in the 1940s, Clark County had only one District Court judge. When Claiborne arrived in 1943, it was George E. Marshall. A United States Marine

57 Nevada Lawyer (Reno and Las Vegas: State Bar of Nevada), April 2003, 23-25.
58 Reno Evening Gazette, November 4, 1952; Nevada State Journal, November 5, 1952; Thomas W.
    Miller, Memoirs of Thomas Woodnutt Miller: A Public Spirited Citizen of Delaware and Nevada,
    interview by Mary Ellen Glass (Reno: University of Nevada, 1966) 101; David C. Frederick, Rugged
    Justice: The Ninth Circuit Court of Appeals and the American West, 1891-1941 (Berkeley: University
    of California Press, 1994) 130-131; In Memoriam: Frank H. Norcross, 69 Nev. 355, (1952); Nevada
    Lawyer, April 2003, 23-25.
59 Harry Hunt Atkinson, Tonopah and Reno Memories of a Nevada Attorney, interview by Barbara C.
    Thornton (Reno: University of Nevada Oral History Program, 1970), 71-73.

in the First World War, Marshall was wounded in the crucial battle
at Belleau Wood, which stopped the German advance on Paris. After
recuperating, he returned to active duty, but was again wounded during
hand-to-hand combat at Mont Blanc Ridge. In 1946, Marshall resigned
from the bench to unsuccessfully run for the U. S. Senate. In 1958, Clark
County voters returned him to the District Court bench, where he served
until retirement in 1966.[60]

Claiborne had many dealings with Marshall over the years. He described Marshall as an "old timer" in the Las Vegas area who was very
popular with the voters, and for good reason he believed. In Claiborne's
view, Marshall was a good judge; knowledgeable, usually with a good
temperament on the bench, and as accommodating as a judge could be
without passing over the line. "But for some reason, and it might have
been just as much my fault in looking back, he didn't like me. I could
walk into court and his whole temperament changed. He just couldn't
stand me," Claiborne remembered. One incident characterized their
relationship as well as the casual manner in which some Nevada judges
conducted their business. Claiborne went to the courthouse to get an order signed, but could not find Marshall and had it signed by Judge Clar-
ence Sundean instead. At the next court appearance in the case, Marshall
glared at Claiborne and announced, "Before we start, I want an explanation from you why you went to another Judge to get this order signed."
The courtroom was full of lawyers. Claiborne asked if he wanted an
explanation right then, and Marshall said he did. When asked if he was
sure, Marshall demanded an answer. Claiborne replied, "I went over to
your chambers, and it was early in the afternoon as you can see from the
file stamp and you weren't there. I inquired where you were and nobody
knew. So I went and got Judge Sundean to sign the order. I found out
later that you were at the Horseshoe (Casino) Bar that afternoon and
didn't come back to your office. If you'd stay in your office on Friday
afternoons, lawyers would be able to find you and we wouldn't have this
difficulty." "His face got deep red. He got so damn mad," Claiborne

60 Review-Journal, March 24, 1980, Obituaries; Sun, March 24, 1980, Obituaries; Political History,
    294, 336, 297, 301.

delighted in recalling.[61]

While in the District Attorney's office in the late 1940s, Claiborne had a criminal jury trial with Marshall, who was in private practice at the time. A girl on the witness stand testified against Marshall's client. She was a prostitute at the infamous brothel named Roxie's, and Marshall knew it. According to Claiborne, Marshall's cross-examination went something like this, "Young lady, what is your occupation?" "I'm a waitress." "What restaurant do you work at?" She said, "Well, I'm unemployed at the present." "What was the last restaurant that you worked at?" "I don't remember." Marshall said, "Oh, come off of it," in a loud voice. "What do you mean, you don't remember it? You must remember the last restaurant you worked at." She looked at Marshall and said, "Come off of it, George." Called him by his first name. She continued, "You know I'm a whore at Roxie's, you've been out there enough." The jury's reaction can only be imagined.[62]

Claiborne's anecdotal recollections of Marshall and the other judges and lawyers during and after the war illustrated the frontier and, to those in other states, the roguish nature of Las Vegas, Reno, and the state itself in the 20th century. Claiborne's legal career repeatedly demonstrates this point, but his experiences as a military policeman in downtown Las Vegas helped prepare him for life in one of American's most bizarre cities. The military transferred Claiborne to Las Vegas in 1943 to serve as prison officer at the air base and as the officer in charge of the downtown Military Police. Basically, he ran the base prison and supervised the MPs in the downtown area. Nellis Air Force Base, originally the civilian airport for Western Air Express, was first called Las Vegas Army Air Corps Gunnery School and later Las Vegas Army Airfield. It has provided Southern Nevada with a significant and stable economic stimulus from the war years to the present. Initially established in 1941 for the "training of aerial gunners to the degree of proficiency that will qualify them for combat duty," the base more than doubled in population less than a month after construction began. From 1942 through 1945, 600 gunnery

61 Claiborne interview, 237; Wiener interview, 5.
62 Claiborne interview, 112.

students and 215 co-pilots graduated from the base every five weeks. By 1945, the military base population reached nearly 11,000 officers and enlisted people. The city fathers recognized the importance of keeping the military leaders comfortable with their selection of Southern Nevada and tried to accommodate their uneasiness over local conditions. Creating a military base in an environment where 24-hour gambling, liquor sales, and prostitution were legal concerned the military. In an effort to control problems created by servicemen on leave in Las Vegas, the Army established a military police force at the gunnery school.[63]

Claiborne's unit principally addressed the commanding officer's concerns regarding prostitution. "That's why we were here, really. That's why there was a cadre of MPs working nights downtown. Colonel George Henry had a thing about prostitutes. In fact, he had a war all the time going about prostitutes in Las Vegas. He even got the Commanding General into the fight."[64] Previously, under pressure from the War Department, the Las Vegas City Commission closed Block 16 in 1942 through daily raids by the police department under the direction of city attorney Paul Ralli. Although Ralli claimed his raids made it "unprofitable and prohibitive for the prostitutes to carry on either in the open or under cover, and so came the end of the red-light district in Las Vegas," prostitution in various forms continued to flourish in Clark County as it always had. Both the policing of the downtown area and the involvement of the military justice system in Las Vegas outside the physical confines of the military base offer some insight into the influence the military could, and did, exert over community affairs.[65]

Claiborne's anecdotal memories of this period illustrate this point, along with the fluid nature of policing wartime Las Vegas. For example, Claiborne had eight men working every night, but the town was still small and he really did not need that many men. Since most of his men had girlfriends, Claiborne normally gave four of them the night off after 8:00 p.m. Someone reported this to the commanding officer, who in turn re-

63 Insider Viewpoint of Las Vegas, "The Military History of Nellis Air Force Base," www.insidervlv.com/nellisairbase.html. (Accessed April 30, 2007).
64 Claiborne interview, 33.
65 Ralli, Nevada Lawyer: A Story of Life and Love in Las Vegas, 40.

ported it to Colonel George Henry. One night, the Colonel decided to determine how many MPs were actually on duty. When he was eventually tipped off, Claiborne already had let four men go home early. He talked to the remaining four men and they devised a plan. As the Colonel drove down the street, he saw two men coming down one side of the street and two coming down the other side of the street. When the Colonel passed, they ran through a club, came out on the other end and walked down the street again. The Colonel counted the same four men all night. Claiborne never heard anymore about it.[66]

To put it mildly, the military's policing operations in Las Vegas were loose, especially when Claiborne was on duty. Despite being in charge of the downtown MPs and the prison officer, Claiborne also served as defense attorney in a number of court martial cases. At Colonel Henry's request, he tried approximately ten cases. Essentially, Claiborne defended the same people his unit arrested. The obvious conflict of interest never seemed to concern anyone. [67]

Military justice was rife with local characters. One court martial case involved a used car dealer called "Madman" Pizinger. His business, called the Used Car Asylum, was located at 510 Fremont Street. Claiborne represented a soldier who stole one of Pizingers cars and drove it to Alabama. The FBI arrested him and sought a court martial. Pizinger often ran newspaper ads in which he described himself as "the craziest man in town. Crazy Pizinger." The army prosecutor, Captain Lou Smith, called Pizinger as a witness and Claiborne objected, claiming he was incompetent to testify. When asked why, he said, "He's crazy." Colonel Henry, the presiding judge, ruled that Claiborne had to prove that Pizinger was insane. Claiborne asked Pizinger, "Don't you regularly advance to the general public, as well as the whole world that you are crazy? Don't you even advertise in the newspaper that you're crazy?" Pizinger acknowledged it. Claiborne then asked, "What further proof do you need? The man's not only crazy, but he advertises it." The judge

66 Claiborne interview, 32.
67 Ibid., 152.

declared a recess. The prosecutor was flabbergasted: "You're in the car business and run those ads that you're crazy to attract attention to your car lots?" He said, "Yes." "You don't do that for any other purpose, do you?" He said, "No." Claiborne then asked, "Weren't you at the El Rancho Hotel for a war bond drive?" "Yes." "Were you out there selling cars?" He said, "Of course not." "You went up there to make a contribution?" "Yes." "Didn't you jump up on the stage and say that you were the craziest man in Nevada?" He said, "Yes." "And that wasn't part of your sales pitch, was it?" "No." Claiborne said, "That's all I have." Captain Smith did not know what to do. Colonel Henry told Pizinger, "Get out of here! We don't want to mess with you!" Some time after Claiborne mustered out of the Army, he met Pizinger on the street. Pizinger shouted at him, "Goddamn you. You know I'm not crazy." Claiborne confessed, "No, I don't know that. All I know is what you say."[68]

---

[68] Ibid., 208; For an example of Pizinger's advertisement, see Review-Journal, November 23, 1944, 15.

Photo Courtesy of Las Vegas News Bureau

50

Photo Courtesy of the Claiborne Family

CHAPTER THREE

POLICE OFFICER AND ADMINISTRATOR

The Army transferred Claiborne from Las Vegas to West Overfield, Massachusetts, in September 1945, and discharged him that December. Given a train ticket to Little Rock and $800 in mustering out pay, he rode to Chicago. At first, he did not plan to settle in the West, much less Las Vegas. But just before boarding the Missouri-Pacific train to Little Rock, Claiborne heard the announcement for the Union Pacific's "City of Los Angeles," and made an instant decision to return to Las Vegas and practice law there. Several days later, on the night of December 4, 1945, Claiborne arrived in town. The Nevada Bar Association required a one-year residency before an applicant could take the examination, making it necessary for him to find work as a non-lawyer. The next morning, he immediately went to the police station seeking a job and met George Thompson, newly appointed Chief of Police, coming out the door. As an MP, Claiborne had worked with Thompson and they were friends. At the time, training for Las Vegas policemen was still very informal, if it existed at all. Thompson hired him on the spot, and Claiborne reported to work that afternoon. He rode his first shift the night of December 5, 1945 with Bill Hanlon, who later became the Captain of Detectives.[69]

Claiborne's experience with the Military Police, coupled with his legal education, gave him a unique perspective regarding law enforcement in a small town environment. As an MP, Claiborne had not concerned himself with the local policies and politics of a community that was not

---

69 Claiborne interview, 34; Wiener interview, 1; Dennis N. Griffin, Policing Las Vegas; A History Of Law Enforcement In Southern Nevada (Las Vegas: Huntington Press, 2005), 11-12.

his home. Now, he looked at the same issues and people from a different and arguably expanded point of view. His law enforcement experiences in post-war Las Vegas gave him a background that he later drew upon in his law practice. It also instilled in him a sense of "camaraderie" with his fellow police officers, which influenced not only the types of cases he handled, but also gave him a healthy skepticism of the "evidence" often uncovered in police investigations.

With the establishment of Las Vegas in 1905 came the need for law enforcement, which initially consisted of a group of men know as night watchmen. In a town comprised mainly of railroaders and miners, coupled with open prostitution, law enforcement was a dangerous job. Within the first year, one watchman was killed and several others severely beaten. The saloon owners demanded that the city hire the toughest man they could find - that was Sam Gay, a six foot, 260 pound former miner and bouncer who shunned the use of a gun in favor of his fists. Gay was the first in a long line of Las Vegas police chiefs who perhaps were more practical than political because it was not until 1945 that the first chief of police left office on his own accord, Harry Miller. The others were all fired. By 1940, the department consisted of 14 officers, which included two relief patrolmen.[70]

The Las Vegas Police Department of 1945 reflected the small town atmosphere and the "good ole boy" system of the community itself. The force consisted of approximately 25 officers (six of whom served in the detective bureau) and three vehicles, Claiborne estimated. In the late 1940s, the Clark County Sheriff's Department and city police departments of Las Vegas and newly created North Las Vegas handled local law enforcement. Apart from jurisdictional issues, they were similar in composition and sophistication. Yet, the community was in rapid transition, thanks to the post-war population explosion. Although the character of law enforcement and the community changed rapidly over the next several years, the remnants of an entrenched small town mentality remained for many more.

When Claiborne arrived in 1945, V. Gray Gubler was the Clark County

70 Griffin, Policing Las Vegas, 1-16.

District Attorney. Gubler had numerous problems with the Las Vegas Police Department. He was a stickler for proper legal procedures and thought most of the officers were just a bunch of stupid cowboys - an opinion partly shared by Claiborne. They did not give a "damn about the rules. They caught the bad guys and did not care how." After starting as a patrolman, Claiborne soon transferred to the detective bureau. His colleagues were Allie Swark, Pete Reid, Bill Hanlon, Joe Bremser, Iram Powell, and Marl Hopkins, whom they called a "super sleuth" because he smoked a crooked stemmed pipe much like Basil Rathbone did as Sherlock Holmes. Claiborne described them as "good men and delightful." He served as the liaison with Gubler's office and reviewed all investigations and prepared the evidence before submitting cases to the district attorney for prosecution.[71]

Claiborne and Gubler worked well together, although they got off to a strained start. Gubler suffered from a chronic eye condition that caused him to blink his right eye all the time. During their first meeting, Claiborne recalled that Gubler "began to wink at me." When Claiborne got back to the police station, the captain asked how the meeting went. Claiborne responded that "I got along with him fine but I kept my distance. That son-of-a-bitch is a fag." The captain then told him of Gubler's eye problem.[72]

Claiborne's reminiscence about public drunkenness further exemplifies the small town character of post-war Las Vegas. Chet Morrison, Inspector of the Police Department, was a former Hollywood movie actor, who, because he looked mean and tough, often played the bad guy in western movies during the Tom Mix era. Claiborne recalled seeing an old black and white western movie where Morrison was raiding a stagecoach. He surmised that Morrison had been a prize fighter at one time because his nose was so broken up. He had a "face like a sledgehammer had hit him." Though a genial person, Morrison was "no rocket scientist," as Claiborne put it. Claiborne recalled that Morrison once gathered the police force together a day after they arrested a local man for drunkenness. Morrison

71 Claiborne interview, 35-36.
72 Claiborne interview, 35.

laid down the law and declared, "By God, there better not be anymore of this." Everyone looked at each other because they did not know what he meant. He continued, "The next one of you who arrests any local residents for being drunk or driving drunk is going to get fired the next day." One policeman asked why and Morrison retorted, "Because all of my Goddamned friends are drunks. Does that answer your question?" And that was the policy. The police department became a taxi service. If a local got inebriated (and many of them did given the 24-hour atmosphere of the town) an officer drove him home. Fortunately, little driving was involved, because in the 1940s almost everyone walked downtown.[73]

Until the creation of the Metropolitan Police Department in July 1973, the Las Vegas Police Department and the Clark County Sheriff's Office continually wrestled with jurisdictional issues, some serious, others humorous. On one occasion the Chief of Detectives ordered Claiborne and Joe Bremser to investigate reports of a body hanging from a tree in the desert. They soon located the body. As they approached, the odor hit them. Sickened by the stench, Claiborne decided to let the Sheriff's Office handle the matter. They returned to the car and drove to a gas station where Claiborne called the Sheriff's department. "My name is Herbert Thompson," he announced, "and there is a body hanging in a tree." Roy Trahan, a good friend of Claiborne's, answered the telephone but did not recognize his voice. Trahan asked where he lived and Claiborne responded, "Never mind," and hung up. When they returned to the police station, the chief asked Claiborne, "Okay, what is the deal?" and Claiborne replied, "The Sheriff is taking care of it."[74]

While hardly a super cop, Claiborne occasionally collared a major criminal - although these incidents sometimes contained a touch of humor. In one case, Ben Shaffer escaped from the Wyoming State Prison and stole a car. The police put out an "all points bulletin" for him. A 22 x 14 inch wanted poster hung on the wall of the detective's office, warning officers to approach Shaffer with care because he was believed to be armed and dangerous. It gradually became a joke. When the detectives left for

73 Claiborne interview, 36, 223; Wiener interview, 52.
74 Claiborne interview, 186.

the State Café to get some coffee, they often told the Captain: "We're going out to pick up Shaffer." The Captain would just smile and wave. One day when Bremer and Claiborne decided to go to the Café for coffee, they told the captain: "Well, we're going out and see if we can locate Shaffer." As usual, the Captain waved. They went and had coffee, and as they came walking out, Bremer suddenly stopped. "Jesus Christ! Look, look. Coming down the street. Do you recognize that guy?" he asked Claiborne. It was Shaffer. Claiborne immediately reminded Bremer, "The poster says he's armed, arrest with caution." "I don't think I'm up to a gun battle in the street," Bremer declared and Claiborne agreed, "I'm not either." Claiborne later remembered that they nearly walked away. But finally, he told Bremer, "Well, we have to take him. We'll take him from behind. He'll stop at the intersection at the light. We'll take him from behind. I'll take the left arm and you take the right and we'll do it so fast he won't have a chance." That's exactly what they did. When they took him to the police station in handcuffs, they marched right up to the Captain's desk and matter-of-factly told him, "We'd like you to meet Ben Shaffer." The Captain looked at them incredulously and asked, "How did you do this?" The fast-thinking Claiborne responded, "Hell, we've been working on this case for a week." The disgruntled Shaffer contradicted him: "You Goddamned liar. I've been in town for less than an hour."[75]

Wyoming had posted a reward for Shaffer's capture. In those days, police officers could still accept rewards, and Claiborne and Bremer did. The reward check came to the police station along with a letter of praise from the State of Wyoming Department of Corrections. Chet Morrison told Claiborne and Bremer that it was customary - not mandatory, however - to split reward money with the Police Widows and Orphans Fund. They, of course, wanted to do the right thing, and did. Claiborne recalled feeling good about his decision, because even though he was not yet married, he would appreciate it if his widow received some money if he got killed.

Years later, detective Billy Woofter died and left a wife and several children. Roy Woofter, who later became the District Attorney in Clark

---

75 Claiborne interview, 247-248; Wiener interview, 25.

County, was his nephew. Claiborne went to the funeral and while he was paying his respects to Mrs. Woofter, she wondered aloud what she was going to do for money. She was destitute. A sympathetic Claiborne told her, "I don't know if you know about it, but there's a Widows Fund. I don't know how much is in it, but I will find out first thing in the morning." But Morrison was no longer working for the police department, and just as Claiborne should have suspected, no such fund existed. Inspector Morrison had simply pocketed their money.[76]

Any discussion of early Las Vegas law enforcement would not be complete without the "Blue Room." Built in 1908, the corrugated-iron jail was built on Stewart Avenue between First and Second streets. Interestingly, the women's jail, constructed later, was called the "Pink Room." Often compared to the Black Hole of Calcutta, the Blue Room was a greater deterrent to crime than the police department. It was the only holding tank in the city's police station. Designed for sixteen prisoners, it had one door, one toilet, one wash basin, bunk beds, and no air conditioning. On weekends, when the town was booming, it held eighty to ninety men. It often became so crowded, they could not even sit down. "God, it was awful," Claiborne recalled. "When I was a detective, we used to throw guys in there and we knew they were going to plead guilty within three days. They couldn't stand that damn place. Throwing them in the Blue Room was tantamount to a guilty plea. It took a tough human being to stand even three days. The worst place I've ever seen in my life." When it closed in 1947, the Review-Journal reported, "Historic Blue Room Dies But Mourners Are Few."[77]

In the 1940s, Las Vegas law enforcement had a close relationship with politics, as Claiborne soon came to realize. This was often true in small communities where everyone knew one another, along with their business and social connections. Roy Parrish, who later became Chief of Police in North Las Vegas, was an officer with Claiborne. Claiborne claimed Parrish almost cost him his job. A physically handicapped man was gambling in one of the clubs. Jimmy "Bad Boy" Williams was a local

76 Claiborne interview, 247-248.
77 Claiborne interview, 165-166; Wiener interview, 23; Griffin, Policing Las Vegas, 3, 154;
      Review-Journal, August 19, 1947.

prize fighter and a bully. Williams walked up to the man, took a handful of his chips and gambled them away. When he came back for more, the man called the casino floorman, who told Williams to return the chips. Williams knocked the floorman down. The casino called the police and Parrish and Whitey Bunker responded. Both were big men. They handcuffed Williams, took him to jail, put him in the Blue Room, wrote their report, and were ready to go off shift when Williams started beating the other prisoners. They were all on the top bunk beds trying to get away from him. The jailer opened the door and Parrish walked in. Williams picked Parrish up and threw him against the wall, breaking his leg. The police could not get Parrish out. Claiborne got a call to go to the jail at once. When he arrived, Claiborne saw some unfinished riot sticks, three feet long and made of hickory. He also asked the captain for a sap, a leather bag containing metal BB's. Claiborne planned to occupy Williams while the others got Parrish out. When Claiborne stepped in, Williams had his back to him and was banging a prisoner's head on the bottom bunk. Williams turned around and as Claiborne later told it, "I hit him just like I would hit a fastball." Williams went down and the police dragged Parrish out. The riot stick shattered and Williams started to get up. Claiborne jumped on him and started hitting him in the head with the sap. Pat Clark, a city commissioner and prominent businessman, who owned a car dealership and a beverage company, walked in as he was pounding Williams. Claiborne hit him so hard with the sap that the leather case split and the BB's flew all over the jail. He finally knocked Williams out. As Claiborne started to leave, Clark said, "There's no need for that. You be in the mayor's office in the morning."

Las Vegas Mayor Ernie Cragin and Claiborne met with Clark and Bob Baskin, another commissioner. Cragin said, "Mr. Clark related what he saw at the station yesterday and he's asked that you be fired." Claiborne explained the situation, but Clark still wanted him fired. They took a vote and it was three to one against firing him. Claiborne recalled, "I thought I was real close to getting fired but I found out later that I could have killed the guy and they wouldn't have charged me. I found out years later

78 Claiborne interview, 165-167.

that Williams' mother and Clark were very good friends."[78]

Just as Claiborne experienced a sense of camaraderie with his fellow policemen, he had similar feelings for fellow war veterans. Veterans, he believed, owed a bond of honesty toward each other, and a breach of that bond infuriated him. In 1946, Las Vegas converted Helldorado Village, a complex of western buildings used for an annual celebration, into lodging for war veterans. Many soldiers relocated to the city after the war looking for work in the blossoming resort city. The municipal government provided nearly forty army cots, blankets, shaving material, and towels so the men could be comfortable until they found a job. On one occasion, the Chief of Police sent Claiborne to investigate thefts at the village. Claiborne obtained a roster of the men staying there, studied it and soon realized that only one man was present during all of the burglaries. But the district attorney wanted more evidence for court. Claiborne was incensed. He drove to the Village in his police car, found the man and told him, "Get your gear together. You and I are taking a trip." Claiborne put him in the car, drove north on Highway 95 toward Reno and said, "Get out. Don't you ever come back to Las Vegas. Ever. If I ever find out you're back, I'll kill you." The man believed it. He hitchhiked to Reno, went to the United States Attorney's Office and reported what happened. Several days later, an FBI agent came into the Las Vegas Detective's office with the man's written statement. Claiborne was present with Bill Hanlon, Billy Woofter, and others. The agent handed them the statement, which recited verbatim what Claiborne told the man. It also described the policeman. "My own mother could not have described me as well," Claiborne admitted. The statement even noted, "He had an accent like he comes from Texas, Arkansas or Oklahoma." Claiborne said, "You can't get much closer than that." But the officers all agreed: "Nope, that doesn't sound like any of us." Detective Jack Holliday turned around to Claiborne and asked, "How about you Claiborne?" Claiborne answered, "I don't know him." The agent just grinned and walked out. Of course, he and the others knew it was Claiborne all the time. But nothing more was heard of the matter.[79]

79 Claiborne interview, 246-247; Wiener interview, 25.

As a policeman, Claiborne learned many things that served him well in his later criminal law practice. One lesson was that eyewitnesses to a crime could be unreliable. Lineups and eye witness identification were a larger part of police work then due to the lack of sophisticated techniques now utilized. In effect, this experience provided an education on the vulnerability of such an identification and how best to challenge it on cross examination as an attorney. This was the case when a restaurant operated by two women on Stewart and 2nd street was robbed. They gave the police a description of the robber. As Claiborne and Hanlon responded, they saw a man they thought might be the robber. They picked him up and took him to the restaurant for the women to identify. They did not use line-ups in those days. They removed the man from the car. Hanlon then stayed with him while Claiborne went inside to see if the women could identify him. They came out and claimed, "That's him. The one with the yellow shirt on." It turned out to be Hanlon. Claiborne went back to the car, got in, and told Hanlon to take the man back to where they picked him up. Afterwards, Hanlon pressed his partner, "They couldn't identify him, huh?" "Oh yeah," Claiborne responded, "they identified the robber - they identified you."[80]

Even after Claiborne started practicing law, he still maintained a close personal relationship with his fellow police officers. The force knew and respected him, and for that reason officers also loved to "rawhide" him whenever he came into court representing defendants they arrested. In an incident that could only have happened in a different era than today, Claiborne, early in his law practice, represented a drunk driver who ran into a wall and knocked it down. When he appeared for trial with his client, the arresting officer, "Tex" Skelton, greeted Claiborne with a grin: "Hi Harry. You bring the guy's fine with you?" Skelton told Claiborne his client was drunk and he would certainly lose the case. Claiborne responded, "All right. Tex, you're so damn sure, I'll bet you 20 dollars. That's about all the money you're worth." Skelton jumped at the bet. They both gave their $20 to a fellow cop, Pete Reid, to hold. The trial began and Skelton testified how drunk the driver was at the time, stag-

80 Claiborne interview, 121-122.

gering, etc. Claiborne cross-examined, "Mr. Skelton, I only have one question for you. Do you have a wager on the outcome of this case?" He looked at Claiborne and angrily responded, "You rotten son-of-a-bitch. Even you wouldn't do this." "Answer the question," Claiborne demanded. Skelton reluctantly said, "Yes." "No further questions." Claiborne snapped, "Your Honor, I move to dismiss. You can't find this man guilty on contaminated evidence. The man is betting on the outcome of this case." The judge looked at the beleaguered witness and said, "That's right, Tex. Case dismissed." Claiborne was leaving the courtroom when he heard a scuffle. Pete Reid and another cop were holding Skelton, who was trying to get away from them and was yelling, "Turn me loose. I'll kill that bastard."[81]

In 1946, while waiting to take the Nevada Bar Examination, Claiborne briefly served as a federal administrator. Rent control began in Las Vegas during World War II. After the war, tenants persuaded city officials to preserve rent control as a means of restraining greedy landlords in a boom town where the growing number of resorts and casinos sparked a population explosion. The Office of Price Administration (OPA) director for Las Vegas, Albert S. "Bert" Henderson, a former school superintendent and longtime attorney, was impressed with Claiborne. In 1946, Henderson anticipated that current District Court Judge Clifford A. Jones would resign and that he would be appointed to replace him on the bench. Henderson wondered if Claiborne wanted the OPA's director position. Claiborne responded enthusiastically, "Sure, more money." Jones did resign, and shortly after Henderson's appointment to the bench, the State OPA Director contacted Claiborne. "I have an agreement with Judge Henderson to appoint you as the director in Las Vegas. Would you accept it?" Claiborne was appointed the next day.[82]

Under the applicable law governing the OPA, landlords had to apply to the agency for permission to raise rents. On numerous occasions, Claiborne took action against those who raised the rent without approval, and irate owners continually flooded the office with complaints. They

81 Ibid., 192.
82 Claiborne interview, 38-39.

knew they could not argue with Henderson, but many thought the young Claiborne could be intimidated. Claiborne admitted it was a miserable job, possibly the worst one he ever had in his life. He went home a "wreck" every night. But, the office was being phased out. The state of Nevada requested discontinuation of rent control in August 1950, and Congress approved the action on September 6, 1950.[83] A relieved Claiborne, however, had resigned several years earlier in December 1946, after learning he had passed the Nevada Bar Examination.[84] Claiborne was about to affect his times.

83 Review-Journal, July 1, 1946, September 7, 1950; Claiborne interview, 39-40.
84 Review-Journal, December 26, 1946.

Photo Courtesy of the Claiborne Family

CHAPTER FOUR

A BUDDING LEGAL CAREER

Although Claiborne worked as a policeman and with the OPA, his
ultimate goal was to practice law in Nevada. As stated, the Bar Association required a one-year residency before an applicant could take the
examination. Review courses for the test were not available, so applicants studied on their own or with a friend. Claiborne spent the summer
studying with Milton Keefer, a former FBI agent, who later became a
respected Las Vegas attorney and eventually served as Chairman of the
Nevada Gaming Commission.[85]

Nevada gave the Bar Examination once a year in Reno. Claiborne and
Keefer traveled there and roomed together at the Palace Hotel. The day
before the test, Claiborne had his first encounter with George Franklin.
Franklin approached Claiborne and Keefer in the hotel lobby and told
them: "I got a tip on a question ... on the Bar exam tomorrow, be prepared for it. (You are) going to get a question on the Apex Doctrine."
Off he went. Claiborne looked at Keefer and asked, "What the hell is the
Apex Doctrine?" Keefer confessed, "Hell, I don't know." About that time
Bill Woodburn, a prominent Reno lawyer, walked in. Keefer knew him
and introduced Claiborne. Keefer asked, "Mr. Woodburn, what the hell is
the Apex Doctrine?" He said it was a mining principle and explained it to
them. Back in their room that night, they looked at the list of authorized
potential subjects on the examination. Mining law was not on it. Franklin was clearly playing mind games with them. This marked the beginning of what would become a long and contentious relationship between

85 Review-Journal, January 8, 1999, Obituaries.

Claiborne and Franklin.[86]

George Edward Franklin, Jr. held many political positions, including
Clark County Commissioner, City Attorney for North Las Vegas, City
Attorney for Boulder City, state legislator, and Clark County District
Attorney.[87] He was hardly an admirer of Claiborne, whom he described
years later as "all sizzle and no steak." As Franklin told listeners, Claiborne "was colorful and flamboyant, but not very successful. Do you
ever remember a case he won?"[88]

Claiborne acknowledged that Franklin hated him until the day he died,
and for good reason. Franklin never attended law school, but instead
studied law through the La Salle correspondence school while working
as a guide at Hoover Dam. The two men would later be in the courtroom
together arguing some issue, and Franklin would cite a case as legal
authority for his client's position. When the Judge asked Claiborne what
he thought about it, he would invariably quip: "Well, it must be correct because Mr. Franklin graduated first in his class. Commencement
exercises were held at the post office." The judges always laughed and
Franklin never forgave him.[89] Nor did it help that both were flamboyant
courtroom performers, and ambitious young men competing in what was
still a small town headed for status as a big city.

In 1946, Claiborne passed the state Bar Examination and was admitted by the Nevada Supreme Court on December 12. The Report of the
Board of Bar Examiners dated December 12, 1946 recorded that 17 of the
32 applicants passed, a success rate of 53% , which compares favorably
with recent success rates. Interestingly, in that year, only 5 applicants
took the Bar Examination for the first time, while 25 others were already
members of Bar Associations in other states. So, 78% of those who took
the examination with Claiborne were out-of-state lawyers who had recently moved to Nevada.[90]

86 Gordon Morris Bakken, The Mining Law of 1872: Past, Politics, and Prospects (Albuquerque:
    University of New Mexico Press, 2008), 62-71; Bruce Alverson, "The Limits of Power: Comstock
    Litigation, 1859-1864," Nevada Historical Society Quarterly, Volume 43, No. 1 (2000), 74-99;
    Claiborne interview, 41-42.
87 Martindale-Hubbell, Inc. (Chicago: Reed Reference Publishing Company), Vol. III, 1972, 200B.
88 Sun, July 13, 1986.
89 Claiborne interview, 41; Wiener interview, 79.
90 Nevada State Bar Journal, January 1947, Vol. 12, No. 1, 7-8.

Claiborne was part of a significant post-war population shift triggered by the growth-promoting effects of World War II and its aftermath. Lawyers migrated especially to the West where new hydroelectric dams provided the energy for defense and civilian industries that supported much larger populations. Unlike the 1930s, when the Great Depression forced many low-income and unemployed workers to move to the region, the post-war movement often involved established professionals looking for better opportunities, not just an opportunity. The war's disruption of their lives and money derived from the G. I. Bill gave many a chance to start a new career in the West. The Bar statistics reflect this population relocation, albeit in a small yet well-defined segment of the workplace.

Because Claiborne was a licensed attorney in Arkansas when the Army transferred him to Las Vegas in 1943, the Clark County Bar Association invited him to its meetings. By the time he passed the Bar two years later, he knew all the lawyers in town. The County Bar in the 1940s and 1950s consisted of a small and close knit group of attorneys. Claiborne recalled, "It was the most amazing Bar you ever saw in your whole life. Half the lawyers in town ate breakfast together every morning. The same thing at lunch. No lawyer ever missed the monthly Bar Association meeting. If a lawyer wasn't there, we knew he was sick and half-dead."[91] Contemporaries of Claiborne, such as Ralph Denton, confirm the congeniality of the local Bar. The established lawyers looked after the younger ones and often referred cases to them to help them get started.[92] Partly because of this, Claiborne claimed he never struggled in private practice as a lawyer. He had a good income from the day he opened his office.[93] After he became established, he referred cases out as well.

As was common in county seats across the nation before the days of computerized legal research, all local law firms maintained offices near the courthouse. In Clark County, downtown Las Vegas was the hub of legal activity. The county had the most accessible and complete law library in town and the local lawyers needed to have ready access to it. As a result, attorneys clustered in offices near each other. The local Bar

91 Claiborne interview, 265.
92 Ibid., 37.
93 Ibid., 223.

was almost as informal a group of individuals as the city's police force. In the 1940s and early 1950s, many lawyers ate breakfast together at the Melody Lane Restaurant on Fremont and Third Street. One Friday each month, at noon, the Clark County Bar Association met at the Green Shack Restaurant near the intersection of Fremont Street and Charleston Boulevard on Boulder Highway. These meetings could last seven or eight hours. The restaurant always provided a separate bar for them. The Hickory Wood Barbeque on Fremont Street was a favorite lunch spot for the lawyers, with its inviting barbeque in the front window facing Fremont Street. The attorneys even swam together after lunch on many hot days at the Elwell Hotel on Bridger Street. In fact, Claiborne was in court one day when the opposing attorney failed to appear for the hearing. After a brief discussion, the judge learned that he was still swimming at the Elwell. It was a gathering place in the evening as well after a long day in the courthouse and office.[94]

Before the arrival of television in Las Vegas in 1953, the courts frequently provided entertainment for the community. The more colorful trials, covered daily by the local newspaper reporters, often amused their reading public and spectators alike. The old Clark County Courthouse grounds provided a pleasant setting, surrounded with nearly 40 cottonwood trees towering forty to fifty feet high. The courts often scheduled closing arguments in the evening, regardless of when the testimony finished. Court personnel raised the courtroom's windows. The townspeople came with drinks, blankets, and food and lay on the grass under the trees while they listened to closing arguments. For many people, it was the only show in town. There was no time limit on closing arguments; lawyers could argue as long as they wanted. Claiborne remembered that "we all gave them their money's worth." Arguments would last an hour and a half to two hours for each side. " Those were the days of the courtroom orators, too."[95]

Claiborne's growing reputation in the community soon brought him to the attention of Las Vegas' power elite. Jones, Wiener and Jones was

94 Ibid., 222-223.
95 Ibid., 99.

the most politically connected law firm in post-war Las Vegas. It began in 1938 when Clifford Jones opened his law practice. Louis Wiener and Robert "Bob" Jones later joined him to form a partnership. For years, the firm represented all the major businesses in town, thanks in part to their close connection with U. S. Senator Pat McCarran. Cliff Jones was not only the kingpin of the firm, but McCarran's spokesman in the community.[96] Aware of Jones' ambitions, McCarran once said, "Cliff wants to be the Thatcher Woodburn (the politically powerful law firm in Reno) of Southern Nevada," the political boss.[97] His sister, Florence Lee Jones, was married to Review-Journal managing editor John Cahlan. Besides being the sister-in-law of editor Al Cahlan, she was also a major reporter for the newspaper. But her brother's connection with Nevada's senior senator was paramount. As Claiborne recalled, there was no doubt that McCarran ran the state. There was no middle ground; you were either a McCarranite or you were his enemy, as far as he was concerned. Due to his ties to McCarran, Jones was probably the next most powerful figure in Clark County in 1946, and he was still a young man.[98]

All three major partners in the firm possessed interesting backgrounds and their prominence illustrates the degree of upward mobility that mid-century Las Vegas offered to talented professionals. Clifford Aaron Jones initially came to Las Vegas to work on the construction of Hoover Dam. Admitted to the Nevada Bar in 1938, he immediately became politically active. After serving as the majority leader in the Nevada State Assembly, Jones briefly served as District Court judge in Clark County, then re-signed to run for Lt. Governor, a position he held for eight years. As a co-owner of the Thunderbird Hotel, which opened on the Strip in 1948, he was an enthusiastic supporter of the creation of Paradise and Winchester townships in 1950 and 1951, respectively.

96 Claiborne interview, 74.
97 Ralph Denton, A Liberal Conscience: Ralph Denton, Nevadan, interview by Michael S. Green, (Reno: University of Nevada Oral History Program, 2001), 172.
98 Claiborne, 43; Jerome E. Edwards, Pat McCarran: Political Boss of Nevada (Reno: University of Nevada Press, 1982), 149-161; Michael Ybarra, Washington Gone Crazy: Senator Pat McCarran and the Great American Communist Hunt (Hanover: Steerforth Press, 2004), 661-692; Jack E. Sheehan, The Players: The Men Who Made Las Vegas (Reno: University of Nevada Press, 1997), 23-34.

Louis Wiener moved to Las Vegas from Pennsylvania as a boy. Admitted to the Nevada Bar in 1941, he was one of only 16 attorneys in Las Vegas. Jewish gaming figures such as Moe Dalitz and Benjamin "Bugsy" Siegel would soon transform the former whistlestop into a national resort mecca. In early Las Vegas, anti-Semitism was not the obstacle it was in many other American towns. Wiener, Hank Greenspun, and other Jews would have no trouble launching their professional careers in Southern Nevada's gambling hub. Indeed, Wiener served as the Las Vegas City Attorney before becoming a special prosecutor in the District Attorney's office. His more famous clients included Siegel, Howard Hughes, Kirk Kerkorian and Frank Sinatra during a 55-year legal career that extended into business, land, and media ownership. Wiener typically arrived at his office by 4 a.m. to handle his busy law practice.[99]

Siegel's retention of Wiener as his lawyer graphically illustrates the informal, if not folksy, legal environment of the time. Not to mention the personal relationships developed between lawyers, judges and court staff seen only in small communities. By 1945, Siegel and his group controlled the Western Union race wire service that reported the horse racing results to Las Vegas. They monitored the results and simulated the races themselves for the sport books, which made it more exciting for gamblers who preferred hearing the replays to merely reading the results. One Friday afternoon, Judge George Marshall signed a restraining order at the behest of Siegel's group which prevented the Northern Club from receiving race results. This essentially put them out of business. The Northern Club's owner, Dave Stearns, called Wiener for help. At 5 p.m., Wiener reached Marshall and persuaded him to lift the restraining order, but the judge was going hunting in Ely for two weeks, and was leaving at 3 a.m. Marshall promised Wiener he would sign an order lifting the restraint if Wiener could get the paperwork to him before he left. Wiener returned to his office, typed the petition and order himself, then drove to Marshall's home to get it signed. It was 3 a.m. and Marshall was anxious to leave, but he signed the order. Wiener then called a court clerk who met

99 Review-Journal, February 7, 1996, Obituaries; Clark County School District, "Louis Wiener, Jr.," http://ccsd.net/schools/wiener/index_files/Page326.htm. (Accessed April 30, 2006).

him at the courthouse at 4 a.m., and opened it so Wiener could file Marshall's order in the clerk's office. The Northern Club was back in business before sunrise. Siegel "went bananas," according to Wiener, when he learned what happened, but Wiener's effort and connections impressed him. Within six months, Siegel visited Wiener's office and offered him a $25,000 annual retainer, telling Wiener that he never wanted him representing the opposing side again. Wiener was Siegel's lawyer until the gangster's assassination on June 20, 1947.[100]

Unlike many American cities, Las Vegas mob figures like Siegel mixed openly with the local politicians and police and enjoyed a good relationship with the town's legal and judicial communities – a fact that antagonized federal judges and law enforcement officials from other states who considered Nevada a rogue state. Most Las Vegans who knew Siegel liked him, according to Paul Ralli. He freely mingled with businessmen and other residents. In the code of the frontier town, no questions were asked and people accepted one another at face value. As Ralli recalled, Siegel followed the local practice of taking a nap from nine to 11 p.m., to be ready for an active night life that often lasted until dawn, indulging in regular steam baths and massages, followed by 15-minute periods of calisthenics, Ralli remembered.[101]

The firm's third partner, Robert (Bob) E. Jones, was an equally capable attorney. One barometer of the power of the law firm's founders was their successful effort to oust Clark County District Attorney Gray Gubler. Wiener had experienced difficulties with Gubler and went to Cliff Jones about the problem. Jones vowed to "get rid" of Gubler. They could not find anyone to run against the incumbent in the next election, so Cliff persuaded his partner, Bob Jones, to enter the race. Jones understood that he could quit the office any time he wanted after the election, but they wanted to replace Gubler. And they did. On election day, voters selected Jones.[102]

The change in leadership hardly affected Claiborne. Gubler had

100 Wiener interview, 42-43.
101 Ralli, Nevada Lawyer: A Story of Life and Love in Las Vegas, 280-281.
102 Claiborne interview, 43. Claiborne never knew the reason for the dispute between Wiener and Gubler. "I inquired of a lot of people and I never did find out.."

promised Claiborne earlier that he would hire him as his Deputy District
Attorney once he passed the Bar Examination. But after Bob Jones was
elected, Cliff Jones walked into Claiborne's office at the OPA, put both of
his long legs on the desk, leaned back in the chair and said, "You're Bob's
new deputy," to which Claiborne responded, "How did this come about,
Cliff? I haven't heard anything about this. I don't know Bob Jones."
Cliff Jones calmly reassured Claiborne, "You don't have to know him.
He will be calling you. I gotta go." He took his feet off the desk, got up,
and out the door he went. The next day, Bob Jones called Claiborne and
urged him to become his deputy. Claiborne never told him that Gubler
had made him the same offer. Once Claiborne learned that he passed the
Bar Examination, he called Jones, accepted the position, and was sworn
in as Deputy District Attorney on January 5, 1947. The Clark County
District Attorney's office now consisted only of Bob Jones and Harry Claiborne. As Claiborne later quipped, he immediately worked his way up to
Chief Deputy.[103] Claiborne's working relationship with one of Las Vegas'
brightest and well-connected attorneys would give the young lawyer valuable experience that would benefit him in his later career.

Although his office consisted of only two attorneys in 1947, the Clark
County District Attorney was a powerful individual because his office
represented all of the growing county's legal interests. Between the
two of them, Jones and Claiborne had little or no practical training in
municipal legal affairs and no outside assistance or consultants. They
rendered legal advice on a broad range of subjects that included bonding
and financing, municipal operations, as well as represented the State of
Nevada in all criminal matters ranging from routine misdemeanors to
major felonies.

Claiborne worked in the District Attorney's office from January 5, 1947
to June 1, 1948. During this time, he began developing the trial skills
and techniques that eventually made him one of the most effective trial
lawyers in Nevada's history. Hank Greenspun, publisher of the Las Vegas
Sun and himself a lawyer, recalled that Claiborne lost only one out of the
90 felony cases he tried while in the District Attorney's office. Greenspun

103 Ibid., 43-44.

regarded Claiborne as the greatest single deterrent to crime in Southern Nevada because local criminals actually feared him.[104]   After only five days in the office, Claiborne made the local newspaper for handling nine court matters in two hours. But in later years he laughingly dismissed the article because the court appearances were merely arraignments and calendar calls. He regarded them as nothing of significance - items that demonstrated the lack of newsworthy events in the community and the newspaper reporter's lackadaisical approach in selecting substantive matters to report.[105]

However, some of his cases were significant even by today's standards. In February 1947, one month after joining the Bar, Claiborne began the trial of Frederick Teeter. This case was the first time in Nevada history that the state Supreme Court reversed a criminal conviction based on prosecutorial misconduct for improper remarks to the jury. After Teeter and his partner robbed a jewelry store, they argued, and Teeter pulled out his gun and shot his companion, who died two days later. During closing arguments, defense attorney John Bonner declared, "We have fought a war. A lot of people had given up their lives and shed their blood so that democracy and the system of justice would prevail forever." Claiborne responded that he agreed, but "I know something about service in World War II. I have knowledge of the reasons that we fought the war and it just so happens that one of the reasons we fought the war was to rid the world of international criminals. I am just bringing that doctrine down to Las Vegas to get rid of Mr. Teeter." The Supreme Court determined those remarks were improper and reversed the conviction. Because it was a landmark decision that limited a prosecutor's arguments, prosecuting attorneys needled Claiborne for the rest of his career. Years later, Claiborne chuckled when he recalled how they taunted him with such comments as: "Now, here's State versus Teeter, you remember that (case), don't you, Mr. Claiborne?"[106]

Entrenched business and political interests exist in communities of all sizes, and post-war Las Vegas was no exception. The gaming fraternity in

104 Sun, September 3, 1964.
105 Review-Journal, January 10, 1947; Claiborne interview, 44.
106 Teeter v. State of Nevada, 65 Nev. 584 (1948); Claiborne interview, 46-48.

the late 1940s was already very powerful and, when necessary, could exert tremendous pressure to promote its interests. Claiborne learned this first hand after only three months on the job when a high profile murder occurred at the Las Vegas Club.

Lester Ben "Benny" Binion moved to Las Vegas under forced circumstances in 1946. Born and reared in Texas, his family were farmers, stock raisers, and horse traders near El Paso, Dallas, and Sweetwater. Binion developed an interest in gambling in his early teens by traveling to farmtown "trade days" where card and number games were popular. Binion gradually established himself as an illegal gaming operator in the Dallas area until a newly elected District Attorney forced him out of town in 1946. Claiborne heard rumors that Binion had two suitcases full of money when he arrived in Las Vegas, but he was sure it was more than just two. Binion immediately purchased a half interest in the Las Vegas Club with J. Kell Houssels and eventually became one of the more colorful and important casino owners in Las Vegas history.[107]

As Claiborne noted, Houssels was the major businessman in Las Vegas at the time and a loyal supporter of Mayor Ernie Cragin and most of the city commission. In fact, some reformers such as the Las Vegas Taxpayer's Association president Charles Pipkin spoke of a "Houssels Machine" at City Hall during the late 1940s. Houssels owned a large part of the El Cortez Hotel and operated the largest taxi cab company in town, the Grey Line, as well as many other businesses. Eventually, he co-owned and operated the Tropicana Hotel. He later sold a one-half interest in the Las Vegas Club to Binion because he was too busy to monitor his businesses and wanted someone with experience to run the casino. It was a wise choice.[108]

Binion replaced the original Las Vegas workers with his own people. Wearing cowboy boots and speaking with Texas accents, the "Texans took over" the Las Vegas Club. Having fought violently with other Dallas operators, Binion even brought his personal body guard to town.

107 Claiborne interview, 52; Lester Ben "Benny" Binion, Some Recollections of a Texas and Las Vegas Gaming Operator, interview by Mary Ellen Glass (Reno: University of Nevada Oral History Program, (1976), iii-iv.
108 Claiborne interview, 52; Moehring, Resort City, 71.

Claiborne described Binion's guard as "a cold blooded, vicious, son-of-a-bitch. He strutted around like a peacock all of the time wearing two silver forty-five caliber pistols in his holster and always dressed in black." His name was Clifford Duane Helm, and Binion depended on him for protection.[109]

But not all of Binion's roughnecks got along. It was a recipe for disaster. Frank Ferroni, Jr., a.k.a. John Beasley, had a violent past. Ferroni and Helm both worked at the Las Vegas Club. For years, they worked and traveled together. On orders from Binion, Helm told Ferroni to leave Las Vegas. On March 25, 1947, Helm and Ferroni met in the boiler room at the rear of the casino and a struggle ensued. As Binion later described it, Helm eventually knocked Ferroni down and shot him in the head, killing him. In Helm's mind, according to Binion, he had to kill Ferroni sometime "since this (was) the most dangerous son of a gun in the world. So he just went ahead and done a good job of it."[110]

Deputy District Attorney Claiborne received an urgent call at home from detective Pete Reid. He explained, "Harry, I'm sitting here with Bill Hanlon. We have a problem. The bodyguard at the Vegas Club shot and killed a man and Binion and Houssels will not let us go in and investigate it. We don't know what to do." Claiborne rushed to the club and encountered Binion and Houssels. The body was still lying in the hallway. Claiborne explained, "Mr. Houssels, I understand somebody's been shot in your club and that his body is back here somewhere. The detectives are here to investigate and I understand you won't let them back there." Houssels told him, "Harry, we take care of our own. That's the way it's always been and that's the way it will be." But Claiborne challenged the notion of the county's jurisdiction ending at the casino's door and said, "I don't know anything about that. I haven't lived here long enough to know about that. It may be the way it used to be, it will not be the way it is now, believe me. Times have changed, Mr. Houssels, and you have to change with it." But Houssels was unmoved and insisted, "They can't go back." Claiborne turned to Detective Reid and said, "Call Captain Pat-

109 Claiborne interview, 52-53.
110 Binion interview, 27.

terson. Get me two uniformed policeman down here." Within minutes, they arrived. Claiborne said, "Go wake up Jake Von Tobel (owner of a hardware store). Check the front doors, I don't know how many chains you'll need, but check on the front doors and go down and get as many chains as you need and as many padlocks as you need. When you get back, I want everybody out of here and I want the doors padlocked." Houssels could not believe that Claiborne would close the casino, telling him "You don't dare." "Wait and see," was Claiborne's reply.

Forty-five minutes later the police arrived with the chains and locks. Claiborne then gave them orders, "All right, get everybody out. That includes you and Mr. Binion, that includes everybody." Houssels left and the police began their investigation, which revealed that although a pocket knife with a two inch long blade was found on the boiler room floor, no weapon was found on Ferroni. Helm, however, had a knife in his possession. Also, Helm's necktie and shirt were cut.[111] The police identified a witness who was in the boiler room and saw most of the fight. Claiborne knew his testimony would be critical in prosecuting Helm.

The young Deputy District Attorney waited at the detective bureau and eventually the detectives led Helm into the room. They had the knife that was found in the boiler room in a plastic bag. Claiborne asked what happened and Helm responded, "He attacked me with a knife and I tried to beat him off me and I couldn't. I finally had to shoot him. He cut my tie." Claiborne asked, "Do you have a knife, Cliff?" "Yes," Helm replied. He handed his knife to Claiborne who dropped it in another plastic bag. Helm asked, "Why did you take my knife?" Claiborne said, "I think you cut your own tie. I think you held your tie and cut it with your own knife. If a guy swiped at you and stabbed at you with a knife, it wouldn't cut your tie in that manner, I don't think." Helm scoffed at Claiborne's reasoning.

The District Attorney's office filed first degree murder charges against Helm. According to Claiborne, Houssels and Binion used their political influence to try to get the charges dismissed, but to no avail. Helm had a stable of the most prominent attorneys in the county represent-

111 Helm v. State of Nevada, 66 Nev 286 (1949).

ing him, including future District Court judge Ryland G. Taylor, former District Attorney Gray Gubler, longtime attorney Leo McNamee, and FBI agent turned attorney G. William Coulthard. The defense team received $25,000, according to rumors, a significant fee in 1947. Houssels retained the lawyers on behalf of Helm. Bob Jones, Louis Wiener, and Claiborne prosecuted the case.[112]

At the hearing to set bail for Helm, Judge Henderson expressed doubt that the state could prove premeditated murder and said if the case were submitted to the jury "today, I do not believe they would find first degree murder." Claiborne argued that Helm deliberately chose the boiler room for the assault "because it is the noisiest part of the building and shots are least likely to be heard from there." This fact, Claiborne asserted, showed that the killing was premeditated. The judge released Helm on $25,000 bail, which Binion and Houssels had posted.[113]

The jury trial began on September 15, 1947. Helm testified that he met Ferroni in the boiler room at the rear of the casino and an argument began. As a special police officer for the casino, Helm carried a gun. Helm further testified that Ferroni attacked him with a knife and, during the ensuing struggle, he shot the victim at least once. As the fight continued, Helm struck Ferroni over the head with the gun and knocked him to his knees. Another special officer for the casino testified that he heard two or three shots, went through the hallway from the casino to the boiler room, opened the door, and met Ferroni coming through the door toward the casino. Helm ordered him to stop Ferroni, which the officer did, holding Ferroni in the hallway. He was later assisted by one or more other men, but Ferroni still moved toward the casino. Another witness testified that Ferroni pleaded with the officers, "Don't let him kill me." Another witness, Fred Merrill, yelled to Helm, "Don't, Cliff." Helm then shot Ferroni in the back of the neck, but Ferroni still moved down the hallway toward the casino. Helm fired two more shots, one through the aorta, and Ferroni fell to the floor dead.[114]

Claiborne believed the defense never knew about the eyewitness in the

112 Binion interview, 28.
113 Review-Journal, April, 17, 1947.
114 Helm v. State, at 296.

boiler room, Henry Moody. Moody testified that Ferroni had his hands
in his pockets when Moody heard the first shots. Since Helm claimed
self defense, this surprise testimony drastically hurt his case. Next, FBI
chemist Roy H. McDaniel compared cloth fragments from Helm's tie and
shirt with Helm's knife and found fibers on the knife that matched the tie
and shirt. Although Helm claimed that Ferroni attacked him, Ferroni's
knife showed no similar fibers. McDaniel concluded that Helm's knife
cut his own shirt and tie. No evidence linked Ferroni's knife to the clothing.[115]

The jury convicted Helm of first degree murder, and fixed the punishment at life imprisonment. It came within one vote of recommending
the death penalty. The girlfriend of South City Bar owner Sid Martin was
on the prosecution's challenge list of jurors. But when jury selection got
down to the State's last challenge, there was a potential juror who worried the prosecutors more. So, they excused him and accepted her. She
was the holdout juror.[116]

A juror later told Claiborne that the knife and fibers convinced them
of Helm's guilt. Another juror disliked Helm's demeanor during the trial
because he came to court every morning in a new Western suit, and fancy
cowboy boots, and looked at the jury as if they were dirt under his feet.
Despite that impression, he also confirmed that the jury convicted Helm
because he used his own knife to cut his tie and then tried to claim self
defense.[117]

Claiborne recalled that the political heat on him was intense and un-
relenting - a clear indication of the influence that powerful casino operators like Binion and Houssels could wield in the "casino city." Claiborne
received threatening telephone calls. Detectives Bill Hanlon and Pete
Reid told him that they feared for his life.[118] During the trial, the Review-

115 Review-Journal, September 15, to October 3, 1947.
116 Wiener interview, 10; In Nevada, as soon as women were accorded the right to vote in 1914, their
    right to serve on juries was automatically established. Burnita Shelton Matthews, "The Woman
    Juror," Women Lawyers' Journal, XV, No. 2 (April 1927); In 1916, Helen Stewart became the first
    woman to sit on a jury in Clark County. A.D. Hopkin and K.J. Evans, eds., The First 100: Portraits of
    the Men and Women Who Shaped Las Vegas, 12-14.
117 Claiborne interview, 52-55; Review-Journal, October 3, 1947; Helm v. State, at 290 (1949); Arthur
    Bernard, Nevada Mine Inspector and Prison Warden, interview by Victoria Ford (Reno: University of
    Nevada Oral History Program, 2003), 200.
118 Claiborne interview, 57.

Journal printed a story that a high official in Texas contacted the Nevada governor's office trying to intervene on Helm's behalf. The Texas official reportedly acted on behalf of a politically powerful figure who was "enlisted by local (Texas) residents who are quite well known." Binion later admitted that it was probably him, because "I had a lot of very high, influential friends in Texas."[119]

Even after the conviction, the pressure continued. Virgil Wedge, later a named partner in the Woodburn firm in Reno, handled Helm's appeal. By now, Claiborne was out of the DA's office, but Wedge nevertheless asked Claiborne for an affidavit in support of Helm's appeal. Claiborne stubbornly refused. McCarran himself called Claiborne and asked for the affidavit and Claiborne again refused. McCarran also requested a similar affidavit from Clark County District Attorney Roger D. Foley who had succeeded Bob Jones, but he also refused. Claiborne never knew if it was a coincidence, but two or three months after McCarran's requests were turned down, the IRS audited both Claiborne and Foley.[120]

Arthur Bernard, former Nevada State Prison warden, provided a different perspective on Helm's prosecution. He served as warden while Helm was in prison and took a liking to him. Helm was already a prominent inmate and, with Bernard's approval, he practically had his choice of activities outside the prison. Bernard put him in charge of the horse stables, where he rode the warden's horses and even took Bernard's wife and friends riding.

E. C. "Ted" Cupid was the first person to head Nevada's newly-created position within the jurisdiction of the Parole Board to supervise convicted criminals who were placed on probation. A former investigator with the Clark County District Attorney's office, he worked with Claiborne. Although Claiborne claimed that Governor Vail Pittman appointed Cupid to the position based on his recommendation, Bernard claimed credit for Cupid's appointment. According to Bernard, because Cupid "knew how he got the job," he often asked Bernard's advice regarding certain supervision matters. During business discussions between Bernard and Cupid,

119 Binion interview, 29-30.
120 Claiborne interview, 75.

Helm's name occasionally came up. When that happened, according to
Bernard, Cupid would get a funny look on his face and change the subject. One day Bernard confronted Cupid, who confessed to having spent
"many a sleepless night" wondering if he should tell Bernard what he
knew about Helm's prosecution. Cupid claimed that his brother-in-law,
a Las Vegas policeman at the time, helped furnish a safe house where the
prosecution held a "very secretive" meeting. At the meeting, an assistant
prosecutor stripped some threads from Helm's tie, put them on Helm's
knife, and then sent it to the FBI. Claiborne and Wiener were the assistant prosecutors. Based on that information, Bernard did some investigating of his own. He spoke with Cupid's brother-in-law and obtained a
written statement to that effect. He even interviewed certain jurors, and
concluded that the jury convicted Helm upon the belief that Helm used
his own knife to cut his tie and then tried to make it look like self defense.
In the jury's view, the necktie and shirt fibers in Helm's knife supported
this conclusion.[121]

The Chief Justice of the Supreme Court, the Governor and the Attorney
General comprised the Pardons Board. Bernard presented the results of
his investigation to Chief Justice Milton B. Badt, who was skeptical and,
despite assuring Bernard that the Board would give his petition serious
consideration, delayed the matter. Helm died in prison before Badt acted
on the petition. Badt then simply dropped the matter.[122]

Most of Claiborne's assignments in the District Attorney's office did not
involve such powerful figures. Many were ordinary people whose cases
reflected the smallness of the office at the time and the legal system's lack
of sophistication. In one instance, Claiborne had to transport a prisoner
named William Crosby from Carson City to Las Vegas. Tall, scholarly,
and polite, Crosby was one of the most courteous prisoners in the Clark
County jail, according to District Attorney Jones. But he escaped from
the jail and later the prison hospital in Carson City. Deputy District Attorney Claiborne and detective Al Kennedy went up to the capital, got the
prisoner, and drove him from Carson City to Las Vegas. The use of an

121 Claiborne interview, 85; Bernard, 200.
122 Bernard, 195-205.

attorney and a detective to transport a prisoner was common in post-war Nevada when small staffs and meager budgets justified such procedures. When they arrived in Beatty, Claiborne and Kennedy decided to eat. Kennedy told Claiborne to stay in the car and guard Crosby. But Claiborne dismissed the idea, telling Kennedy to "take the shackles off him and we'll go in and eat." Kennedy argued, "This son-of-a-bitch has escaped two jails, Harry." "What do you want to do? Go over and lock him up in jail so we can go in and eat?" Claiborne asked. Kennedy retorted, "No, you and I will go in and eat. One of us will stay with him while the other is eating. We'll bring him something. I ain't taking his shackles off of him." But Claiborne persisted, "Aw, come on. I'd hate to admit that the two of us will let this guy get away." So they took the shackles off. They all went in and Crosby was well behaved. They ate, came out, and all of a sudden Crosby pushed Kennedy into Claiborne and they both staggered back. Off ran Crosby. When the prisoner looked back to check their whereabouts, he ran right into a parked car. Before Crosby got off the ground, they were on him. The rest of the trip was uneventful, but the episode speaks volumes about the primitive state of Nevada's criminal justice system at the time.[123]

The county's legal issues were essentially the same as those faced by the local city governments, with which Claiborne also had experience. In January 1948, attorney George Rudiak resigned as North Las Vegas City Attorney. By coincidence, Rudiak and Claiborne were stationed together in the Army at Santa Ana. Claiborne remembered, "When I was First Sergeant, he was in my company. Every time he went in the office to see the captain, I'd tell him he could not see the captain. I'd be sitting with my feet propped up on the desk, smoking a cigar, and I always asked him, 'What's your name." According to Claiborne, Rudiak always claimed that Claiborne could never pronounce his name, but called him "Ruduco."[124]

The North Las Vegas mayor asked Clark County District Attorney Bob Jones if someone in his office could work for the city on a temporary basis. Although the person could not draw a salary from North Las Vegas

123 Claiborne interview, 62-64; Review-Journal, November 28, 1947.
124 Claiborne interview, 63.

and Clark County at the same time, Jones said he would talk to Claiborne, who agreed to help. Through the County, he had already gained some experience in municipal matters. "I had drawn the first County bond issue for the hospital. I did all the legal work on that. As a Chief Deputy, I did nearly all the civil work for the county. So it was nothing new."[125] After Claiborne worked in North Las Vegas for some time, Jones realized that he must be sworn into office as City Attorney. Claiborne did and so while he held two government positions at the same time, he received only one paycheck.[126] Such was the fluid, almost casual nature of governmental administration in Las Vegas at the time.

Claiborne estimated that North Las Vegas's population in 1948 was about 2,000, so "they didn't have a hell of a lot of business."[127] For the most part, he prosecuted misdemeanors and wrote opinions for the city council.[128] In the 1940s, the position demanded relatively little knowledge or skill. "I sat with them during the meetings and they referred their municipal questions to me. Most of the opinions were off the cuff. Only about half of the time did I know what I was talking about. But I found out early down there, it's not what you know that counts, it's how you say it." In April 1951, the newly-elected city fathers "canned all of us" during what the newspaper described as a "shake up among employees."[129]

North Las Vegas was only the first of three Southern Nevada cities that Claiborne eventually represented. He became Henderson City Attorney in January 1955 at the request of Mayor James French, who had just taken office. After initially declining the job offer due to time concerns, Claiborne agreed to fill the position for six months, but stayed for French's entire term as mayor. After winning a bitter political battle to force him to resign, Claiborne quit as Henderson City Attorney on June 22, 1959. Politics, Claiborne explained, had nothing to do with it.[130] French was a physician and first met Claiborne in connection with a medical mal-

125 Claiborne interview, 62.
126 Review-Journal, January 15, 1948.
127 Claiborne interview, 62.
128 Ibid., 164.
129 Claiborne interview, 164; Review Journal, May 15, 1951.
130 Review-Journal, June 23, 1959.

practice lawsuit. A patient had cut his finger and gangrene forced an amputation. The nurse prepared the wrong finger for surgery and French amputated it. When the patient recovered and saw the mistake, he immediately told the nurse. French still had to remove the infected finger. The patient sued and French hired Claiborne to defend him. That started a relationship that lasted not only through French's single term as Mayor of Henderson, but also for a time after French became a councilman in Boulder City.[131]

Claiborne's position as City Attorney of Boulder City in 1965 was short lived. He resigned after just three weeks, officially blaming time restraints and the distance from his office in Las Vegas. Claiming that he initially believed that he could adjust his time to serve the City and not disrupt his practice, he was unable to do so. While Claiborne told the mayor that he was overwhelmed by the time-consuming legal work required involving water and power contracts,[132] he quit because French and Councilmen Bob Broadbent, then a pharmacist and later a major local power as a county manager and airport manager, fought over everything. Claiborne recalled it was one of the worst jobs he ever held. He told French that life was "too precious" to tolerate that situation. His predecessor, George Franklin, had faced similar problems with the "split council," and he too had left.[133] But this was a common problem in the budding metropolitan area at the time. City governments tended to promote from within and political influence often divided the council; the subsequent political infighting eventually forced resignations. In the 1950s, the City of Las Vegas went through six city managers in less than a decade, and other municipal offices were filled even more frequently than that. Mavericks and strong personalities were not limited to the legal profession.

Opportunities and ambition result in productive competition among men. Strong economic factors in Nevada provided unlimited potential for a unique group of newcomers to the area. The men returning from the war brought life experiences far beyond their years, and coupled with

131 Claiborne interview, 189-190; Review-Journal, January 5, 1955.
132 Claiborne interview, 269.
133 Claiborne interview, 190-191; Review-Journal, October 10, 1965.

the never-before available educational opportunities offered by the GI
Bill, a group of community leaders emerged who were far different than
the country had ever produced before. Educated, self-confident, and
self-sufficient, they applied themselves to the economic opportunities in
Nevada to create the momentum for growth in the state that lasted for
several decades. Population in Nevada increased from 160,000 in 1950
to 800,500 in 1980, the end of the Claiborne "era," reflecting growth
rates from the preceding decade of 78%, 71%, and 63%.[134]

134 Political History, 67.

Photo Courtesy of the Claiborne Family

CHAPTER FIVE

THE CALL OF POLITICS

Claiborne left the District Attorney's office on June 1, 1948, to run for the state Assembly. Cliff Jones had urged him to do it, and he jumped at the opportunity. Because state law prohibited any candidate from running for office while holding an appointed position such as Deputy District Attorney, Claiborne resigned. Claiborne later noted, a political "request" from Jones, then Nevada's Lieutenant Governor, was basically an order that could not be ignored. Nonetheless, he "was very, very interested in politics. Always was. I had the fever, it was in my blood," he admitted.[135] After a hectic campaign, Claiborne won the election for Assembly District 2. Although he garnered only 15% of the total votes cast in a field of nine candidates, he received 152 more votes than the second place candidate, Assemblyman Harley Harmon, an insurance agent, lifelong Las Vegan, and the son of a former district attorney and gubernatorial candidate.[136]

In 1948, soon after his election, rumors began circulating in the media that Claiborne planned to run for Speaker of the Assembly in his first legislative session. Three weeks after the election, the Clark County Bar Association unanimously endorsed him for the Speaker's post at its regularly scheduled meeting at the Nevada Biltmore Hotel.[137] Claiborne's chances were enhanced by a telephone call he received from a Reno Assemblyman who wanted to oust current speaker Peter Burke. Even though a group of Assemblymen asked Claiborne to accept the posi-

135 Review-Journal, June 1, 1948; Claiborne interview, 83, 141.
136 Review-Journal, November 3, 1948.
137 Ibid., November 28, 1948.

tion, he rejected their overtures. He later explained that as a freshman legislator, he did not fully understand how the process functioned, and therefore he felt that he was not qualified for the job. While his promoters persisted a while longer, Claiborne ultimately halted their campaign. However, once the session began, he accepted a leadership role, agreeing to serve as Chairman of the Judiciary Committee and floor leader for the Democrats.[138]

The sales tax bill was a major issue in the 1949 legislature. By 1948, more people were moving to the Las Vegas area and neither the schools nor other governmental services could keep up with the growth. K. O. Knudson, an educator who ultimately organized the local junior high school system and advocacy groups for the blind and the retired, originally proposed the idea of a state sales tax to finance the construction and improvement of Nevada's schools. Without the tax, Knudson claimed, education would be a worsening problem in Clark County. Claiborne supported the idea, and between November 1948 and January 1949, he frequently met with Knudson and Harley Harmon to strategize about how to propose the tax that everyone knew the state's gaming community and big property owners would oppose. In a speech before the Las Vegas Optimists Club in January, Claiborne described the most pressing problem for the legislators as raising additional revenue to finance the expansion of state and local services in a post-war era fraught with continued population growth in Reno and particularly in Las Vegas.[139]

At that time, Nevada lured potential new business and residents by boasting that it had "no sales tax, no income tax." As the Democratic leader in the assembly, Claiborne claimed to have pulled every "shenanigan" he could to get the votes to pass the sales tax law in the Assembly, but failed. To his disappointment, the Assembly voted to table the sales tax bill. Claiborne was the only Clark County delegate to vote against side-stepping the issue. The sales tax was important, but more important to Claiborne was that legislators have the "intestinal fortitude and courage to face the issues," and not avoid them. Claiborne told the

138 Claiborne interview, 85, 87.
139 Review-Journal, January 11, 1949; Claiborne interview, 87-88.

press that legislators must be capable of meeting the issues squarely.[140] Only days later, in what was described "as slick a maneuver as has been seen this session," Claiborne removed the sales tax bill from the "table" and referred it to the joint Ways and Means and Taxation Committee. With only seven days left in the session, leaders in both houses admitted they could not agree on a definite financial program.[141] When it became evident that the sales tax would fail, White Pine County Assemblyman Jim Johnson proposed a graduated tax upon the privilege of engaging in business in Nevada, and introduced it jointly with Claiborne. The sponsors estimated it would generate in excess of $2 million annually, but Nevada's cautious lawmakers were not yet willing to raise taxes. Johnson paid the price for his bold foresightedness, suffering a defeat in his next election for his efforts.[142]

Claiborne returned home one weekend and received a telephone call from the editor of the Review-Journal, Al Cahlan, who was a political ally of McCarran, an influential businessman, and himself a former assemblyman. He did not ask Claiborne to come down to his office, but ordered him down. At the meeting, Cahlan was furious, "Have you lost your Goddamn mind? You are gonna tax business, what the hell is the matter with you?" Claiborne took a beating in the newspapers. One editorial even suggested that the casino owners had gotten to him and Claiborne was trying to avoid taxing casinos.[143]

A wary Governor Vail Pittman, himself a supporter of the state's casino industry, took no position on the sales tax. Upon reflection, Claiborne believed that Pittman's support would have passed the bill. Nevertheless, Claiborne stubbornly persisted, simply because he saw no other way to financially support the state's growth.[144] However, few legislators were willing to risk their political future on the issue and the sales tax bill died.[145]

Claiborne's efforts were premature. In 1949, the anti-tax mentality

140 Review-Journal, March 2, 1949.
141 Review-Journal, March 10, 1949.
142 Claiborne interview, 87-88; Review-Journal, March 3, 1949.
143 Claiborne interview, 88-89.
144 Review-Journal, April, 27, 1949.
145 Claiborne interview, 87-89, 140-41.

was too ingrained in Nevada's electorate and legislative leaders. Since the 1930s, the anti-tax proponents had promoted Nevada as "one sound state," and as the "cyclone cellar for the tax weary." Despite studies and polls from as early as 1951 that supported increased taxation for school improvements, the legislature postponed passage of a sales tax until 1955, when the need for more schools to educate Nevada's baby boomers gave Assemblywoman Maude Frazier and other school advocates enough leverage to push a tax bill through. Even then, a group calling itself "Volunteers in Politics" circulated a petition for a referendum on the sales tax law just weeks after its passage, asking voters to affirm or reject the new law. Despite questions about the legality of the petition itself, opponents agreed not to challenge it in court, but allowed the voters to express their opinion. Thanks to the vigorous support of Governor Charles Russell, who argued that the revenues were necessary to upgrade the state's notoriously weak schools, nearly 70% of the voters approved the sales tax.[146]

To be sure, the legislature was not an entirely satisfying experience for Claiborne. Although voted "the most handsome and most forceful member of the Assembly" by the legislative staff, who conducted a poll during the opening days of the session,[147] Claiborne was not pleased with the legislature's accomplishments during the session. On April 26, 1949, he spoke at a Lions Club dinner in Henderson and criticized the caliber of the state lawmakers. If Clark County voters were smart, he told his audience, they would not return a single lawmaker in the next biennium. Claiborne felt that most legislators were "not big enough for the job." They were too beholden to special interests such as labor, livestock raisers, and mining to represent the people properly. Claiborne saw a financial crisis looming and predicted that unless new sources of revenue could be identified, the state would be bankrupt before the next session. He observed that Nevada's motto of "One Sound State" was an "absolutely false statement" and that even the Reno newspapers had dropped it as their slogan. Nuisance or vice taxes were no panacea, because revenues derived from such items as cigarettes, liquor, and gambling fluctuated

146 Mary Ellen Glass, Nevada's Turbulent '50s: Decade of Political and Economic Change (Reno: University of Nevada Press, 1989), 50, 57-60.
147 Review-Journal, January 21, 1949.

too much and did not provide a stable and constant tax base. Relying on these taxes, he insisted, was not sound fiscal policy. Only the enactment of a sales tax could provide enough revenue to finance school construction and the expansion of other services in the growing state. Claiborne also rejected an income tax, because it would take six years to amend the constitution to permit an income tax and there would be no state government left by that time, he told them. Still, he conceded that this was not the least productive legislature in Nevada history because others actually had worse records.[148]

Claiborne's time in the Assembly fed his growing political aspirations. Rather than seeking re-election, he wanted to serve in the state senate and then run for Attorney General.[149] Ultimately, he had his eye on the Governor's mansion.[150] On May 5, 1950, he formally announced his candidacy for Clark County's state senate seat on the Democratic ticket. B. Mahlon Brown was his opponent.[151]

In opposing Brown, Claiborne faced a formidable challenge. Brown moved to Las Vegas at age nine. His grandfather, Dr. Halle Hewetson, came to Las Vegas with the construction of the railroad in 1904 and was the town's first doctor. His mother managed the Clark County Sheriff's office from 1935 to the early 1950s. Brown was a member of Las Vegas High School's first football team and an all-state selection in his final year. He served as student body president in his senior year. He was a home grown boy with deep ties to the community.[152]

But Brown also faced a formidable challenge in the ever-resourceful Claiborne. During the 1950 campaign, Claiborne heard a little ditty on Los Angeles radio advertising household tips. The announcer called himself "Helpful Harry and his Helpful Household Hints." He sang little household suggestions. Claiborne thought it would be a great campaign gimmick and ultimately secured the rights to use the tune. He con-

148 Review-Journal, April 27, 1949; Although prohibited by statute in 1949, the Nevada Constitution was not amended to prohibit a state personal income tax until 1988. Political History of Nevada, 321.
149 Claiborne interview, 141-42.
150 Claiborne interview, 83.
151 Review-Journal, May 5, 1950, 2, September 1, 1950.
152 Nevada Senate Concurrent resolution memorializing former Senator B. Mahlon Brown, November 22, 1995; Nevada Lawyer, June 2003, 22-24; Russell McDonald Collection.

tacted KLAS, one of the three radio stations in Las Vegas at the time, and bought air time to run the song. Fifteen times a day listeners would hear the announcer begin with, "Helpful Harry and His Helpful Household Hints," the song would begin, and soon Claiborne's voice would break in and say, "Vote for Harry Claiborne for your Senator." Everyone thought Claiborne was singing the ditty. Years after the campaign, Claiborne recalled, he still got calls from local residents seeking advice about how to get rid of grape juice stains from a sweater and other household hints.[153]

Claiborne attacked Dick King, publisher of The North Las Vegas News, who penned an editorial critical of him. Claiborne referred to King's newspaper in his radio broadcast as "one of those yellow sheets, throw away papers." Claiborne later conceded "I probably had a few drinks that night on my way out to the radio station" where he commented on King.[154] An outraged King retained Claiborne's old nemesis George Franklin to file a lawsuit. The newspaper headlines read: "Claiborne accused of Libel in Suit filed by Publisher."[155] The complaint claimed that Claiborne called King a "Russian-born editor of a two-bit scandal sheet down in North Las Vegas." These statements , according to King, inferred "that he was and is a member of the communist party or a so-called fellow-traveler." The lawsuit also included KLAS radio as a defendant because the station failed to exercise due care in preventing the broadcasting of Claiborne's statements. Although conceding that he "really blasted" King and did refer to him as a Russian, Claiborne denied calling him a communist but later said, "I did implicate him, just a little bit." King eventually dropped the case.[156]

In his campaign against Brown in the Democratic primary, Claiborne emphasized his experience and ability. His campaign literature touted legislation he had sponsored in the Assembly to extend the state's civil service code to cover police and fire departments. His promotional material particularly highlighted courage and leadership on controversial but necessary legislation in the Assembly. Newspaper advertisements

153 Claiborne interview, 157-58.
154 Claiborne interview, 83, 157.
155 Review-Journal, September 14, 1950.
156 Claiborne interview, 158.

claimed that his "record as a lawyer and as a legislator proves that he has the courage to take a stand. He is no fence-straddler. He is not a pussy footer. He has a proven reputation as a fighter."[157]

Despite running against a longtime resident and hometown favorite, Claiborne made a good showing, receiving 4,774 votes, just 551 short of Brown's tally. Brown went on to defeat Las Vegas department store owner Richard Ronzone, later an influential county commissioner, in the general election. For his part, Claiborne put politics aside for the next 14 years and began what would become a long and storied career as a private attorney.[158]

During the 1950 campaign, Claiborne successfully sponsored a referendum question that placed on the ballot a law allowing probation for persons convicted of a crime. Upon reflection, he declared, "I said this a thousand times, if I said it once. I don't think I contributed a damn thing in my whole life, really worthwhile to mention, save and except one thing. It's something of great pride to me. I used my own money and campaigned the whole summer (of 1950), formed committees all over the state and worked like a dog to get it passed."[159]

In 1951, the legislature passed a bill allowing probation. Before enactment, a convicted person served a mandatory prison sentence regardless of the extenuating circumstances. Although routinely accepted today as a necessary option for judges, probation was a controversial issue in the early 1950s. On many occasions, Claiborne had discussed the need for such a law with Clark County District Court Judge Frank McNamee, the younger brother and onetime law partner of Leo McNamee, Claiborne's opponent in the Helm case. After Claiborne's election, but before he went to Carson City, McNamee urged him to work on its enactment. McNamee was instrumental in eventually getting the bill passed through a word of mouth campaign.[160]

Claiborne had predicted that the legislature would never pass a proba-

157 Review-Journal, September 1, 1950.
158 Review-Journal, September 6, 1950.
159 Claiborne interview, 85.
160 Friedman, Crime and Punishment in American History, 162-163, 406-409; Claiborne interview, 85-86.

tion law. Indeed, he could never get it through the 1949 Assembly, even though he chaired the Judiciary Committee. There was never a public outcry against probation, instead, opponents worked behind the scenes. In a later reminiscence, Claiborne attributed the lack of support to Nevada's conservative atmosphere at that time. But his prediction proved incorrect. During the summer of 1950, while campaigning for the state senate, Claiborne spoke at many union meetings. Bill Carter, head of the Teamsters Union, supported his efforts and Claiborne credited him for convincing the union members to support the bill. "He got every organized labor member in the state supporting it. Truly, that's what passed it."[161]

Governor Vail Pittman signed the bill in Claiborne's presence. The Governor never realized that Nevada lacked some type of probation provision in the law. That admission, coming from the Governor, amazed Claiborne. Several days later at dinner, the Governor asked Claiborne to help form the probation panel. At Claiborne's suggestion, Pittman appointed E. C. "Ted" Cupid the first probation officer and head of the newly created probation department, which was placed within the jurisdiction of the Parole Department. Claiborne and Cupid, who later assisted in the attempted release of Cliff Helm from prison, traveled to California about five times to confer with the head of its probation program, then came back, drafted regulations, and formed the probation department. "I've always considered that as the only really meaningful thing that I did in my life. I have a lot of pride in that."[162]

Claiborne first recognized the need for this law while in the District Attorney's office. He was not sure, but maybe one case particularly opened his eyes. It involved a rooming house on Garces Street, called the White House, where some casino workers lived. A young California man was walking toward the highway to hitchhike back home. When he got to the White House, he saw the lights on, walked in and entered a room belonging to the woman who owned the place. She was lying in bed reading a book. He put a knife to her throat, took her money, and ran down the

161 Claiborne interview, 86.
162 Claiborne interview, 143.

hallway to leave when a renter came in, tackled him, and held him for the police. At his subsequent trial, attorney Roland Wiley defended him. Claiborne recalled that Wiley, a former Clark County District Attorney, was a cagey "old bastard and taught me a lesson that day." In his closing remarks, Wiley made the perfect argument for a probation law in Nevada.

Wiley suffered from migraine headaches. Just as he began his closing argument, he told the presiding judge, "Your Honor, I have a terrible migraine headache. I just don't feel like standing up and making my argument. Could I just pull a chair up in front of the jury and make my argument?" Judge Henderson said, "Why sure." Claiborne recalled that Wiley's closing argument went something like this:

> Now we don't have any probation law in Nevada. They do
> have in California where this young man is from. Now if
> you convict him, then he goes to the penitentiary. That's the
> law. If he had committed this crime in California, where he's
> from, the court would turn it over to the probation depart-
> ment. They'd send a probation investigator out into the field
> and make an investigation of the boy. They would find out
> that he's a good kid. That he's never been in trouble. They'd
> go talk to his pastor and he'd find out he's a good boy. Goes
> to church regularly. He'd go to his high school and talk to his
> teachers. They'd say he was a good student and he never has
> been in trouble. He's a nice kid. The probation investiga-
> tor would go back to the judge and say, 'Judge, this is a good
> kid.' The Judge would say, 'All right, bring him in.' They
> would bring him in the court for sentencing and the Judge
> is going to say, 'You're a good kid. I don't know why you did
> this, but it's contrary to your character. I'm going to give you
> a second chance and I'm going to put you on probation. At
> the end of the probation, if you keep your nose clean, I'm go-
> ing to wipe this off your record. So you won't have a criminal
> record in the future when you get married and have a family.
> This won't be hanging over you.'

Claiborne remembered that the jury stared at the boy, then at Claiborne, then at Wiley. He continued,

> You know what will happen to him now? You find this young
> man guilty, and the Judge sentences him to the penitentiary,
> for what? Not less than two nor more than 10 years. For one
> mistake in his life. How many of you in here made mistakes?
> Some maybe not as grave as this, but some, maybe worse.
> I bleed inside today when I think about this young man's
> future. I'm going to ask you to do something really, really
> unusual. I'm going to ask you to unofficially place this young
> man on probation. The only way you can do that is to find
> him not guilty. I'm going to check on him constantly through
> the years as his unofficial probation officer. Mr. Claiborne,
> this young lawyer here, does a fine job. It's not his fault what
> the law is. I know in his heart he would like to see this young
> man put on probation, if he possibly could, under the law.

Wiley put the chair back and sat down. According to Claiborne, everyone in the courtroom was looking at each other. Claiborne got up, looked at Wiley, looked at the defendant, stared at the jury and thought to himself, "What in the hell am I going to say?" He finally sputtered, "Mr. Wiley is asking you to violate your oath. I have no other alternative but to file charges against the young man and to prosecute him. We're here today because I had no other alternative. Because it's my obligation and my responsibility under my oath to do this. Otherwise, I violate the terms of my oath. Unfortunately, as much as you'd like to, you cannot grant Mr. Wiley's request. You just can't do it." The jury did it anyway and acquitted the defendant. That was the only case Claiborne lost while he was in the District Attorney's office.[163]

Claiborne sometimes called on Nevada's congressional delegation to intervene on behalf of his clients. In fact, some of McCarran's power plays involved Claiborne. McCarran was arguably Nevada's most power-

163 Claiborne interview, 68, 70-71.

ful politician in the 20th century. After serving as Nye County District Attorney and Nevada Supreme Court Justice, McCarran fought the dominance of George Wingfield's political machine for nearly two decades until he won a seat in the United States Senate in 1932 and served until his death in 1954. Not only was he politically powerful, but McCarran ruthlessly wielded his considerable influence to advance his own career. During the Roosevelt Administration, he established a patronage system that produced a supportive following of young Nevada lawyers known as the "McCarran Boys." McCarran ensured that powerful Nevada interests were protected at the federal level, whatever the costs. He indirectly manipulated the system to determine which candidate would (or could) run for political office in the Silver State. Details of Claiborne's experiences with him shed light on McCarran's backroom deals and hardball approach to politics. They also illustrate the power he wielded and his willingness to use it.

As Nevada's senior senator after Key Pittman's death in 1940, McCarran made many political appointments and wasted little time forwarding his nominations to the White House. He once told Claiborne over a drink that he always acted quickly to keep his friends from getting mad. McCarran would tell someone who wanted the just-filled position, "Jesus Christ, I didn't know you wanted the position. If I had known that, you'd have gotten it, you know that." He gave that line to everyone. The politically astute Senator gave no one time to apply or even speak with him before making the appointment.[164] He also told one "McCarran Boy" that every time he made an appointment, the result was "one ingrate and nine enemies." Senator Alan Bible had the same experience, telling Bruce Thompson prior to nominating him to a federal judgeship, "Now I've got this problem of appointing a new U. S. Judge. The longer I wait, the more enemies I am going to make. I just want to do it in a hurry, ... "[165]

Claiborne once represented three Barstow men who wanted to buy land on the Nevada-California line where Whiskey Pete's is located today. Claiborne had difficulty with government red tape and decided to go to

---

164 Claiborne interview, 39.
165 Bruce Rutherford Thompson, interview by J. G. Sourwine on February 10, 1988, 35.

Washington to confer with the Assistant Secretary of the Interior. While in Washington, he stopped by McCarran's office to say hello. After showing Claiborne around, McCarran invited him to eat in the Senate restaurant. Claiborne was direct: "I want a favor." McCarran responded, "You got it," without even asking what it was. After hearing about Claiborne's difficulties in acquiring the land, McCarran returned to his office with Claiborne, McCarran picked up the telephone and called the Department of Interior officials. The Senator was indignant, telling one bureaucrat: "You people have been jacking Claiborne around long enough. I'm getting very angry about it. He's in my office right now and I'm sending him over there and, by God, the buck stops with you." Claiborne then went to the Interior Department and got full cooperation. A week later he received the patent for the acreage.[166]

Reno gambler Ernest Primm, for whom the area is now named, eventually purchased the property from Claiborne's clients. He reportedly contemplated developing a large resort area with at least one hotel casino on the several hundred acres. Everything depended upon the success of the water drilling tests. In March 1954, Claiborne announced the future construction of a super gas station, restaurant and tourist court nearby in partnership with others, and hoped to complete the $100,000 project by the summer. In a story, the Review-Journal referred to this development as a "new" Strip.[167]

It was not long, however, before McCarran expected something in return: "Nobody gets anything for nothing. You know that, Harry." Claiborne agreed. McCarran then went on, "C.D. Baker (the state senator from Clark County at the time) is going to announce that he is going to run for governor. I want that son-of-a-bitch buried. I understand you and Baker didn't get along in the legislature. I also understand he dislikes you very much and that he is scared to death of you. When he starts putting the word out that he is going to run for governor, I want you to announce that you are going to run too. I will tell you when to run. That will back him off as sure as I am sitting here." Claiborne responded, "All

166 Claiborne interview, 178, 179.
167 Review-Journal, March 31, 1954.

right, I don't have much choice." McCarran just laughed.[168]

Claiborne's history with Las Vegas' future mayor began in the 1949 Nevada legislative session. Claiborne wanted to pass a civil service bill for the police and firemen. Baker, a former city engineer and at the time Clark County's state senator, opposed him on this bill. Although it passed the Assembly, Baker blocked the measure in the Senate. Later in the session, a bill creating a Board of Engineers crossed Claiborne's desk before going to the Judiciary Committee. But it never got there. Claiborne locked the bill in his desk. The session ran into May. The legislature put black-out paper over the clock as a gesture to prevent the statutory time limitation on the legislative session from expiring. The delay was primarily over the sales tax issue. Claiborne remembered that every day he wondered when Baker would look into the status of the engineering bill. Finally, Baker walked over to Claiborne's desk and asked why he was not acting on his bill. Claiborne told him: "Go back over to the Senate and get the civil service bill on the floor, pass it, and the minute it hits the Assembly's desk, I will pull your bill out and we will pass it within an hour." Baker angrily replied, "You can't do a thing like this." But Claiborne did just that. About three days later, Baker returned and told Claiborne, "We just passed your Goddamned civil service board bill and it's on the way to the Governor's desk." The next day, Claiborne passed the engineering bill within an hour, as he promised.[169]

After his conversation with McCarran, Claiborne read in the Review-Journal that Baker would run for governor in 1954. The next morning, McCarran called Claiborne and told him to announce his candidacy for governor immediately. Later that day, Claiborne got a call from Al Cahlan, who kept his finger on the pulse of Las Vegas for the senator. He told Claiborne to come to his office. Cahlan asked, "Did you talk to the Senator?" When told he had, Cahlan released Claiborne's "announcement" that he would run for governor after three days of conferences in Northern Nevada with both Democrats and Republicans. The news release claimed that the one factor influencing his decision to run was to

168 Claiborne interview, 78, 179-180.
169 Claiborne interview, 142-43.

beat C.D. Baker.[170] Baker withdrew his intention to run for governor on April 9, 1954 and never filed, nor did Claiborne. McCarran knew what he was doing, Claiborne concluded.[171]

McCarran hated Baker, who was a rarity in Nevada: a politician who was not taking orders from McCarran. Worse, Baker defeated Ernie Cragin, a McCarran man, for Las Vegas Mayor in 1951. Then, Baker sided with Hank Greenspun when McCarran "prompted" nearly every casino in Las Vegas to boycott the Sun and pull its advertising in retaliation for Greenspun's support of Thomas B. Mechling in the democratic primary race for U. S. Senate against a "McCarran boy," Alan Bible. Mechling beat Bible by 475 votes in the primary, then lost to incumbent Senator Malone in the general election. Greenspun's support included scathing articles against McCarran and his tactics. Upon learning of the boycott, Mayor Baker summoned Greenspun and three resort representatives to his office and demanded to know what was going on between the casinos and the Sun. After initial denials by Thunderbird owner Cliff Jones, Monte Carlo Club owner Fred Soly and the Boulder Club's owner Kell Houssels contradicted Jones and admitted McCarran's involvement. Steaming, the crusty Baker declared, "Neither the gambling industry nor any politician in Washington will be permitted to destroy a legitimate enterprise in this community."

Greenspun filed a million-dollar lawsuit against McCarran, Eva Adams who was director of McCarran's Washington office and future director of the U. S. Mint, and fourteen casino owners, charging that they had engaged in a conspiracy in violation of the Sherman Anti-Trust Act and were attempting to monopolize the local daily newspaper business in Las Vegas. In Roger T. Foley's courtroom, a McCarran recommendation to the bench, Baker, in a dramatic appearance at the hearing, contradicted the testimony of several casino owners when he recounted the conversation in his office when two of the defendants admitted to him that "outside pressure" played a part in the advertising cancellations. Although he did not directly implicate McCarran, it was clear that no one else wielded

170 Review-Journal, March 5, 1954; Claiborne interview, 179-180.
171 Claiborne interview, 78; Sun, April 9, 1954.

such power over the casinos. Foley granted Greenspun's preliminary injunction on June 6, 1952, and ordered the defendants to place advertising in the Sun under specific guidelines. He later ruled that there was sufficient evidence for McCarran to personally remain as a defendant in the case.

The trial began in February, 1953. On the second day of trial, Greenspun introduced a "mystery witness," a secretary in the office next to Hicks, general manager of the Thunderbird, on the day he allegedly received the telephone from McCarran. When asked by Greenspun's lawyers if she was present "when the call was received from Washington," the defendant's attorneys strenuously objected and Foley abruptly announced a recess until the following day. The trial never resumed. The case settled and despite its confidentlially, news leaked that the settlement ordered the casino to pay Greenspun $80,000, continue with their advertising, and although McCarran admitted no guilt, neither was he exonerated. There was also pressure to settle the case to deflect attention away from Nevada's huge gaming industry.[172]

Confirming Claiborne's suggestion of McCarran's power, the application of Bonanza Airlines to the Civil Aeronautics Board (CAB) in 1950 provides a brazen example. Bonanza, Nevada's first commercial airline, sought approval to exchange passengers and air freight with other airlines, but the agency delayed approval. While the application was pending, CAB officials appeared before McCarran's appropriations subcommittee for funding. Prior to the hearing, McCarran asked these officials why the Bonanza application had not been approved. When told they were too busy to act on it, McCarran instructed them to go to the back of the room and consider the application before the hearing began. Fifteen minutes later, they approved Bonanza's application.[173]

McCarran's influence extended to private corporations as well. The senator, for instance, was fond of Las Vegas attorney Calvin Cory, another

172 Ybarra, Washington Gone Crazy, 673- 679; Edwards, Pat McCarran, 158-166; Political History, 299, 337; Federal Reporter, Greenspun v. McCarran et al., 105 F. Supp. 662 (1952); Nevada State Journal, January 18, 1953; Sun, February 4-7, 1953; For a detailed account, see also Hank Greenspun with Alex Pelle, Where I Stand: The Record of a Reckless Man. (New York: David McKay Co., Inc., 1966), 193-206, 222-228.
173 Review-Journal, April 4, 2004.

beneficiary of his law school patronage. When a vacancy for regional counsel for the Union Pacific Railroad opened up, McCarran called the president of the railroad and announced, "You will appoint Cal Cory in Las Vegas as legal counsel." Not wanting to antagonize the powerful Senator, he did. Cory held that position until the day he died.[174]

---

[174] Claiborne interview, 74-75.

Photo Courtesy of the Claiborne Family

CHAPTER SIX

PRACTICING LAW IN MID-CENTURY LAS VEGAS

If the late 1940s was the period for post-war readjustment and resettlement, the 1950s reflected the growing realization of Nevada's economic potential. Between 1950 and 1960, the state's population grew from 160,083 to 285,278, an increase of 78.2%. Population in Las Vegas more than doubled. The resort industry began a growth trend that continued into the next century. Before 1950, Las Vegas had six resorts hotels and by 1960 the number grew to nineteen. The Nevada Test Site became a significant economic contributor in the 1950s with the commencement of nuclear testing. The Korean War, the Cold War, and growing unrest in Southeast Asia contributed to the growth of Nellis Air Force Base during the 1950s. The state legal community grew as well, expanding from 284 lawyers to 383, while the number of Las Vegas lawyers increased from 65 to 141. It was also a time of political transition as McCarran began to lose his grip on power and Southern Nevada began to achieve some degree of political primacy. Yet rural Nevadans continued to occupy the governor's mansion. Vail Pittman and Charles Russell were from Ely. While northern Nevadans held key federal posts in Washington (Pat McCarran, George W. "Molly" Malone, and Walter Baring). But, by the late 1950s, Southern Nevada held one of the two U. S. Senate positions when Howard Cannon was elected in 1958, starting a trend which gradually moved political power to the south.[175]

In February 1945, Judge Frank Norcross finally announced his long anticipated retirement from the federal bench, effective June 30. The

175 Political History, 67, 106; The Nevada State Bar Journal, Vol. 15, No. 2, April 1950, 96; Vol. 25, No. 1, January 1960, 40.

United States Justice Department informally asked McCarran if he would accept the judgeship. McCarran told reporters he was seriously considering the offer, which would allow him to complete his days on the federal bench and avoid many of the "obnoxious" details of politics. The Roosevelt Administration's motives were obvious: it wanted the fiercely independent McCarran, the newly ensconced chairman of the important Judiciary Committee, out of the Senate. It is doubtful, however, that the Senator was seriously tempted, because even though he was 68 years old, he had just won a third term and enjoyed a reputation for being one of the dominant powers in national politics. Furthermore, he detested Governor E. P. Carville, a fellow Democrat who would choose his successor. In a characteristic display of ego, McCarran implied that he was indispensable in the Senate and his work in that chamber was too important to abandon. In February, he issued a public statement that he would remain in his present position.[176]

McCarran then visited Nevada's other U. S. Senator James Scrugham in Overton, and advised him that he would let Scrugham appoint Norcross' replacement.[177] Other reports, however, indicated that the two senators jointly selected Roger T. Foley. They agreed to appoint someone who would not create a vacancy in any state office, because they did not want Carville filling it. Foley was relatively unknown at the time when compared to the attorneys whose names were mentioned for the appointment.[178] However, at the 1944 Nevada Democratic Convention, Foley had supported McCarran in his bitter primary race against Vail Pittman, and this surely influenced McCarran's thinking in selecting Foley.[179]

When Norcross announced his retirement, Foley immediately circulated petitions to have Nevada Supreme Court Justice William Orr named to the vacancy. But McCarran told Foley that he had other plans for Orr (whom McCarran later recommended to the U.S. Court of Appeals for

176 Jerome E. Edwards, Pat McCarran: Political Boss of Nevada, 133.
177 Norman H. Biltz, Memoirs of "Duke of Nevada:" Developments of Lake Tahoe, California and Nevada; Reminiscences of Nevada Political and Financial Life, interview by Mary Ellen Glass, (Reno: University of Nevada Oral History Program, 1969), 137.
178 Jerome Edwards, Pat McCarran, 133.
179 Peter C. Petersen, Reminiscences of My Work in Nevada Labor, Politics, Post Office, and Gaming Control, interview by Mary Ellen Glass (Reno: University of Nevada Oral History Program, 1970), 52-53.

the Ninth Circuit) and instead wanted Foley for the position.[180] Within a week after McCarran's visit with Scrugham, they recommended Foley.[181] Franklin Roosevelt nominated the Las Vegan shortly before the President's death in April 1945, and President Harry Truman appointed him to the federal bench on May 2, 1945. As one of Roosevelt's last judicial nominations and probably the first federal judge commissioned by Truman,[182] Foley's selection marked the beginning of a half century of Foley family representation in Nevada's federal judiciary.

Born in 1886, Foley joined his father's law practice in Goldfield after graduating from the Chicago Law School. He won election as District Attorney for Esmeralda County, but lost his bid for re-election eight years later. Foley moved to Las Vegas, became Justice of the Peace and, later was elected District Attorney in Clark County. After two years as District Court judge for Clark County, he returned to private practice until his appointment to the federal bench in 1945. Foley assumed senior status on April 1, 1957, but actively heard matters until just before his death at the age of 88.[183]

Claiborne had many dealings with Judge Foley over the years and remembered him as the "grandest gentleman you ever saw. A terrific Judge. He was a hard knocker. A lot of lawyers did not like him. But the only lawyers that did not like him were the lawyers who came into his court unprepared." Claiborne said, "You better be prepared when you went into Foley's court. A lot of lawyers thought he picked on them. He did pick on them if they came to court and did not know anything about the case. You were going out with your tail between your legs. They all said how tough he was." But Claiborne had a different experience. "I never found him tough, I found him good and knowledgeable. He was quick to see where a lawyer was going with his case. He believed in letting you try your case. He, never one single time, embarrassed me."[184]

Roger T. Foley had five sons, all lawyers. As far as Claiborne was con-

180 Formal Dedication Ceremony of the Foley Federal Building and United States Courthouse, 615 F. Supp. LXVI, LXXVIII (1984).
181 Biltz, 137.
182 Formal Dedication, LXXIX.
183 Review-Journal, October 10, 1974; Sun, October 10, 1974.
184 Claiborne interview, 76.

cerned, "George, of all the Foley boys, was the best lawyer. All of them, except John, had a very high temper. But most of the time, that temper worked in their favor. They were never out of line. I guess Joe had the highest temper of all. John was not one of the high-tempered Foley boys. Gracious man. Good lawyer. Could try a good case. Had a good temperament for the courtroom. They were a great family and good to me."[185] All had accomplished careers in their own right. At various times, his sons were Clark County District Attorney (Roger and George), District Court Judge for Clark County (Tom), Nevada State Senator (John) and University of Nevada Board of Regent (Joe).

In 1962, Roger T. Foley had the honor of swearing in his successor to the federal bench in Southern Nevada, his eldest son, Roger D. Foley. Born in Goldfield, Roger studied to be a priest after growing up in Las Vegas. He served in the Army Air Corps during World War II and flew fifty combat missions over Europe as a Bombardier/Navigator. Following his discharge, Foley followed in his father's and grandfather's footsteps and pursued a legal career. He ran for District Attorney, defeating Oscar Bryan, father of future Nevada Governor and United States Senator Richard Bryan.[186] Voters elected Foley Attorney General and he served until his federal appointment to the bench four years later.

Roger D. Foley and Bruce Thompson, appointed to the federal bench in Reno less than a year after Foley's appointment, had issues with each other. While Foley was Attorney General, he appointed Thompson as special assistant in two important cases. While Foley was being considered for the federal judgeship, friends circulated a petition among lawyers in his support for presentation to Senator Bible. Thompson refused to sign it, and proceeded to tell Foley why he was not qualified to be a federal judge - it was primarily based on Foley's "political tactics as Attorney General in many matters." Foley admitted, "In several administrative proceedings where the political stakes were very high, I often went to the jugular, sometimes ignoring the rules of evidence and orderly procedure; frequently I tried the case in the newspaper." He noted that in

185 Claiborne interview, 136.
186 Review-Journal, January 1, 1996, Obituaries; Sun, January 8, 1996, Obituaries.

one political and highly publicized case, "I was doing the governor (Grant Sawyer) a favor that he had requested of me personally in conducting an administrative proceeding ... It was very important to my political ambitions at the time for higher political office that I look good to the voters. I had to come down on the side of motherhood and apple pie. Bruce deplored this conduct. He may have thought that it would carry over to the bench if I were ever appointed," Foley admitted. Eventually, the hostility diminished and a deep friendship developed between the two Nevada federal judges.[187]

In 1982, Foley went on senior status, which allowed him to select the cases he would hear. His death in 1996 ended a fifty-year era of Foley family representation on the Nevada federal bench. This time span is amplified when considering that between Roger D. Foley's appointment in 1962 and his father's active retirement in 1970, both Foleys sat on the bench at the same time, effectively expanding their combined service an additional eight years. Incredibly, through 1996, at least one Foley sat on the federal bench in excess of 40 percent of the time since Nevada's statehood in 1864.

Claiborne believed that Roger D. Foley "never received the recognition he should have received on the federal bench." They worked together in the District Attorney's office in 1947, and later served as U. S. District Court judges at the same time. He "was a good lawyer," Claiborne remembered, "not spectacular, but good. Conscientious. He was a fine Federal judge. He did not have writing skills but his decisions were to the point. He had excellent judgment."[188]

Two other judges also influenced Claiborne's early career. When Claiborne began practicing law in 1946, Frank McNamee and Albert (Bert) Scott Henderson were the two District Court judges in Clark County. Because most of the jury trials in a community occur in state court, rather than federal court, Claiborne spent much of his early trial years in front of one of these two judges. In the process, he formed a strong relationship with both of them. The McNamee family's roots in

187 Federal Reporter, In Memoriam: Honorable Bruce R. Thompson, LXVIII-LXIX.
188 Claiborne interview, 136.

Las Vegas ran deep. Born in Lincoln County, Frank McNamee served as
Municipal Judge of the City of Las Vegas. Three years later, he began the
full time practice of law with his brother, Leo, until he joined the Army
in 1942. Appointed to the Clark County District Court on July 11, 1946,
McNamee served until elevated to the Nevada Supreme Court on December 15, 1958.[189] The McNamee family had a long association with the
legal profession in Nevada. Frank's father, Frank R. McNamee, Sr., was
a widely acclaimed attorney and represented many of the leading mining concerns in central and Southern Nevada at the turn of the century.
He was the Nevada attorney for the San Pedro, Los Angeles, Salt Lake
Railroad Company, later the Union Pacific, a prestigious client. The law
firm of McNamee and McNamee began in 1914 when Leo A. McNamee,
Frank Jr.'s brother, joined his father's practice. Frank McNamee, Jr.
joined the firm nearly 20 years later, upon his father's death. The family
law firm continued with the later addition of two of Leo's sons, John and
Joseph.[190]

While Claiborne and others remembered Leo McNamee as the "leading
lawyer" and the dean of the Bar in Las Vegas in the mid-1940s and 1950s,
Frank, Jr. was less prominent - but, according to Claiborne, he was the
smartest. "You seldom will meet anybody in your lifetime as brilliant as
him. Masterful Judge." Claiborne thought McNamee was a better trial
court judge than he was a Supreme Court justice.[191] He knew because he
spent a lot of time arguing cases before him. Despite his respect for the
man, Claiborne was not above engaging in his usual courtroom antics before him. For example, McNamee's courtroom had a drinking fountain
that Claiborne used to his advantage for 10 years before McNamee caught
on to him. Sometimes when a prosecutor was in the middle of closing
argument and making points against his client, Claiborne would walk
over to the fountain and in the process of supposedly getting a drink, intentionally sprayed water all over himself. He then took his handkerchief
from his pocket and wiped his face, all with a great flourish, hoping the

189 In Memoriam: Albert (Bert) Scott Henderson, 85 Nev. 731 (1970); Nevada State Bar Journal,
       October,1970, Vol. 35, No. 4, 6-7.
190 Nevada State Bar Journal, Oct, 1958, Vol. 23, No. 4, 121.
191 Claiborne interview, 51; Wiener interview, 20.

jury would watch his misadventure and not pay attention to the prosecutor's argument. McNamee eventually grasped the situation and without
telling Claiborne, ordered the water fountain removed, leaving only the
stubbed pipe. At the next trial, "I went over to the water fountain to do
my thing and I looked down - the water fountain was gone! I must have
looked dumbfounded . When I looked up, McNamee had his head down
laughing, as did the Court Clerk and the Court Reporter. They were all in
on it. I've always said that was Frank McNamee's finest hour."[192]

Claiborne also tried many cases before another long-time Nevada
judge, Albert (Bert) Henderson, who attended public schools in Eureka
before enrolling at the University of Nevada for two years. He qualified
for the Bar by studying law in the Eureka office of Judge Peter Breen,
patriarch of a longtime northern Nevada judicial family. Henderson's
early career exemplifies the fluid nature of a frontier society in the early
20th century, when it was still relatively easy to change positions without
much formal education. After serving as District Attorney for Eureka
County, he moved to Las Vegas in 1910 as the first principal of Las Vegas
High School. After two years, Henderson started his law practice. He
served three terms in the Nevada State Assembly and one in the Nevada
State Senate. After seven years as Las Vegas City Attorney, Henderson
became Clark County District Attorney for two terms. He was appointed
Clark County District Court Judge in 1946, remaining for 14 years.[193]

Claiborne remembered Henderson as "pretty weak on the law. But he
was a hell of an equity judge. They used to say his decisions were always
right, but always for the wrong reason."[194] Claiborne recalled a story
people told about Henderson in his youth which provides considerable
insight into his character and perhaps his strength on the bench. He was
a United States Marshal stationed in Elko, Nevada. A local doctor owned
a thoroughbred horse which he used to make house calls to the surrounding ranches until someone stole the animal. The doctor was obviously

---

192 Claiborne interview, 252-253; Review-Journal, August 16, 1978.
193 Nevada State Bar Journal, October, 1962, Vol. 27, No. 4; James G. Scrugham, ed., Nevada:
    A Narrative of the Conquest of a Frontier Land (Chicago and New York: The American Historical
    Society, Inc., 1935), Vol. II, 69-70; Communique: Official Journal of the Clark County Bar
    Association (Las Vegas: Clark County Bar Association), October 1995, 13.
194 Claiborne interview, 161.

upset, so Henderson promised to retrieve his horse. He tracked the horse thief south to Beatty, Nevada and into Death Valley, hundreds of miles away. Henderson finally caught up with him. The thief was frying bacon when Henderson rode up, got off his horse, and said, "The jig's up. I'm the United States Marshal." The thief said, "Yeah, I know who you are, Bert. It just so happens that you don't have any jurisdiction. Right down there, that clump of bushes, is the California line. You don't have any jurisdiction. There's not a damn thing you can do." Henderson pulled out his pistol and shouted angrily, "All right, get up and turn around. I'm a United States Marshal. I ain't no damn surveyor. I don't know where the lines are. As far as I'm concerned, we're still in Nevada." And he took him in.[195]

While Claiborne was still in the District Attorney's office, an older lawyer, John Cope, took him under his wing and treated him like a son. Cope was a World War I veteran and moved to Las Vegas in 1941 to practice law. Calling him a "fine old gentleman, a wonderful lawyer," Claiborne claimed Cope gave him the best advice he ever received, none of which he ever followed.[196] It was while dining with Cope and Henderson that Claiborne first met "Bugsy" Siegel. On that occasion, Cope asked Claiborne to join Judge Henderson and him for dinner at the Flamingo Hotel. He agreed. During dinner, Siegel approached them. Claiborne recalled him as "really a good looking guy. Nattily dressed. You'd never believe that he was a gangster and killed something like 20 people. Soft spoken, just a very nice man." After introducing himself, Siegel sat next to Judge Henderson and talked about Nevada history. "Judge Henderson liked to talk about the history of Nevada about as much as I like to talk about my old cases that I won," Claiborne explained. After 30 minutes, Siegel excused himself and left. It did not register with anyone, except Claiborne, who he was. As they were driving home after dinner, the Judge asked Cope if he knew the man and Cope said he assumed he was one of the hotel executives. The judge asked Claiborne if he knew the man and he replied, "Yeah, Bugsy Siegel." Startled, Henderson lost con-

195 Claiborne interview, 161-162.
196 Claiborne interview, 160; Nevada State Bar Journal, October 1962, Vol. 27, No. 4, 2.

trol of the car, drove off the road, and ran into the desert. The next day, the judge asked Claiborne not to mention to anyone that they had been to the Flamingo the previous night.[197]

Siegel's mere presence in Las Vegas symbolized the city's dramatic transformation during and after World War II. A decade earlier, the closest thing to mobsters in town was a few bootleggers. But, as reformers began clearing gamblers out of Southern California and as soldiers and defense workers confirmed the hopes of Las Vegas promoters that gambling would be the city's salvation, the community began to change. The post-war urbanization of Las Vegas and Reno, along with the shifting reliance upon gaming and tourism rather than ranches, farming, and railroading, brought corresponding changes to Claiborne's future profession as well.

The general post-war migration to western states such as Nevada did not initially affect the Bar, but geographical relocation of lawyers within the state reflected the changing economies within the state's borders. In 1950, the State Bar Association's membership consisted of 284 lawyers. Although the Bar's total membership had increased by only 50 lawyers since 1943, their move to the larger cities was apparent. Las Vegas lawyers increased by 28 and Reno lawyers by 39. The "cow counties" clearly lost attorneys, which reflected the movement of business and population away from the state's fading mining and ranching communities and toward cities expanding through tourism and federal projects.

Bar membership statistics five years later indicated another trend: Las Vegas posted a faster growth rate than Reno. Las Vegas added 31 attorneys during that time while Reno gained only 2. In terms of percentage, 30% of Nevada's attorneys practiced in Las Vegas in 1955, compared with 23% in 1950. The Reno percentages dropped from 57% to 50% during that same time period. This trend continued until 1967. Then, six more attorneys practiced in Las Vegas than Reno.[198]

While the Clark County Bar Association was numerically small, it boasted many capable lawyers, according to Claiborne. Their interaction

197 Claiborne interview,160-162.
198 Nevada State Bar Journal, April 1943, Vol. 8, No. 2, 69-75; April, 1950, Vol. 15, No. 2, 101-108; January 1955, Vol. 20, No. 1, 43-49; January 1967, Vol. 32, No. 1, 58-71.

and antics illustrate the colorful nature of practicing law in Las Vegas during the 1940s and 1950s. Specific anecdotes demonstrate the closeness of the members, revealing a bygone era when lawyers took time to laugh at themselves, and each other, while practicing their profession. Their "war stories" describe a legal environment that faded long ago and will likely never return to Las Vegas.

Madison Graves and Claiborne had several entertaining encounters. Graves was very prominent in Bar activities; President of the Nevada State Bar, Board of Governors for several years, and President of the Clark County Bar Association. Graves was a Harvard Law School graduate and, according to Claiborne, "quickly let everybody know it." Graves thought Arkansas was a wilderness and that "everybody in Arkansas was an ignorant hillbilly." Claiborne was no exception. Graves "had the most magnificent vocabulary that you've ever seen in your life and he loved to expound to juries. The jurors never understood the words, much less being able to pronounce them." When Claiborne had a jury trial against him, "I'd throw that country boy style at him that I used quite often. I found it very appealing to juries. He never got wise." Then he shared a courtroom tactic he found effective against Graves. "I would mispronounce a word deliberately and he would jump up from the counsel table and correct me. I'd always turn around and say, 'I didn't go to Harvard like you did, Mr. Graves, and I'm very sorry that I mispronounced that word.' He never got it. I used to stop him. I'd say, 'Hold it. Hold it. Mr. Graves, what does that word mean?' He would turn around and define the word to me. He never got it. For twenty years, he never got it."[199]

Claiborne and Graves once argued a civil case before Judge Henderson, who took it under advisement. Six months passed and Graves wanted a decision. He proposed to Claiborne that they both call Henderson and push for a decision, but Claiborne did not want to "kick a sleeping dog." Graves contacted Henderson on his own, which, according to Claiborne, really "pissed the judge off," thereby violating a principle understood by nearly all lawyers since time began - never press a judge for a decision. The next day they received a call from the court that the judge was ready

199 Claiborne interview, 72-73; Diamond Jubilee, 62.

to rule. Henderson had the wrong case in front of him, which Graves readily pointed out. When Graves told him the name of the correct case, Henderson wrote it down but never asked his clerk to bring him the file. Henderson proceeded: "Let the record show that Mr. Graves representing the plaintiff is present and Mr. Claiborne representing the defendant is present." Henderson read off the notes he just made. Graves just smiled knowing he was going to win. Henderson continued, "The court finds for the defendant and against the plaintiff together with the defendant's costs." Graves' mouth "flew" open, Claiborne recalled. They went into the hall and Graves was furious. "You knew all the time it was the wrong case, why didn't you join me? Claiborne replied, "Every lawyer in town knows, Maddy, not to interfere with anything you do." Clearly, Henderson ruled against Graves without remembering what the case involved; he only remembered which attorney pressured him to render a decision.[200]

John Bonner was another prominent and colorful Las Vegas lawyer. Born in Ireland, he was the county clerk in White Pine County before obtaining his law degree from a correspondence school. Bonner represented nearly all of the labor unions and union leaders in town at one time or another. In 1962, President John F. Kennedy appointed him United States Attorney for Nevada.[201]

Bonner and Claiborne had many encounters in the courtroom. In one, memorable for the wrong reasons, they were on opposing sides of a criminal matter set for argument and both were preparing in the Clark County Law Library. Bonner had a high stack of law books and marked them with pieces of paper. When Bonner was out of his sight, Claiborne changed all the book marks, assuming that Bonner had written down his legal citations. They appeared in Judge McNamee's court for oral argument. Bonner read half of the first page of a civil case, which of course had nothing to do with the criminal matter. When McNamee began to questioningly look at him, Bonner said, "I don't believe that this is the case." McNamee said, "I'm sure it isn't." So, Bonner put it down

200 Claiborne interview, 162.
201 Claiborne interview, 97; Review-Journal, December 5, 1991.

and started reading another case, without reading it to himself first. He looked up and said, "I don't think this case is it either." He then took the third case and read a little of it. One would think by now that Bonner would look at the case and make sure of its content before reading it, "but not John," Claiborne recalled. Bonner read a portion of it, stopped, and then asked the judge for more time: "Your Honor, I don't know how to explain this. But I need a recess." All the time, McNamee was looking at Claiborne who said, "I'll agree to that, Your Honor. I'll agree to that." McNamee said, "Oh, I'm sure you're happy to do that." He knew immediately what happened to Bonner.[202]

Seven or eight years later, Claiborne and Bonner were in Carson City. The Democratic Central Committee was meeting in Elko and, over lunch, when Claiborne and Bonner discovered each were attending, they agreed to drive from Reno to Elko together. As Claiborne put it,

> So we got in John's car. We got about halfway to Elko, and it begins to snow. I decided to tell John about the books. He threw on the brakes on his car. There was enough snow on the road, about a quarter inch, that the car slid all the way over and off the road. He jumped out. He began to curse me, running around the car. I ran. I didn't want to fight him. Half of the time, I'm running backwards, holding my hands up. I definitely made four, five circles of the car. While I'm at the back, he stopped and got in the car and drove off. He left me on the highway! He never came back for me. I'm there in the highway and it's snowing! I'm looking both ways and I don't see any cars coming from any direction. Finally, a guy comes by in a cattle truck with his kids, and he stopped. He said, 'Say fella, what are you doing out here in the middle of the road?' I had a suit on. I said, 'I was riding with a guy who got mad at me and he put me out of his car and I'm stranded out here.' He said, 'Well, where are you going?' I said, 'Elko.' He said, 'Get in, I'm going there too.' He had

202 Claiborne interview, 231; Wiener interview 8.

been to a cattle sale somewhere. I get into Elko and John wouldn't speak to me. I said to him from a distance, 'John, you still mad at me?' He turned around and walked away. I rode back to Reno with Cliff Jones. I wasn't going to push it and ask John if I could ride back with him.[203]

Stories such as Claiborne misplacing book marks in his case against Bonner, and George Franklin's attempt to misguide Claiborne on Bar exam topics may need some explanation. While some may interpret these as underhanded tricks, or even unethical, lawyers at the time, and presently, generally view them as practical jokes. Stunts to laugh about afterwards, and reminders to "get even" in the future. In general, it is antics like these that contribute to the congeniality of the Bar. As the Bar got larger and more impersonal, these pranks become more restricted to a select few who would take them in the manner intended.

Artemus W. Ham, Sr. was an established attorney in Las Vegas when Claiborne began his practice. He was one of only six lawyers in town when he began practicing in 1916, and the only one with formal legal training. He served as Las Vegas City Attorney from 1924 through 1928. Ham was instrumental in getting the first street paved in Las Vegas, Fremont between Main and Fifth, by getting it designated as part of US Highway 91, then under construction between Los Angeles and Salt Lake City. In addition to his law practice, he actively acquired and developed land and invested in casinos. An original owner of the Frontier Club, one of the first casinos in downtown Las Vegas, he later became a partner and founder of the Golden Nugget Casino. He also built one of the first luxury homes in Las Vegas. Ham's family made large contributions to the University of Nevada, Las Vegas for the construction of Artemus W. Ham Hall and later for Alta Ham Hall.[204]

Claiborne's memories of Ham were not all that favorable. Claiborne remembered that "Art Ham, Sr. hated me. Absolutely hated me. Art Ham was a grouchy, grumpy human being. He envisioned himself as the

203 Claiborne interview, 231.
204 Nevada State Bar Journal, October, 1970, Vol. 35, No. 4, 3-4; Nevada Lawyer, July 2003, 21-23.

best trial lawyer in the world. And he was quick to tell you so." When Claiborne was still with the District Attorney's Office, he had a case with Ham where the judge allowed Ham to withdraw his representation from a criminal defendant. After court, Ham walked up to Claiborne and said, "Well, I guess you're damn happy that I'm out of this thing." Claiborne responded, "What makes you think that? Hell no. I'm not happy. He'll go out now and get a good lawyer!" Ham only spoke to him one time after that.[205]

Sometime later, when Claiborne was in private practice, he heard a thump at the back door to his office which opened on to an alley near the Golden Nugget. He saw Ham lying unconscious in the middle of the alley. He was ill and passed out. Claiborne called an ambulance. Claiborne then began spreading the story that when he saw Ham unconscious in the alley, he was afraid that Ham would get run over by a delivery truck. So he pulled him over against the wall, then went back to work at his office. Five people walked by, turned Ham over, saw who he was, and walked away. Finally, the porter from the Golden Nugget (Ham was a 20% owner in the Nugget) came down the alley, turned him over, recognized him, and called the management. Ham eventually learned about Claiborne's story, and six months later they ran into each other in the same alley, of all places. "Goddamn you! You are a rotten son-of-a-bitch. I always knew you were a no-good bastard. But if I hear of you telling that story about me unconscious in the alley, you're going to hear from me," Ham screamed. "Jesus, Art, sorry you took offense to it. People would ask me what happened to you down there and I told them," Claiborne replied, then just walked away. Ham never spoke to him again.[206]

In contrast, Claiborne regarded Louis Cohn as the best all-round lawyer he ever met when considering attorneys who could try both criminal and civil cases - something few people could do with any degree of success. Not all good criminal lawyers can try a civil case, but Cohn was the exception, Claiborne observed. "Fantastically good lawyer." Louis

205 Claiborne interview, 138.
206 Claiborne interview, 139.

Wiener agreed, remembering Cohn as having a nose "that could hold four rolls of nickels, but he had an expression when he talked that made you think he was handsome. He was the most expressive man you ever saw. He just had personality." Cohn's talent made quite an impression on Claiborne, because Cohn died only three years after Claiborne started practicing.[207]

Harold McKinley Morse may have been the best trial lawyer Claiborne ever encountered.[208] He had a deep bass voice you "could hear for forty miles," as Claiborne put it.[209] Morse graduated from the University of Nebraska Law School, put his legal degree on hold and enlisted in the U. S. Navy during World War I. As a naval aviator, he engaged in aerial combat while flying a wood framed, canvas covered bi-plane aircraft; pilot parachutes were not yet available. After farming in Nebraska and practicing law for a short time in Los Angeles, he moved to Las Vegas, where his two sisters lived. One sister was married to lawyer C.D. Breeze, with whom Morse started sharing office space. The other sister was married to Dr. Raymond D. Balcom, who together with Dr. Roy Martin built and operated the Las Vegas Hospital, which opened in 1931 at Eighth Street and Ogden Avenue and continued to operate into the late 1980s. Nationally recognized as an outstanding trial attorney, Morse was the first in Southern Nevada to be admitted to the prestigious American College of Trial Lawyers. In 1940, Morse formed a partnership with Madison Graves and the firm Morse & Graves was one of Southern Nevada's premier firms for many years. His son William R. Morse (later a District Court judge), and grandson Harold McKinley Morse II, carried on the family name in Clark County legal lore.[210]

Claiborne had many court encounters with Morse, but one case typified the semi-humorous twists a prosecution could sometimes take in Las Vegas. Morse defended a man named Fitch who was accused of killing his wife's boyfriend. Claiborne was the prosecutor. Fitch had been a stand-in for Gregory Peck in some films. His wife eventually moved to Nevada

207 Claiborne interview, 37; Wiener interview, 21-22.
208 Claiborne interview, 37, 72, 293.
209 Wiener interview, 2.
210 Nevada State Bar Journal, April, 1967, Vol. 32, No. 2, 3-4; Nevada Lawyer, August 2003, 19-23.

and filed for a divorce, exploiting the state's liberal waiting period. Fitch
found her living with another man and a violent fight began involving
a gun. Numerous shots were fired, killing the boyfriend. Fitch claimed
the gun accidentally fired during a struggle on the floor. In front of the
jury, both Morse and Claiborne, at one time or another, got on the floor
with the gun to re-enact the struggle. The jury was delighted, as were
the spectators, to see such behavior by the lawyers. In the back row was
a juror named Leavitt. The jury seats were on cast iron spindles about
six inches in diameter. The seats tilted back and forth so a juror could
lean back. Morse began talking to the jury with the gun in his hand. He
pulled the trigger each time the gun was supposedly fired while in the
various positions during the fight. He pulled the trigger for the third shot
and for the fourth shot. All the time, Leavitt leaned way back in his chair
in the jury box. Morse told the jury that such and such shot was fired,
and at the same time as he pulled the trigger, the cast iron spindle in
Leavitt's chair broke, causing a loud bang. Leavitt fell backwards into the
window, landing on his backside with his feet in the air. Morse thought
he shot Leavitt. He said to Graham Butterfield, Clerk of the Court, "My
God, Graham, I thought the gun was empty." Morse dropped the gun on
the clerk's desk. Claiborne knew the gun did not fire because he knew it
was not loaded. But Morse still thought he shot the juror, especially after
they got Leavitt out of the window and saw that he was bleeding profuse-
ly. He cut his head on the window glass. As Claiborne recalled, "It was a
wonderful day for the jury, but justice took a beating."[211]

Paul Ralli was an established lawyer in Las Vegas when Claiborne
arrived. Ralli definitely possessed one of the more interesting backgrounds of any member of the local Bar. He once appeared on stage as
Mae West's leading man in "Diamond Lil," and on screen with Marion
Davies in "Show People." He worked as a lumberjack in Wisconsin, a
steelworker in Chicago, and a common laborer in New York before opt-
ing for a legal career. Born in Cyprus, Ralli moved to America in 1927,
studied law by correspondence, and joined the Nevada Bar. In one of his
books, Ralli recalled his first day in Las Vegas in 1933, when he asked the

211 Claiborne interview, 79-80; Wiener interview, 3.

hotel room clerk how many lawyers were in town. He replied, "I reckon about twenty - and they're all rich men." In the midst of the Depression, that was good news for Ralli, he confessed, and stayed to profit from the Hoover Dam boom. By all accounts, Ralli was one of the more colorful, and popular, attorneys in the Clark County Bar.[212]

In addition to writing two books on the practice of law in Las Vegas, Ralli was "a character, delightful guy." Being Greek, he brought gallons of wine to every Clark County Bar Association meeting at the Green Shack Restaurant. He was famous for making Coffee Diablo, a mixture of several different wines and coffee. Called the "custodian of the wine," Ralli was also the leading divorce attorney in town - even then a very profitable industry. In 1945-47, with so many quickie wartime marriages being dissolved, Claiborne believed some lawyers were handling four or five divorce cases each day. The secretaries did all the work and the lawyers spent less than ten minutes in the courtroom for each divorce. Ralli, Claiborne estimated, handled six or seven a day. Nobody could match him. Since the minimum fee for a divorce was $100, Ralli earned $600 to $700 a day which Claiborne called a "ton of money" for that time.[213]

Ralli was a relatively popular figure on the Las Vegas Strip, where many prospective divorcees stayed, gambled, and partied while they waited out the six-week residency requirement. In the mid-1940s, the Last Frontier and El Rancho, the only hotels then on that stretch of highway, catered to divorcees, and to Ralli. Claiborne laughingly remembered, "You could go out for dinner at either one of those hotels and every hour there would be a page, 'Paging Paul Ralli, the attorney. Paging Mr. Paul Ralli, the attorney.' Ralli was paying the switchboard operators to page him. Wherever you went, everybody knew Paul Ralli was an attorney. The divorcees walking around heard it all the time." He rode around in a big convertible with the top open and was a very good looking man. While Claiborne respected him, he was not above occasionally antagoniz-

212 Nevada Bar Journal, October 1953, Vol. 18, No. 4, 139; Paul Ralli, Nevada Lawyer: A Story of Life and Love in Las Vegas, 2-3.

213 Claiborne interview, 58-59, 98, 222; Wiener interview, 91; Paul Ralli, Nevada Lawyer: A Story of Life and Love in Las Vegas, 1930-1970 (Culver City: Murray and Gee, Inc., 1949); Paul Ralli, Viva Las Vegas (Hollywood: House-Warven, Publishers, 1953).

ing Ralli by making fun of his Greek accent. Claiborne recalled that Ralli frequently said, "I thiiink (sic) that's right," when asked his opinion on matters, which emphasized his accent. "I'm in court with him one time and he said something and I looked around and I said, 'Yeah, I thiiink that's right.' He didn't like me either; he joined George Franklin."[214] Of course, not all of the lawyers in Las Vegas were men. Nelle Price, the daughter of an Ohio judge, was one of the town's first women lawyers. She moved to Las Vegas at age 15 to help her mother operate a tea house on a "dirty desert road" near Fremont Street. They were described by some as "two prim and proper Eastern-bred ladies," something of a novelty in the frontier town at the time. Price joined the Bar in 1947 and practiced in Las Vegas for 22 years. "Nelle was a real good attorney. You could pass by Nelle's law office on many late nights and see her working. She was also a gracious woman," Claiborne remembered. A stickler for fine fashion, she browsed the finest apparel shops in Los Angeles and was noted for her stunning courtroom attire. Claiborne remembered her as "a very smart young lady. Pretty. Very attractive. She went into law practice with Paul Ralli. They eventually got married and divorced. She left Ralli and went into law practice with Roland Wiley. I guess it was habit forming for her to marry the lawyer whose office she was in. So she married Roland." Price and Wiley were married and divorced four times.

Price unsuccessfully ran for District Judge in 1966. She later told her family that her opponent "looks more like a judge than I do." At that time, she had been married and divorced five times, Claiborne believed. He had been married and divorced three times. Both obviously took advantage of Nevada's liberal divorce and marriage laws. When she came into Claiborne's office seeking his support just before the election, he confessed that he was already committed to another candidate. Disappointed, she lashed out, "You don't like me, do you, Harry." He responded, "Nelle, I love you. I really do. I don't want anything ever to happen to you. If it does, then I'd be the most married and divorced lawyer in the community. She stormed out of my office." She was married to a

214 Claiborne interview, 58-59.

total of eight different men – some, like Wiley, more than once. She was, according to her daughter, "a very romantic woman. She fell in love very easily."[215]

Emilie Wanderer also started practicing law in Las Vegas after passing the Bar in 1947, and was the oldest living member of the Nevada Bar when she died in 2005 at age 102. Wanderer worked in Madison Graves' office as a legal assistant before passing the Bar and starting her own practice. She was best known for her work in civil rights, having served as counsel for the NAACP during the 1950s, and was a driving force in establishing the Clark County Family Court system. Claiborne recalled that she represented many clients free of charge. "She was very smart, and I think she was a very, very fine lawyer. She was knowledgeable." In describing one case against her, "she fought like a tiger."[216, 217]

The pursuit of clients by male and female lawyers is as old as the practice of law itself. Before the United States Supreme Court authorized attorney advertising for clients, enterprising attorneys used business cards as their sole marketing material, but often did it in a very aggressive manner. Many believed that promptness in presenting one's business card to a potential client was the key. The small and close legal community allowed a relationship where judges would readily share humorous cases with favorite attorneys, even at the expense of the other members of the Bar. One day Judge McNamee called Claiborne and asked him to come to his Chambers, where he showed him the actual trial transcript reflecting this testimony: Attorney Charles E. Catt, a standout college football player who was active in Democratic politics, hustled personal injury cases "left and right." A woman fell from a bus one day, sustained injuries and sued the bus company for her damages. At trial,

215 Claiborne interview, 68-69, 134; Sun, June 30, 1998; Review-Journal, November 7, 1947.

216 Review-Journal, March 23, 2003; Sun September 25, 1999, March 4, 2005.

217 Although Price and Wanderer were pioneers in a profession that in Nevada was dominated by men, they were not the state's first female lawyers. The first woman attorney of record in Nevada was Laura M. Tilden, admitted in 1893. Alfreda Noland was the first woman lawyer in Las Vegas. Admitted in 1930, she was one of only three applicants to pass the Bar exam out of 11 who took it. The Nevada Bar's records reflect that Price and Wanderer were among the first 25 women to practice law in Nevada, and both, according to Claiborne, were excellent attorneys. Sun, March 4, 2005, September 25, 1999; Review Journal, April 17, 2003; Diamond Jubilee, 35, citing Las Vegas Evening Review & Journal, October 1, 1930.

Catt asked his client, "Did you hit on the ground?" "Yes." "Were you rendered unconscious?" She asked, "What is that?" "Were you knocked out?" "Yes." Catt asked, "When you came to, what is the first thing that you recall?" Catt expected her to say her head hurt and she was in great pain. She asked, "The first thing?" "Yes, the first thing you recall when you came to." She said, "You were standing over me with your card in your hand."[218]

Helldorado and other social activities sponsored by the community illustrate the frontier life style of "old Las Vegas" that was still part of the town into the 1980s. In 1947, a group of fifty horsemen, consisting, in part, of prominent businessmen and civic leaders in the area, formed the Clark County Mounted Posse. They performed in parades, represented Las Vegas, and the state, at many events, and owned a facility known as the "Posse House," where Cashman Field is presently located. Claiborne, a member for 15 years, recalled that the group spent a lot of time together and that there was "no meeting, just socialization." Like many of the town's leading contemporaries, Claiborne spent time at the Posse House three or four nights a week.[219]

Sometimes, the group represented the town in various festivities, and occasionally the results were unexpected. In 1953, for instance, thirty-six members of the Posse traveled to Washington to represent Nevada in the parade for President Dwight Eisenhower's inauguration. The inaugural parade committee allowed one group from each state to participate, and the Posse was Nevada's entry. They hired a special train with parlor cars, and special cars for their horses. The members dressed in blue and white uniforms, white hats, and blue and white cowboy boots. They also carried a brace of .45's, but no live ammunition. On the day of the inaugural parade, the weather was ten degrees above zero. The Posse members wore long underwear and gloves, but they could not cover their Posse suit with a coat without looking strange and detracting from their intended look. They froze. While waiting for the parade to begin, Claiborne and Jimmy Schuyler, fellow Posse member and general manager of the Thun-

218 Wiener interview, 4; Claiborne interview, 46.
219 Claiborne interview, 265; Griffin, Policing Las Vegas, 32-33.

derbird Hotel, decided to get a drink to warm up. They rode down the street and found the Neptune Bar & Grill. As a patron came out, Claiborne yelled, "Hold the door open." He stepped back with the door open and the two rode their horses into the bar. Claiborne ordered a double Jack Daniels, and Schuyler ordered the same. But the bartender refused to serve them while sitting on their horses because the law required customers be seated at the bar. So they got off their horses and sat on bar stools, and while still holding the reins, got their drinks. The bartender was so nervous, he poured "Jack" all over Claiborne. They drank up, put the glasses back on the bar and turned their horses around. On the way out, Schuyler's horse spooked and kicked out some tile on the wall. A person in the bar said: "Wait. Wait. What is your name?" Claiborne told him, and even spelled it for him, not knowing he was a newspaper reporter. Claiborne also told him they were the Las Vegas Posse from Nevada. Claiborne and Schuyler returned to where they left the Posse, galloped into formation and finished the parade.

After he returned home, Claiborne received a letter from a Washington lawyer demanding $650 for damage to the bar. The owner had obtained their names from a newspaper article in the Washington Post, which referred to them as "two cowboys from Nevada." Claiborne never replied. A week later, Schuyler met a representative from a New York television station who was interested in reenacting the story, and so they called Claiborne who met them at Schuyler's office. He explained that, "We do a program called Interesting People In The News. We have as one of our guests the guy who owned the bar. He's going to be on and we're to interview him and ask him what happened when you guys rode into his bar on horses. We'd like some live pictures of you two on your horses." He had his television crew with him, and wanted to film them in the same posse suits they were wearing and on the same horses. The man also hoped to find a good place in the desert for the photo shoot, but Claiborne suggested they use his pasture which was closer and more convenient. When asked, "Will that look like we're out in the Wild West," Claiborne replied, "Well, moderately so." They filmed for an hour. Later, the man

gave them two large photos. Claiborne never heard from the bar owner
again about the damages. Claiborne speculated that he was so happy
to be on television and deemed an interesting person, that he forgot the
lawsuit.[220]

This episode illustrates the dramatic contrast between what typical
Nevadans and Easterners consider normal. The "frontier behavior" of a
western town's leading citizens did not seem particularly unusual to the
Nevadans. Indeed, riding horses into Nevada bars happened with some
frequency during that era. But it shocked Easterners. Indeed, from the
perspective of the eastern news media, the Posse members' behavior was
significant enough to earn them recognition as "interesting people" - so
much so that the television reporters wanted to capture on film these
interesting people in their natural "Wild West" environment. For Claiborne, as a "Posse" member and as a lawyer, Las Vegas did indeed have
all the earmarks of the Wild West. But the story of the West is also the
story of urbanization and professionalization, and Claiborne had a part to
play in that, too.

Claiborne's self-confidence, willingness to take risks on behalf of
himself and others, and maybe even some recklessness, if he thought it
was right thing to do (all elements in his later decision to take on federal
agents) came together in an astonishing story of a hunting trip. No one
could tell the story better than Claiborne in his own words:

> I hunted in either Northern British Columbia or the South-
> west Territories Alaska every year for, I guess, 18 consecutive
> years. I skipped a couple of years when my hunting buddy
> got phlebitis in both legs. So we skipped a couple of years
> and I guess then I hunted 5 or 6 years after that. We had an
> outfitter, it was an Indian guy who was very well known, by
> the name of George Ezerdza. He was a full blooded Indian.
> We arranged to hunt with him in a little place called Lincoln
> Lake in Northern British Columbia. Beautiful country. We

---

220 Claiborne interview, 258, 263-265; Sun, September 23, 1973.

made arrangements for a pilot to fly us up to Lincoln Lake. I presumed Lincoln Lake was about 80 miles away, maybe. He flew us down to the lake and we made camp. We had one of Ezerdza's sons with us as a guide. The pilot was Ralph. Going back, he crashed. He had some plane trouble, he had a pontoon plane and he tried to land in some stream and I guess it was too shallow. He wrecked his plane. He had some injuries but he walked back. He was supposed to pick us up in 10 days. We knocked camp down on the 10th morning. We got up and knocked the camp down and got our fishing gear. We're fishing around in the lake waiting for him and he didn't show. This is in the last week in August and already it had begun to spit a little snow. Eleventh day he didn't show. We began to get a little anxious. Joe Bellow, a rancher from up in Caliente, was with me. Joe and I talked with the guide. There was two other hunters in the camp besides us. He said, "Well, that happens quite frequently. Pilots are all independent contractors and they work out of this lake and they haul hunters and something gets wrong with their plane and they can't go get hunters and are delayed several days." The guide says, "But, he'll be here. You can bet on that, he's a very reliable guy. He'll be here." Well, it got around the 13th or 14th day. Joe and I woke up one morning and there was about 2 inches of snow on the ground. Joe and I got to talking that morning while we were eating our breakfast. "That son-of-a-bitch ain't coming, something's happened." So we took a walk with the guide. I told him, "I don't think the guy's coming back." We had a radio, but on the second day we were there, it went out. So he says, "Well, let's go to work on the radio." We went back to camp and we spent the whole day, I don't know a damn thing about radios. Joe knew a little bit of something, but not much. We couldn't get it functioning. Going out to Lincoln Lake, I rode up next to the pilot in this single engine

plane and no other seats other than the pilot and seat one to
his right, and the rest was cargo space. He was equipped to
haul hunters and their game. So, I'm sitting up there with
him and I'm talking about the country that we're flying over.
I knew we were flying into the sun all morning - the whole
trip. We flew over a place and I saw it was a lake and I said,
"Is that it?" He said, "No, that's a lake called Surprise Lake."
I looked and I saw buildings. He said there was a mine there.
By now, he said, they're closed down and they leave just a
caretaker there. When the weather starts getting bad, they
pull out. So I remembered that and I remember that we were
flying right into the sun all the way. I didn't know the
distance. Joe and I started talking that night. We couldn't
fix the radio. I said, "We can't be marooned in this Goddamned place. That's all there is to it." He said, "Somebody's going to have to walk out of here." I said, "I know
how, I know where there's a mine and there's a caretaker on
the lake. We flew over it. And I know damn well it's due
west of here." I said, "Somebody's got to walk out and get
some help. I think you and I should do it." There was
another guy with us, R.L. Jefferson, here from Las Vegas, and
2 or 3 other hunters. But in the morning we got up early and
we went to the guide and told him we're going to walk out of
here and get some help. He said, "Well, I can't go with you. I
have to stay with my hunters and I can't leave these guys
here. I don't want you guys to try cause you don't know
where in the hell you are." I said, "Well, I think I can find
that damn mine." I knew I could. You just go due west. I
asked him, I said, "What do you think the distance is?" He
didn't know. We had practically run out of provisions
because we planned it that way, we were going to leave. So
we had gone out and knocked down a moose calf. We hung
the meat in the trees, and there are not a lot of trees in that
area. But we hung up the meat in the tree and there was a

whole tenderloin that we had out. So I went and cooked the
tenderloin. One of the guys had a backpack, so we took a
blanket each and I wrapped the tenderloin in some plastic
that was there. Put it in the backpack and took the remaining coffee we had. We started out. It didn't get dark in that
country until somewhere around 9:00 o'clock, 9:30 at night
at that time of the year. So we could get a full day's march in
pretty good. The weather was good. On the second day, it
began to spit a little snow. We had trouble seeing the sun,
but enough that we weren't worried. That second night, a
grizzly. We saw a little clump of cedar or a juniper bush of
some kind. It was only about that high and about 8 or 10 of
them in this little circle. So we went in there and camped for
the night. I sleep like a log. A burglar could carry me right
out of my house and I'd never know it. He started punching
me in the ribs and I said, "Yep?" He said, "We have a visi-
tor." Then I heard it. It was a grizzly moving around in those
bushes - sounded just like a hog. Course we both had our
rifles. I reached over and I got mine. I loaded it and I'm
ready if we had to use it. He went away. Next morning we
looked and he had made about 8 or 10 circles around our
little clump of spruce. Joe got up and he went to relieve
himself and somehow during that he took his watch off. I
guess in order to wash up in this creek, and he left it. His
kids worked and saved their money and bought him this
watch for his birthday. We got about two hours out that
morning and he said, "My God, I left my watch back there."
He said, "Well, I've got to go back and get it. I'm sorry, but I
gotta go back and get it." Well, it was spitting a little snow
and I was concerned about the day. I thought, well, is there a
storm coming up or what have you. I said, "Joe, I'll buy you a
watch when you get into Anchorage." He said, "No. I gotta
go get that watch." I said, "I'm not going to wait for you, I'm

going with you. If it starts snowing and we get separated that's the worst thing that can happen. I'm going with you." So we walked back to get his watch. Hell, we didn't go a hundred yards and that god-damn bear was following us. That son-of-a-bitch was stalking us right in our tracks. Oh brother. He was a good size and the son-of-a-bitch was stalking us. He had gone off of our trail that's why we went about 100 yards before we picked up his tracks. He was off to the right of the trail. I guess he gave it up. But it spooked us the rest of the day, we kept walking and looking back. Got his watch and, of course, we lost about 4 hours. The third day out was cold and clear. It was clear as a bell that day, but it was cold as hell. And uncomfortable even walking. About 4:00 o'clock that afternoon, Joe said, "Hey, we should have hit that lake." I said, "Well, I don't know." He said, "What do you think we've been doing - how many miles a day." I said, "Well, I guess we been doing about 20." He said, "Oh. Well the guide said he thought it was about 60 air miles." He said, "We should have hit it by now." I said, "I don't know. I don't think so." I said, "Alright, I tell you what, we'll go two more hours before we decide what we're going to do." Joe said, "Well, did you ever think that it would be easy for us to miss it?" And I said, "Yeah." He said, "Maybe we've missed it." I said, "I don't think we've reached it yet." He said, "Well, every two hours, you go south for an hour and I'll go north for an hour and then we'll come back and meet. In my opinion, we've either passed it or we are getting close to it and that way we won't miss it." I said, "Alright." I knew when we started out it was going to be a hit or miss proposition. So we started to do it. I walked my hour and I came back and he was sitting there. I said, "Well you walked pretty fast, huh?" He said, "I found the lake." He said, "It's about a quarter of a mile in this direction. It's right at the bottom of that ridge." So we walked to the ridge and we looked down.

We got down there and we walked around the lake before we got to the buildings. It began to get dark on us. I had already told Joe there was a caretaker there and that I didn't want to walk in on him there in the nighttime. So we slept on the lake bank that night. And we were damn glad to do it. We had scored. I know that we were both doubting that we won't be able to pull it off. But by this time we knew we were goddamn lucky - we were damn near dead on. We got up early the next morning and we walked down and all we saw was two iron corrugated buildings. That's all the buildings was there. I said, "Well, hell, there's no damn caretaker here. But, we know one thing - there's a road in here. They're hauling ore out of here somewhere." He said, "Yeah." I said, "It will be quite easy to walk until we find a settlement or something." Joe said, "Well, you know, maybe there's a vehicle in one of these dumps." He said, "I don't understand this, I don't see no goddamn mine. But maybe there's a vehicle." The reason we didn't see any mine is because where we were was, hell, a quarter of a mile away from the mine. But he said, "I'm going to knock off this goddamn lock if I can find something and we'll look inside there." He finally found an iron bar somewhere and he come back. The caretaker walked up around the corner and he says, "What are you guys doing?" We turned around, of course, we were damn happy to see him. We said, "Jesus Christ, we've walked all the way from Lincoln Lake!" He said, "The hell you have!" I said, "Yeah." I said, "We got marooned over there. The guy that was supposed to fly us out never came back." He said, "Who's that?" And I said, "Ralph", whatever his name was. He said, "Jesus Christ, he's as reliable as hell." He said, "Hell, I've seen a lot of goddamn planes around here. Maybe he crashed somewhere." He said, "He could have had some trouble and set down, or something, but I've seen a lot of planes flying and obviously looking for him, probably." He knew him well. So he says, "Come on you guys. Are you hungry?" I said, "We're starving." He said, "Well, come on down to my place." We went on down and it's the funniest thing I ever saw in my goddamn life. Wood all around each wall to the ceiling. It was partitioned off. On one end was a gray horse. Big son-of-a-bitch. One of those draft horses, you know, in one end of that building. And the other end was his living quarters. God, we ate like it was our last meal, the end of the world. He took us into a trader's store and the owner, Lowell Ford, drove us all the way into Atlin. They hadn't found Ralph yet. We drove from there into White Horse in the Yukon Territory. Talked to George Ezerdza. The pilot had shown up. I think a day or two days after we flew out of there to White Horse. Goddamnest experience I ever had in my whole life. Joe never knew it, but about midway of the second day, I began to think, you know, this ain't going to work. The odds are against us finding that damn lake. Because that day it began to get cold and it wasn't snowing hard but it was just like a mixture between ice and snow. Just barely. The air was kind of full of it but barely coming down. I began to get scared. I never showed it, I'm not going to let him think that I'm scared. But obviously he was thinking the same thing because the next day he was the first one to mention that he'd thought we'd missed it.[221]

Such was a day in the life of Harry Claiborne.

---

221 Claiborne interview, 23-27.

Photo Courtesy of the Claiborne Family

131

The Early Years. In October 1948, the Clark County Bar Association gathered for a cocktail and dinner meeting at the Green Shack. This may be the first unofficial photo of the CCBA. Standing left to right: John Cope, Unidentified, Neubar Wright, William Compton, George Franklin Jr., Judge Frank McNamee, Clifford Jones, Royal Stewart, Milton Keefer, Herb Jones, Paul Ralli. Far left table, facing camera: Marion Earl, Judge L.O. Hawkins, Judge Rylan Taylor, George Rudiak (facing them). Head table, l. to r.: Art Ham Sr., Harold Morse I, Judge A. S. Henderson, Judge Roger T. Foley, Madison Graves, Leo A. McNamee, George Marshall, C.D. Breeze. Middle table, facing camera, l. to r.: Rulon Earl, William Coulthard, Unidentified, George Gilson, Charlie Catt; Back to camera, l. to r.: Art Ham Jr., Robert E. Jones, Joe Hufford, Norman Cornwall, Oscar Bryan. Front table, facing camera, l. to r.: David Zenoff, Roger D. Foley, Mahlon Brown I; back to camera, Herb Gamble, Harry Austin. Photo courtesy of the Clark County Bar Association and Roger D. Foley

Judge Roger T. Foley

Judge R. S. Henderson

Judge Frank Mc Namee

Judge William Orr

John Bonner

Howard Cannon

Charles Catt

Harry Claiborne

Prominent figures from the 1955 Clark County Bar Association.
Photos Courtesy of the Clark County Bar Association

133

John Cope   George Dickerson   Roger D. Foley

George Franklin   Madison Graves   V. Gray Gubler

A. W. Ham   Clifford Jones

Prominent figures from the 1955 Clark County Bar Association.
Photos Courtesy of the Clark County Bar Association

George Marshall   Harold Morse   Nellie Price

Louis Weiner Jr.   Roland Wiley

Prominent figures from the 1955 Clark County Bar Association.
Photos Courtesy of the Clark County Bar Association

Richard Bryan   Lloyd D. George   Oscar Goodman

Herbert Jones   John Mowbray   Annette Quintana

Harry Reid   George Rudiak

Prominent figures from the 1965 Clark County Bar Association.
Photos Courtesy of the Clark County Bar Association

Photo Courtesy of Las Vegas News Bureau

CHAPTER SEVEN

FAMOUS CLIENTS

In a significant career move, Claiborne left the District Attorney's office on June 1, 1948. He planned to run for the Assembly and, more important for his future career, he opened his own law office. He decided early in his career that he would specialize in trial work. He was convinced that the uncontested divorce business was so lucrative for Las Vegas lawyers that they would not want to go to trial in many cases. It was too much work and they were making enough money processing uncontested divorces. Claiborne came out of the District Attorney's office with a "very, very good reputation as a trial lawyer," he believed. Soon, lawyers began referring cases to him for trial if they could not get them settled or otherwise resolved. By specializing in trial work, he could make a good living by doing the thing he liked best. "So pretty soon I became the leading trial lawyer, civil and criminal, in town. I know that everybody thinks of me as just a criminal lawyer, but it wasn't up until the last 15 years that I was active that I was handling nothing but criminal cases. I was pretty well balanced with civil trial work. But civil trials never made the newspaper and criminal cases always did."[222]

A clear indication of how the maverick nature of Las Vegas society influenced even its legal profession was Claiborne's decision to locate his first office in the Las Vegas Club, owned by Kell Houssels and Benny Binion, who had resisted his aggressive prosecution of Cliff Helm. But they respected Claiborne's ability, and like all casino operators in all eras, sought to recruit the town's best legal talent. Several days before

222 Claiborne interview, 98.

his resignation, Claiborne met Farmer Page on the street. Page, one of the owners of the Pioneer Club, was talking to Binion. Page said, "Hey, Harry, I hear you resigned." "Yeah, I resigned yesterday. It's effective Friday. I'm going into private practice and I'm going to run for public office." Page said, "You know Benny?" Claiborne responded that he had seen him and they shook hands. Following this brief introduction, Binion wasted no time putting him to work. "I want to hire you." When Claiborne asked what kind of trouble he was in, Binion replied, "Well, you're still in the damn DA's office today aren't you?" Claiborne said he was until 5:00 p.m. on Friday. Binion said he would see him after Friday, "I got some troubles coming from Texas." Claiborne retorted, "Well, Mr. Binion, from all I hear, you don't like me very well." During the Helm case, Claiborne felt that Binion "dumped" on him. Binion looked directly at him and quipped, "Well I didn't know there was a Goddamn law that said you had to fall in love with your lawyer." They laughed and shook hands, and Claiborne represented Binion for the rest of his life. Indeed, from that day forward, the two forged a life-long friendship.[223]

Binion was clearly one of Fremont Street's most flamboyant operators. As noted earlier, he began his gaming empire in Dallas. Binion's illegal casino occupied a suite of rooms in various Dallas hotels during the 1930s and 1940s. The enterprising Binion furnished the suites with gaming tables and a bar and made arrangements with various restaurants to deliver food. The Southland Hotel was the most famous location, but he used the Blue Bonnet and the Maurice as well. Everyone knew about his operations, Binion bragged, and no one complained. They operated "just like right here" in Las Vegas, he once declared. When asked to confirm rumors that the Mafia tried to move into Dallas but found that Binion's organization was too strong to penetrate, Binion shrugged off the question: "I wouldn't want to go into that."[224]

Claiborne believed that, while in Dallas, Binion operated with the sheriff's approval as well as the district attorney's. After World War II, a reform campaign to clean up Dallas resulted in the election of a new sheriff

223 Claiborne interview, 56.
224 Binion, 16-17.

and district attorney. Binion asked the new district attorney whether he could operate on the same terms as in the past or whether he had to shut down. There are two versions to the story. According to Binion, he had an agreement with the newly-elected district attorney that if he would voluntarily leave Texas permanently, he would not be prosecuted for any past criminal violations that were still within the statute of limitations. The reform-minded district attorney, however, denied the story and publicly declared he would prosecute Binion for all his gambling violations in Texas. This was the "trouble" that Binion mentioned to Claiborne at their meeting with Farmer Page on the street.[225] This decision, along with a series of gangland slayings, drove Binion to Las Vegas in 1946.[226]

Claiborne built his early reputation on extradition cases, beginning with Binion.[227] Prior to adoption of the Uniform Extradition Act, an accused defendant could go behind the charging state's (i.e., the state that wanted physical possession of the defendant) indictment and force the state to prove that he or she had actually committed a crime there. That resulted in a full-blown trial within the framework of a habeas corpus proceeding in the state where the defendant was physically located. Moreover, no limitation existed on the number of habeas corpus writs (trials) an accused could file. If a defendant lost in one county's jurisdiction, he could file in another county and get a new trial. Theoretically, a defendant could have seventeen trials in Nevada. It is obvious why a Uniform Act throughout the United States was necessary.

Claiborne exploited this loophole to the fullest in his defense of Binion. Texas tried to extradite the casino operator five different times to face various gambling-related charges. Whenever Texas notified Nevada's governor of an extradition action, Claiborne asked the governor for a few days before he signed the extradition warrant, which he usually did. That gave Claiborne time to prepare and file a writ of habeas corpus in state District Court to block the extradition. It was a clever strategy. If

225 Claiborne interview, 100.
226 For more on Binion, see A. D. Hopkins, "Benny Binion: He Who Has the Gold Makes the Rules", in Jack Sheehen, ed., The Players: The Men Who Made Las Vegas (Reno: The University Of Nevada Press, 1997), 48-67.
227 Claiborne interview, 159.

Claiborne won, Texas would drop that case and file a different one. If Claiborne lost, he would file a writ in the same case in a different county. If he lost there, he would go to another county. "I had seventeen shots (one for each county). We didn't have to take them all, but I did have to take five or six. I finally prevailed," Claiborne recalled. The statute of limitations allowed Texas to go back only four years on the charges. It was hard to prove a gambling offense in Nevada, given the prevailing atmosphere and attitude regarding gambling. Despite many attempts over a four year period, Texas failed to extradite Binion.[228]

Because of his success with Binion, Claiborne began handling other extradition cases, but not always with the same success. Indeed, Texas gambler Bert Wakefield was less fortunate than Binion. Wakefield surrendered himself to Clark County Sheriff's deputies on April 8, 1954, on a Texas grand jury indictment charging him with operating a gambling establishment in Texas. While Claiborne was representing Wakefield in Judge McNamee's court, two Texas policemen bodily carried Wakefield out of the courtroom and returned him to Texas.[229] Wakefield threw Claiborne the keys to his room as he was going out the door, with Claiborne pleading to the judge: "Order to stop, order to stop, your Honor." Although convinced that McNamee knew it was going to happen, Claiborne had to take the judge at his word when he protested: "Oh, Harry, I should have done something quicker but I was so shocked, astounded about what happened, I just could not collect myself to stop this thing. My God, I hope you'll forgive me." All Claiborne could say was: "I'll talk to Mr. Wakefield about it. Maybe he'll forgive you." The next and last time Claiborne heard from Wakefield was to retrieve his clothes from his client's hotel room.[230]

Joseph "Doc" Stacher was the subject of an extradition case that involved some of Nevada's top lawyers, with cross allegations of misconduct and bribery. Claiborne represented the Sands Hotel and "Joseph Stacher, alias Doc Harris, alias ten thousand other names," a high roller at the resort. Stacher, whom some considered a hidden part owner of the

228 Claiborne interview, 101-102.
229 Review-Journal, April 8, 1951, May 28, 1951.
230 Claiborne interview, 159.

Thunderbird Hotel, supposedly expressed interest in purchasing Reno's Golden Hotel and the Bank Club. A preliminary investigation of Stacher by the Nevada Tax Commission suggested "mob" connections. Stacher never filed a formal application for licensing, but state gaming authorities believed some applicants were fronts for Stacher.[231]

In 1952, New York indicted Stacher on 25 criminal counts based on his alleged illegal activities at the Saratoga race track. He was in Las Vegas gambling at the Sands Hotel when the police arrested him. Claiborne secured bail for his release from custody. An unidentified man then warned Claiborne that two New York state policemen planned to kidnap Stacher and take him back to New York. Nevada Governor Charles Russell received New York's request for Stacher's extradition and issued his own warrant authorizing the suspect's return. Claiborne learned of Russell's action and surrendered Stacher to the custody of Las Vegas township constable Woody Cole, who was also a special deputy sheriff. Claiborne then hurried to the county clerk's office and filed an application for a writ of habeas corpus. Judge Henderson set a hearing on the writ. This action meant it was no longer possible for the New York officers to take Stacher from Nevada because the writ commanded the Clark County sheriff to produce Stacher in Henderson's courtroom for the hearing on the writ. Stacher posted a $5,000 cash bail, as required by the writ, and was released until the hearing. Seizure of Stacher by the New York authorities after this legal maneuver would be kidnaping.[232]

Claiborne then drove to Ely and filed another writ and bond. That was the court where Claiborne wanted the trial. Claiborne selected White Pine County because Judge Harry Watson had a reputation for denying extradition. Ely attorney C.E. "Dutch" Horton, a former State Bar president, worked with Claiborne on the case.[233] The state had high-powered representation. Jack Streeter was the district attorney in Reno. George Dickerson was the Clark County district attorney and later president of

231 Robbins E. Cahill, Recollections of Work in State Politics Government, Taxation, Gaming Control, Clark County Administration, and the Nevada Resort Association, interview by Mary Ellen Glass (Reno: University of Nevada Oral History Program, 1977), 709-713, 718; Claiborne interview, 172-173
232 Review-Journal, November 23, 1952.
233 Review-Journal, November 23, 1952; Claiborne interview, 172-73; Diamond Julibee, 62.

the Clark County Bar and the State Bar as well. Jon Collins, a "McCarran boy", and future District Court judge, Supreme Court justice and founding partner in Nevada's largest law firm, was the district attorney in White Pine County. All three represented the State in this case.[234]

After court one day, Claiborne was lying on his bed. "I rolled over. I was just resting before I went to dinner and my ear hit the radiator pipe that ran down through the building. I heard voices when my ear hit this pipe. So I put my ear up against it. I listened and I recognized Streeter, Dickerson and the DA from New York. They are talking about kidnaping him. They're saying, 'We've lost, we've lost this case.' They're talking about the two guys (kidnappers) being on the way and the best way to do it would be to just take him out of his room in the nighttime. They're going to get some help. I listened to all this." The two New Yorkers were expected the next day. Because no airlines flew to Ely, a White Pine County deputy sheriff arranged to meet the plane in Salt Lake City and drive them to Ely.

Colen E. "Bud" Bodell was Claiborne's private detective. Bodell was a legend in Clark County in his own right. A World War I veteran, Deputy United States Marshal, undercover agent for the United States Secret Service and a former operator of the Boulder Club in Las Vegas, Bodell was among "the toughest of the tough men" building Hoover Dam. He became head of enforcement for the Six Companies, the general contractor building Hoover Dam.[235] Bodell switched rooms with Stacher. About 2:00 that morning, there was a knock on the door. Bodell grabbed his pistol, went to the door and asked, "Who is it?" A voice responded, "I'm the bell clerk." The hotel did not have bell clerks. The voice continued, "I have an important message for you." Bodell opened the door, pointed the gun at the two New Yorkers, and demanded, "What are you guys trying to pull?" They pleaded: "Don't shoot us! Don't shoot us! Don't shoot us." They probably thought Bodell was one of the mob, Claiborne believed.

Claiborne appeared in court the next morning and reported the attempted kidnapping to Judge Watson. Claiborne demanded that Streeter

234 Communique, September/October 2003, 20; In Memoriam: Jon R. Collins, 105 Nev. 939 (1989).
235 Paul Ralli, Viva Las Vegas (Hollywood: House-Warven, Publishers, 1953), 239; Joseph Stevens, Hoover Dam: An American Adventure (Norman: University of Oklahoma Press, 1988), 154.

and Dickerson take the witness stand and answer questions under oath. Watson replied, "Well, that won't be necessary. They are all officers of the court. Let me hear about this thing from you." Dickerson and Streeter denied knowing anything about it. Watson ruled in Claiborne's favor on the writ of habeas corpus and ordered Stacher's release. The judge determined that the criminal indictment was not properly prepared because it did not state in "plain and concise terms" the nature of each overt act that it claimed to be illegal. Watson also noted, on the record, the New York agents' effort to "spirit" Stacher out of Nevada and remove him from the jurisdiction of the Nevada courts.[236] An angry Streeter wanted an investigation of the judge, intimating that he had been bribed. For his part, Claiborne concluded that they "just got their ass whipped, not by just a margin or two, they got pounded. They were both good lawyers but they just got pounded."[237] In 1964, Stacher pleaded guilty to two federal tax code violations and exiled himself to Israel.[238]

In 1955, Claiborne began representing the Thunderbird Hotel in the first, and probably the most significant, challenge to the state's authority to regulate gaming licenses. The legal issues, although procedural in nature, were critical to the state's ability to enforce its decisions. The issue was clear: specifically, what standards, if any, must the state follow in considering the suitability of holders of gaming licenses, and what role, if any, should the courts have in overseeing gaming control issues? The case had a long and suspenseful history. It began with a "sting" operation, then a hearing before the state's regulatory agency at the time (the Nevada Tax Commission), followed by a trial in Clark County District Court contesting the agency's ruling, an attempted end run in the 1957 legislature by the Thunderbird lobbyists, and finally a landmark decision by the Nevada Supreme Court in May 1957.[239]

The Nevada legislature re-legalized gambling on March 19, 1931. Although each individual county was responsible for regulating gambling establishments within its own jurisdiction, state legislators gave coun-

236 Ely Record, January 24, 1953.
237 Claiborne interview, 172-173.
238 Pete Earley, Super Casino: Inside the "New" Las Vegas (New York: Bantam Books, 2000), 62.
239 Nevada Tax Commission v. Hicks, 73 Nev. 115 (1957).

ties little or no guidance concerning regulation. As a result, statewide regulation and enforcement were largely non-existent. With no effective regulatory scheme in place and even less state funding available, Nevada's regulatory control of the gaming industry was wholly inadequate. By 1945, everyone recognized the need for uniform regulation at the state level.

In that year, the legislature gave the already overburdened Nevada Tax Commission the task of regulating the gaming industry. Never designed to oversee gaming, the small Commission had administered the state's revenue and tax affairs for decades. The agency, consisting of five commissioners, plus the chairman of the Public Service Commission and the governor, who served as chair, already had enough to do. To demonstrate economic diversity, the commissioners needed a background in one of each of the five basic industries of the state: mining, banking, land values (interpreted as meaning a rancher, developer, or anyone making a living off the land), livestock, and general business. By 1955, with the proliferation of casinos in Reno and especially Las Vegas, the Tax Commission clearly needed help. At the recommendation of Governor Charles Russell, the 1955 legislature established the Gaming Control Board, a three-member investigative unit with a full-time staff. Initially, however, the entire state gaming regulatory division really consisted of just one person.[240]

Robbins E. Cahill was chief administrative officer of the Nevada State Tax Commission from 1945 to 1963, except for 1955 to 1958, when he chaired the Gaming Control Board.[241] He was a central figure in several high profile cases, including the Thunderbird case, which ultimately led Nevada's gaming community to challenge the state's authority to regulate the industry. Aside from Cahill, the case also involved another major public figure, Hank Greenspun. Greenspun, the flamboyant editor-publisher of the Las Vegas Sun, routinely attacked and investigated governmental corruption in Nevada. In the summer of 1954, needing evidence to counter a libel suit against the Sun by Clark County Sheriff Glen Jones,

240 Cahill, 241, 254, 587, 593, 594.
241 Cahill, v-vii, 254.

Greenspun and Sun investigative reporter Ed Reid devised the most famous sting operation in Las Vegas history up to that time, recruiting undercover detective Pierre LaFitte for the job. LaFitte impersonated a notorious gangster who wanted to invest in Las Vegas gaming and other business interests. The purpose of the sting operation was to determine which, if any, Nevada politicians would expose themselves as susceptible to corruption in an attempt to obtain a gaming license for a person clearly not licensable.[242]

Deputy District Attorney Gordon Hawkins and Reid, hiding in a closet at the El Rancho Vegas, recorded conversations between LaFitte and various local politicians and business leaders. Posing as "Louis Tabet," LaFitte met separately with Clark County Sheriff Glen Jones, Clark County Commissioner Rodney Colton, Lieutenant Governor Cliff Jones, and his law partner Louis Wiener, among others. The discussions with Cliff Jones and Wiener focused on using their political connections to obtain a gaming license for "Louis Tabet."

Cahill recalled listening to certain of the audio tapes in Hank Greenspun's house, along with Governor Charles Russell, Tax Commissioner Paul McDermott, and LaFitte. Russell faced a challenge from Vail Pittman in the gubernatorial race that was only months away. Pittman was a decided favorite to oust the incumbent Russell. The tapes, however, recorded boasts by Wiener that once Pittman was Governor, he would remove Cahill from the Tax Commission and gaming applicants with questionable backgrounds would be looked upon more favorably for licensing purposes. Exposing that situation, of course, was the objective of the sting operation. Greenspun demanded to know what Governor Russell and the Tax Commissioners intended to do about this revelation. If Russell took positive action, Greenspun's newspaper would support him in the gubernatorial race. If Russell did not, then Greenspun would attack both Russell and Pittman.[243] When Russell hesitated to act, the Sun began running a series of articles on October 11, 1954, less than a month before the election, detailing the recorded conversations. Years

242 Ralph Denton, 179, fn 2.
243 Cahill, 998-1002; For more on this sting operation, Ed Reid and Ovid Demaris, The Greenfelt Jungle (New York: Trident Press, 1963).

later, this episode became a part of perhaps the most famous expose of Las Vegas ever written, The Green Felt Jungle, authored by Ed Reid and mob specialist, Ovid Demaris.

Marion B. Hicks built the Thunderbird Hotel in 1948, making it the fourth hotel on the Strip, following the El Rancho Vegas, Last Frontier and the Flamingo. Hicks, a contractor and onetime offshore gambling boat operator in Southern California, who had earlier built the El Cortez on Fremont Street, partnered with attorney and former Lieutenant Governor Cliff Jones to buy 1,100 feet of frontage on the Strip for their Navajo Indian-themed casino. Described as a rather straightforward, quiet man who spoke in a low voice, Hicks managed the operations well according to Cahill, and was cooperative with gaming authorities. The Thunderbird operations proved very profitable.[244]

But gaming regulators always suspected that "Lansky" money was in the Thunderbird Hotel. Hicks borrowed $160,000 in 1947 from George Sadlo to construct the hotel. Although it later appeared that Jake Lansky (brother of organized crime leader Meyer Lansky) helped finance the loan, Hicks denied knowledge of Lansky's participation. Hicks repaid the loan in 1954. In 1948, Hicks borrowed another $37,500 from Sadlo to bankroll the gaming operation. There was no evidence that Lansky participated in the second loan, which Hicks repaid in 1952. Hicks told Cahill of these loans, and Cahill advised him that he saw nothing "startling" about them. According to Cahill, these transactions were not an issue at the time. So, he promptly forgot about them. He was "rudely" reminded of it later, as he put it, during the Thunderbird hearings.[245]

The Nevada Tax Commission cited Hicks, Cliff Jones, and others on February 10, 1955, and ordered them to show cause why the state should not revoke their gambling licenses. This would be the first test of the Commission's authority to exercise control over holders of gaming licenses. The response, Cahill recalled, was a long, indignant telegram from Hicks demanding that if they had any evidence of wrongdoing, he wanted it made public. He further demanded the show cause hearing be

244 Moehring, Resort City, 49; Cahill, 991-992, 995.
245 Nevada Tax Commission v. Hicks, at 126; Cahill, 991, 993-994.

conducted as soon as possible. Cahill believed that Jones actually wrote the telegram after conferring with Thunderbird executives. The Commission scheduled the show cause hearings.[246]

Cahill admitted he was never in a more tense setting, before or since, because of the bitter underlying political issues involved and because many gaps in the Tax Commission's case could have weakened the agency's position against Hicks and Jones. The initial hearing, as far as he was concerned, was a fishing expedition by the Commission to get witness statements on the record. It was clear the agency could not conduct a complete hearing and reach a decision within the time frame Hicks requested.[247]

At the recommendation of Wiener and Jones, the Thunderbird license holders retained Claiborne. However, when Jones testified, and Claiborne represented him, many were surprised. Cahill himself had thought that Claiborne and Jones were not friends, but that Jones had retained him simply because of his legal ability and reputation. He remembered kidding Claiborne by quipping, "Well, I never thought I would see Harry Claiborne playing the fiddle for 'Arkansas Slim.'" Claiborne merely grinned and said, "Ain't it hell," and proceeded with his usual vigor.[248] Claiborne claimed, however, that he and Jones were good friends, dating back to their time together in the 1949 legislature when they had adjoining rooms in a Carson City motel.[249]

Cautious in his testimony, Jones testified that he could not remember ever speaking with Tabet. It was apparent that Jones did not know if the Commission had any recordings of his conversations, and he did not want to say anything that might conflict with any possible recorded conversations. Cahill did not believe any such tape recordings existed.[250]

In a more recent remembrance, Cahill noted that as Jones' testimony proceeded, he got more tired and nervous, although nothing significant came from his testimony. Eventually, Jones began saying a little more

246 Nevada Tax Commission v. Hicks, at 117-118; Cahill, 1012-1013.
247 Cahill, 1016-1017.
248 Cahill, 1017.
249 Claiborne interview, 95.
250 Cahill, 1017.

than Claiborne wanted, so during a recess Claiborne cautioned Jones "very vigorously." When they resumed, Jones' demeanor changed considerably. He demanded to see the evidence against him and would answer "no further questions." Other than the considerable sparring on both sides, Cahill believed that no significant testimony resulted from the first hearing.[251]

The second hearing was even more tense, with loud accusations voiced by both sides. By then, Jones had obtained the Tax Commission's records and knew they contained no tapes of his conversations. Claiborne believed the commissioners had a tape, but for some reason refused to play or release it.[252] Now Jones felt more comfortable in testifying and went on the offense by demanding that LaFitte appear and testify. Cahill asked LaFitte to appear, but LaFitte kept hedging until the day before the hearing. Then, he refused to appear. After the second hearing, the Commission took the matter under advisement.[253]

Held in Carson City, the Tax Commission hearings were a "dog-eat-dog fight," Claiborne remembered. After three days, with two more to go, Claiborne conceded that "I got my ass whipped. Those kind of things I usually won." They were staying in the old Riverside Hotel in Reno, and Claiborne recalled, "Someone with a lot of clout went to Marion Hicks and told him that if you will get rid of Claiborne and hire the Woodburn law firm, this thing will go away. Claiborne's got so many of them mad at him, by now, that you're going to lose your license. Hicks woke me up about 1:00 o'clock in the morning and said meet me down in the bar, it's important. So I met him down at the bar." After being told the story, Claiborne replied, "I can tell you what to do. I'm out as of now. You get up early in the morning and go hire the Woodburn firm. Do what the guy says. My objective in this case is to keep them from revoking your license. If me getting out of the case will keep them from revoking your license, then I'm out. My duty is to you."[254] Claiborne also knew that William Woodburn's firm remained the most powerful law firm in Ne-

251 Cahill, 1019-1020.
252 Claiborne interview, 93.
253 Cahill, 1036-1037, 1043.
254 Claiborne interview, 93.

vada, long after its association with George Wingfield's political machine early in the twentieth century.

After breakfast the next morning, Claiborne met Hicks, who said he had an appointment with the Woodburn firm. Claiborne recalled, "I told Marion I thought a lot about this. They are going to revoke your license. He looked stunned. I got up to leave and I turned around to him and said, 'I'm going back and prepare a restraining order. They revoke your licenses, you grab a telephone and you call me. In 10 minutes, I'll be at the courthouse with a court order restraining them from locking your place up. I'll prepare the pleadings and we'll go into District Court and we'll fight this thing. I hope we don't have to, but I've got a feeling that I will be.'" Hicks retained the Woodburn firm and Claiborne returned to Las Vegas. Unfortunately for Hicks, Claiborne's prediction came true.[255]

The Tax Commission rendered a decision on April 25, 1955. It declared Hicks and Jones unsuitable to hold gaming licenses and suspended the licenses of all partners in the business until Hicks and Jones disposed of their partnership interests. On May 18, 1955, the co-partnership, doing business as the Thunderbird Hotel Company, filed a court action seeking to enjoin the enforcement of the suspension order. On that same date, the court issued an order temporarily restraining the suspension, and on June 22, 1955, the court also ordered an injunction against the suspension. The Thunderbird was back in business. The judge scheduled trial for October 17, 1955.[256]

Judge Merwyn Brown of Winnemucca presided over the trial on the injunction while sitting in Las Vegas. Cahill testified at the trial, much to Claiborne's delight. The latter, well-known for his histrionic tactics in a courtroom, was sometimes called "Whispering Harry" - a paradox - because he was never quiet. Claiborne shouted and yelled during his examination of Cahill and Cahill shouted back at him. They had "a pretty good go around." Clark County Sheriff W. E. "Butch" Leypoldt, who would later follow Cahill as one of the state's top gaming regulators, heard the yelling from the third floor of the courthouse and came down to

255 Claiborne interview, 93.
256 Nevada Tax Commission v. Hicks, at 118.

investigate, Cahill remembered.[257] Brown ruled in favor of the Thunderbird Hotel on December 19, 1955, and the Tax Commission appealed.

While the Supreme Court had the appeal under consideration, Jones and Hicks sought help through the 1957 legislature. On February 20, 1957, Senate Majority Leader Rene Lemaire, Senate Minority Leader B. Mahlon Brown, and Senator Walter Whitacre introduced Senate Bill 92, nicknamed the "gamblers' day in court" Bill, which provided a license holder a new trial (de novo) in district court when appealing an adverse finding from the gaming regulators. This was the issue the Supreme Court ultimately refused to read into the existing regulations, but which Judge Brown had allowed at the trial court level. The Bill's preamble declared that the legislature intended to settle certain procedural matters in gaming control, both past and future. The Bill passed the Senate by a vote of 12 to 5 less than a week after its introduction.[258]

It next moved to the Assembly, where the Judiciary Committee conducted hearings, including testimony from the Tax Commission attorneys as well as some casino owners who demanded that gaming regulation should be strengthened, not weakened. The only major casino operators who favored the Bill were the Thunderbird owners, who obviously had a vested stake in the issue. Pushed through the process, the Bill came up for final reading in the Assembly on the evening of March 13, 1957, only three weeks after its introduction, and passed 32 to 13 at 2:30 a.m.

As expected, Governor Russell, a strong supporter of Cahill and state regulation of gaming, vetoed the Bill on March 20 and returned it to the Senate. Russell pointed out that the Thunderbird lawsuit pending before the Supreme Court was subject to influence if the Bill passed. The Bill's proponents were involved in the litigation. Needing six votes to sustain the veto, only five senators opposed the original passage less than three weeks before. The Governor was one senator short. Russell himself later recalled that no other Bill came before him during his eight years as governor with more outside pressure than Senate Bill 92.[259]

The Republican Party, normally a force against strong governmental

257 Cahill, 1054-1055.
258 Glass, Nevada's Turbulent '50s, 34-36.
259 Glass, Nevada's Turbulent '50s, 36.

regulation of business, supported control of Nevada's gaming industry which, at the time, was infested with mobsters. Senator Ralph Lattin, a Churchill County Republican, changed his vote, which sustained the governor's veto by a margin of 6 to 11. This action finished his political career. Lattin did not return to the legislature after the 1957 session, claiming the pressure over SB 92 ruined his health and nerves.[260] But Lattin, like Russell, realized that only through strict regulation of gaming could Nevada deter the federal government from taxing the industry out of existence.

Claiborne, like many Nevada lawyers, followed the process with great interest. Nevada Supreme Court Chief Justice Charles M. Merrill issued the landmark decision in Nevada gaming law on May 3, 1957. It upheld Judge Brown's ruling favoring the Thunderbird and defined standards the state gaming authorities must follow in determining the suitability of licensees as well as the guidelines and jurisdiction of the courts in considering issues relating to gaming control.[261] Specifically, the Supreme Court ruled that the trial court could not conduct a new trial and consider evidence which was not presented during the Commission hearing. Rather than conducting a trial "de novo," the trial court had to confine its consideration to the record made during the Commission hearing. To do otherwise would "completely destroy" the effectiveness of the Commission as an expert investigative board, relegate it to hearing only meaningless or preliminary matters and place upon the courts the full administrative burden of factual determinations. The justices also ruled that the trial court committed error by issuing a temporary injunction against the enforcement of the Commission's suspension order. The applicable statutes clearly provided that the suspension should remain in effect until "reversed or modified" on judicial review. In short, a court could not stay the Commission's suspension order until such time as the judge conducted a hearing on the matter, that is, a judicial review.[262]

The Supreme Court examined in detail the five reasons assigned to

260 Glass, Nevada's Turbulent '50s, 36-37.
261 Nevada Tax Commission v. Hicks.
262 Nevada Tax Commission v. Hicks, at 122-125; San Francisco Chronicle, April 3, 1996, A 17; Nevada Reporter, A Special Session of the Supreme Court of the State of Nevada, 75 Nev. 533 (1959); Nevada Reporter, In Memoriam: Charles M. Merrill, 117 Nev. 999 (2003); Political History, 297.

Hicks and the three reasons assigned to Jones that justified the Tax Commission deeming them "unsuitable" to hold gaming licenses. For both men, the principal reason was the concealment from the Commission of the identity of the interests of certain individuals who should have been reported: namely, the two loans by Sadlo, along with a newspaper report that Jones boasted of hidden interests by the Lansky brothers. After analyzing the record of the Commission's hearing, the Supreme Court concluded that the major offenses alleged were "without substantial evidentiary support" and the trial court correctly set aside the Commission's suspension order.[263]

The powerful Thunderbird owners and Democratic party chieftains, led by Cliff Jones, lost their political bid to influence the pending judicial process and weaken gaming control in Nevada. The defeat of Senate Bill 92, coupled with the subsequent decision of the Supreme Court in the Thunderbird case, were monumental events in Nevada's gaming and regulatory history.

Despite Greenspun's sting operation and Senate Bill 92, Claiborne did not believe these events hurt Cliff Jones' political standing in the community. Although, while Jones remained prominent in the community, he resigned as Democratic national committeeman and never ran for office again. Claiborne believed there was personal animosity between Greenspun and Jones and Wiener, but he did not know why. It was not politics but a personal matter, he thought. It may have just been Greenspun's intense dislike of Jones, who was not only McCarran's right-hand man in Clark County, but very powerful in Nevada in his own right. Furthermore, since Jones was related through his sister's marriage to the editor of the Review-Journal, his great rival, Greenspun certainly had no problem with going on the attack. But as Claiborne observed, "Those kinds of things in Las Vegas in those days didn't hurt anybody. It really didn't. Hank Greenspun built his reputation and the Las Vegas Sun and his ultimate empire by attacking the "good ol' boys" network. Cliff was the golden boy of the powers that be in Nevada. Cliff was their man in Clark County. Hank started attacking everybody that was in the power

263 Nevada Tax Commission v. Hicks, at 126-127, 134-135.

structure."[264]

The Sun's sting operation destroyed Rodney Colton's political career. Colton was a 15 year Clark County Commissioner and a descendent of G. F. Colton, who made the first gold discovery in Searchlight in May 1897, which triggered that town's founding. Commissioner Colton was indicted for accepting a $10,000 bribe from Tabet in exchange for "going along" with Tabet's application for gaming and liquor licenses. Colton met with Tabet on three different occasions, the first on September 8, 1954. He admitted accepting "the finest geiger counter available" from Tabet, after several drinks, but denied offering anything in return. Their conversations were all captured on tape. Colton retained Claiborne, but was convicted after a short trial.[265]

The Tabet tapes also suggested that Clark County Sheriff Glen Jones enjoyed a working relationship with the owners of Roxie's, the notorious brothel at Formyle near today's intersection of Boulder Highway and Sahara Avenue. The actual owners were Eddie and Roxie Clippinger, but Greenspun charged that Sheriff Jones and Wiener also owned a part of it. Wiener claimed he was just their lawyer. One night, according to Claiborne, "there was a superficial raid on Roxie's. Everyone had notice that they were coming. Wiener figured that they were going to grab the money so he runs out and he's taking the money out of the register when the newspaper reporters and the police come in." Wiener secured approximately $175,000 in the cash register. When he walked out and was parallel with the bar, a Sun photographer took his picture. The next day, it was prominently displayed on the front page of Greenspun's newspaper under the caption: "Wiener tending bar at a whorehouse." Greenspun claimed in his column that Wiener was the only person in Roxies at the time of the raid other than the girls, and tongue-in-cheek quipped that it was "not determined if Wiener was representing the girls or merely tending bar," further noting that a quick check of the records indicted that he was not a member of the Bartenders Union. "I was so hot you could have lit a match on me. I was really upset about it," Wiener

264 Claiborne interview, 92-93, 95.
265 Claiborne interview, 110-111; Review-Journal, November 24, 1954; Colton v. Leypoldt, 72 Nev. 83 (1956).

later admitted.[266]

The Thunderbird was not the only big Strip resort that retained Claiborne's services. He also represented the Sands Hotel. Although he was not the lawyer for the original applicant, Mack Kufferman, he represented Jakie Freedman, who purchased the hotel from Kufferman with Claiborne's help. Kufferman, a wealthy liquor businessman from New Jersey, had begun construction of the Sands in 1951. Robbins Cahill soon heard rumblings that Kufferman was a member of the "syndicate" and an associate of Joseph "Doc" Stacher. Kufferman claimed he was building the Sands with his own money and needed no outside financial associates. Cahill remembered when Kufferman appeared before the Tax Commission for licensing in 1952 that he was a large man, hard of hearing, and the most arrogant person he had ever met. Claiborne, who had many dealings with Kufferman, agreed with Cahill.[267] Kufferman's overbearing attitude seemed to confirm the rumors about him. He appeared before the Tax Commission on several occasions and with several different attorneys. A major issue arose when the Sands neared completion, and the Commission refused to issue him a license. As opening day approached, Kufferman became increasingly concerned. In a turnabout, he appeared before the Commission without an attorney, and even assumed a respectful demeanor. Cahill remembered him as rather charming, but very intense as he pleaded his case, even going so far as to say, "I'm getting down on my knees to you." He almost got down on his knees, breaking into tears. He admitted that the license was the only thing in his life that he had ever gone after that he could not obtain. The Commission denied him again.[268]

After the licensing denial, Cahill spoke frankly with Kufferman. Cahill remembered Kufferman responding rather meekly: "I know what you thought of me, and I can understand you thinking that. I'm leaving, I'm going to get out. I've got to tell you that you were entirely wrong, but I cannot blame you for it because I can understand how you would believe the things that you had heard." He gave Cahill information that would

266 Claiborne interview, 111-112; Wiener interview, 47; Sun, April 30, May 1, 1954.
267 Claiborne interview, 108.
268 Cahill, 795-800.

later prove useful in cleaning up the whole licensing process. Many people came to Kufferman claiming they could get him a license for $25,000 to $50,000. Not only did they guarantee the license, but their "fee" was contingent upon it. He believed they were "phonies" and rejected their overtures.[269]

They shook hands and parted amicably. Kufferman, in Cahill's opinion, was an entirely different man than he first saw at the hearings. Cahill even conceded that the Commission may have been wrong in denying Kufferman a license, and that Kufferman's initial arrogance may have unfairly prejudiced their opinion of him.[270]

During his storied career, Claiborne handled many cases involving major Strip hotels. Ballard Baron owned the majority interest in the Last Frontier Hotel. Originally from Ft. Worth, he was a personal friend of Jakie Freedman and Joe Brown, who took over the Horseshoe from Benny Binion when the Texan went to prison on tax charges in 1953. Because Claiborne was Baron's lawyer, he met Freedman and they developed a friendship. Freedman previously had run a Houston gambling operation in a gorgeous, private, old mansion that he had converted into a private club. He furnished it with French antiques. Freedman was well known and liked in Houston, despite being an illegal gambler. Cahill loved Freedman because they could talk together and frankly discuss problems. He described Freedman as one of the great characters of contemporary Las Vegas.[271] During the Kufferman hearings, Claiborne had lunch at the Last Frontier with Baron and Freedman. Baron doubted that Kufferman would ever obtain a gaming license. Several days later, Freedman called Claiborne and informed him that the Tax Commission had rejected Kufferman's license request. So, Freedman wanted to buy the Sands from Kufferman. Claiborne agreed to schedule a meeting and Freedman eventually bought the resort, a deal that contributed mightily to Claiborne's reputation and standing in the legal and business community. Indeed, he served as the Sands' lawyer until the day Howard Hughes bought it. "I was the first person Howard Hughes fired," Clai-

269 Cahill, 801-802.
270 Cahill, 803.
271 Cahill, 803-804, 872.

borne boasted.[272]

In his capacity as the Sands Hotel's lawyer, Claiborne eventually met Frank Sinatra. In the early 1950s, Claiborne received a call from Freedman asking him to represent Sinatra, who was at a low point in his career and owed the federal government $116,000 in taxes. His Los Angeles lawyers had withdrawn from the case, so he had no representation for a scheduled hearing before the appeals section of the Internal Revenue Service in San Francisco. Claiborne protested to Freedman that he knew nothing about taxes, but Freedman persisted. With the hearing only one week away, Claiborne agreed, "All right, I'll go and do my best but I want this guy to know that this is beyond my field." Freedman understood but was adamant: "He knows that, but he can't get anybody else. He doesn't have any money." Claiborne settled the matter for $25,000, which Freedman paid on behalf of Sinatra, who never forgot Claiborne's willingness to help. That case started Claiborne's long relationship with Sinatra. The day after the hearing, Sinatra got a call from a studio telling him he had a part in a movie called "From Here to Eternity," Claiborne recalled. It was the big break that Sinatra needed. He accepted the role and won an Oscar for best supporting actor in 1953. The singer's career skyrocketed overnight and he soon became the biggest draw in the entertainment business.[273]

Claiborne also represented Sinatra in 1954 when the Gaming Commission approved him for a 2% ownership interest in the Sands Hotel and voted to add his name to the Sands' gaming license. Claiborne recalled that gaming regulators kept deferring the hearing to get more information and it took what seemed to be an unreasonable length of time, but Sinatra received his license on February 8, 1954.[274] The Commission hearing raised some interesting issues. Jack Entratter, the Sands' entertainment director, originally signed Sinatra to perform, but now the singer wanted a gaming license. Some of the commissioners balked at his application. It was not because of Sinatra's mob connections in New Jersey, Chicago, and Los Angeles. At the time, the only issues the

272 Claiborne interview, 108-109.
273 Claiborne interview,104-105.
274 Claiborne interview, 105; Review-Journal, February 9, 1954.

commissioners had with Sinatra were his problems with the Internal
Revenue Service and a pending divorce proceeding. Cahill saw no connection between these issues and his right to hold a gaming license. In
fact, two of his commissioners were themselves undergoing tax audits by
the IRS, Cahill noted, and the other commissioner had marital problems.
He believed that some of the commissioners simply wanted to meet and
question Sinatra because of his celebrity status. It was one of the few
times, Cahill recalled, that the commissioners took advantage of the fact
that an applicant was publically well known and they could show the
public how tough they could be, especially when dealing with high profile
applicants.[275]

Commissioner Bob Allen asked about Sinatra's court action and the
amount of money involved. Everyone saw Allen get mad over the answer,
including Sinatra, who asked if he had offended Allen. "What have I said
that's wrong?" Allen would not tell him, but just glared at the singer.
Finally, a one word response by Allen gave a clue. Sinatra made a depre-
cating remark about an amount of money that was small to him, but not
small to Allen or any of the other commissioners. Allen soon remarked
that Sinatra must not care about money to make a remark like that. Sinatra told Allen he worked very hard for his money and was sorry if he had
offended him. Allen just continued to glare. Although it was clear that
Allen would not support Sinatra's application, the commission approved
him for a gaming license.[276]

Claiborne served as Sinatra's attorney for six years until it began to
overwhelm him. "I wasn't equipped to handle it. I wasn't a business
lawyer; he needed the best there was in that field and so I quit him. The
money was good but I never was so miserable as during that period when
I worked for him. You have to know your limitations. When I quit him,
I told him, 'Hey, your business has gone beyond my capabilities and I
dearly love you. My relationship with you has been wonderful but I'm
through.'"[277] Still, the experience demonstrates how flexible Claiborne
was in practicing law and how fluid the profession still was in Las Vegas.

275 Cahill, 807, 809-810.
276 Cahill, 808.
277 Claiborne interview, 101.

Once specialization became more of a prerequisite, Claiborne knew it
was time to hand Sinatra off to someone else. That someone was Mickey
Rudin. Claiborne admitted that hiring Rudin was the best thing that ever
happened to the entertainer. Rudin made Sinatra lots of money, capably
managed his affairs, and became his close personal friend. Later, however, when Sinatra faced the loss of his gaming license for hosting Black
Book member Sam Giancana at the Cal Neva Lodge, the entertainer again
turned to Claiborne for help.[278]

Robbins Cahill no longer headed the Tax Commission. Moreover, in
1959, new Nevada Governor Grant Sawyer had championed a bill though
the legislature that removed gaming regulation from the overburdened
Tax Commission and gave it to a new agency, the Gaming Commission. The law also shifted the Gaming Control Board to this new agency.
Edward A. Olsen was chairman of the Control Board from July 1961
until 1966. Handicapped since birth by a serious physical condition, he
required the aid of a walker. This later became an issue in the Sinatra
matter.[279]

Sinatra purchased an interest in the Cal Neva Lodge at Lake Tahoe,
Nevada, in 1960. Although previously licensed for an interest in the
Sands Hotel in Las Vegas since 1954, he never participated in the operation of that business. However, he intended to be the major owner in the
Cal Neva and in 1961 built a new showroom, the "Celebrity Room," which
better suited his style and performance. By 1962, the gaming authorities
had grown suspicious of the operation. Their investigators reported a
series of "peculiar incidents," as Olsen described them. In one instance,
an automobile killed a man whose wife was a Cal Neva employee. Upon
returning to work, she gave conflicting stories about her relationship
with some of Sinatra's people and indicated the "accident" may have not
been an accident at all. In another episode, a shooting occurred on the
front steps of the Lodge involving an employee who then disappeared
for a week. He was later found in a local hospital severely battered and

278 Claiborne interview, 108.
279 Edward A. Olsen, *My Careers as a Journalist in Oregon, Idaho, and Nevada: in Nevada Gaming
     Control; and the University of Nevada*, interview by Mary Ellen Glass (Reno: University of Nevada
     Oral History Program, 1970), v-vi.

bruised. When the patient explained to the physicians that he fell off a horse, the doctor commented that it must have been an "awfully high" horse. Federal investigations also revealed the transportation of prostitutes from San Francisco to the Lodge.[280]

Mickey Rudin, Sinatra's Hollywood lawyer, promised Nevada gaming authorities that his client would be more careful in the selection of his executives and better monitor the operations. More importantly, he assured them that Salvatore "Sam" Giancana, a.k.a. Salvatore "Momo" Giancana, a.k.a. Sam Moony, had never been in the Lodge. Nevada's Black Book, created in 1960 by order of the new Gaming Commission, listed Giancana as permanently banned from the premises of a licensed casino such as the Lodge.[281] But Olsen received information in July 1963 that Giancana had recently stayed at the Cal Neva. An investigation revealed that he occupied a chalet registered to Phyllis McGuire, a singer performing at the Lodge at the time. A nervous Sinatra called in his old friend Claiborne to help resolve the matter. Claiborne recalled that Sinatra "had a limousine pick (Giancana) up at the airport. This wasn't just one visit that was involved in this. Comped his room and everything." He was also involved in a ruckus. Giancana got into a fist fight with a man, and when he got the worst of it, Giancana solicited the help of an employee to "take care of the gentleman." In the meantime, Sinatra and his valet showed up, personally stopped the fight, and even applied a band-aid to the victim.[282]

At a later meeting with Olsen, Sinatra adamantly denied any knowledge of this incident. When asked if he would deny knowledge of the incident under oath, he declined, explaining that he never talked under oath without consulting with his attorney. Sinatra admitted that Giancana was a friend of his, and that he saw him six to ten times a year and occasionally played golf with him. He also confirmed that Giancana was sometimes a guest at his Palm Springs home. While Sinatra insisted that he would continue his association with him, he assured Olsen that he would not associate with Giancana in Nevada. He agreed with Olsen that

280 Olsen, 372-373.
281 Olsen, 373-375.
282 Olsen, 379-381, 391; Claiborne interview, 107.

his association with people like Giancana not only discredited him, but also reflected badly on Nevada gaming. However, the singer only promised to refrain from fraternizing with people of that type while he was in Nevada; Sinatra insisted that he would continue to associate with whomever he wanted when he was elsewhere. "This is a way of life," Sinatra asserted, " and a man has to lead his own life."[283] Claiborne recalled that Sinatra could not understand why his association with Giancana was a problem. Raised in the Italian district in Hoboken, New Jersey, Sinatra started as a prize fighter and lived in a tough environment where there were strong bonds between friends. In Sinatra's mind, according to Claiborne, "a friend was a friend. If a man was your friend, he could do wrong. It made no difference what he did, he's still your friend." As Sinatra told Claiborne, "Don't they understand, Harry? He's my friend."[284]

Olsen saw it differently. Not satisfied with Sinatra's responses or with the cooperation that Cal Neva executives gave to gaming regulators, Olsen ordered subpoenas issued requiring several individuals associated with the Lodge to appear in Carson City for questioning. By coincidence, a newspaper article in the Chicago Sun-Times written 30 days earlier came to Hank Greenspun's attention. The Sun publisher began making inquiries about whether a Nevada investigation was in progress. When Sinatra learned of Greenspun's articles and the now public investigation, he was furious. He wrongly assumed that Olsen had leaked the information to the press and demanded to see him immediately.[285]

After failing to convince Olsen to visit the Lodge to meet him over dinner and see his show, Sinatra telephoned Olsen on August 31, 1963, and proceeded to malign and vilify him, the gaming authorities and, in general, everyone in the state. Olsen prepared a memo on September 4, 1963, relating the facts of the investigation and the details of his conversation with Sinatra. On that same Labor Day weekend, Cal Neva's manager tried to bribe two Gaming Control Board auditors during a routine observation of the money count in the resort's casino cage. This occurred after

283 Olsen, 381-382.
284 Claiborne interview, 106-107.
285 Olsen, 384-385.

Sinatra instructed the Lodge's manager to "throw the sons of bitches out of here!" Sinatra's attitude regarding compliance with Nevada gaming guidelines quickly led to a show-down between the singer and the state. The issue now became: was Sinatra above Nevada's gaming law?[286]

Olsen responded immediately by seeking revocation of Sinatra's license at both the Cal Neva and the Sands for conducting an unsuitable operation and associating with people who were deleterious to the gaming industry. Governor Grant Sawyer supported him even though he knew Sinatra. Indeed, the singer played an active role in John F. Kennedy's presidential campaign. Sawyer was also a big Kennedy supporter, and Kennedy's people had backed him for governor in 1958. However, Sawyer, like others, understood that Sinatra could be very abusive, set his own rules, violate laws with impunity, and buy his way out of most problems, if he could. Sawyer believed Sinatra would give the state authorities problems when they tried enforcing gaming regulations. When the Board wanted to revoke Sinatra's license, Sawyer told Olsen to "go for it! He's no better than anybody else, and you do with him exactly as you would with anyone in that situation. Do the right thing, and do not be intimidated by him." After authorizing the complaint, Sawyer warned that Olsen had "better be right" regarding his investigation, Olsen recalled. After all, Sinatra was a powerful figure whose prosecution could alienate numerous people if the state's case were weak. Olsen and his colleagues understood the position they were in. But they were confident and so the Commission filed the complaint on September 11, 1963, and as Olsen put it, "all hell broke loose."[287]

The powerful entertainer posed the greatest challenge to the state's regulatory powers since the Thunderbird case, and Claiborne was again in the thick of the battle. On September 27, Claiborne responded on behalf of Sinatra by issuing a subpoena duces tecum demanding that Olsen produce all records in connection with the investigation and appear at his office for a deposition on October 3, 1963. Because Olsen had previously

286 Olsen, 388-394.
287 Grant Sawyer, Hang Tough! Grant Sawyer: An Activist in the Governor's Mansion, interview by Gary Elliott and R. T. King (Reno: University of Nevada Oral History Program, 1993), 93-94; Olson, 394-399.

tangled with Claiborne, he decided to "josh" him a little bit. He appeared at Claiborne's office with the requested documents, including two rolls of blank recording tape. Mickey Rudin was also present. Although Claiborne glanced at the tapes, he never asked about them during the four-hour examination. At the very end, Claiborne asked Olsen if he brought any tapes with him, and Olsen replied that none existed.[288]

A newspaper reporter quoted Sinatra as saying that Ed Olson was "not only crippled in the body, but he's also crippled in his head." The negative public reaction to Sinatra's comment was immediate. The die was cast, according to Claiborne. He had a conference with Sinatra and expressed his concern over the singer's offensive comments about Olsen. For his part, Sinatra regretted what he said, but it was too late; the damage had been done.[289] On October 7, four days after the deposition, Sinatra issued a press statement through Claiborne's office. An accompanying letter from Claiborne to Olsen stated that Sinatra decided to withdraw from Nevada's gaming industry and requested that all gaming licenses issued to him be terminated. The Gaming Commissioners gave Sinatra time to sell his stock in the Sands. Because the Cal Neva Lodge normally closed for the winter; the stock was sold in due course and the matter ended.[290]

Surprisingly, "Rat Pack" member Sammy Davis, Jr., supported Sinatra's ouster. After seeing Davis' performance at the Sands Hotel several months later, Olsen had a chance meeting with Davis in the lobby. When he recognized Olsen, Davis wanted to talk. Olsen assumed a brawl would occur since Davis was a recognized member of the famous "Rat Pack." Instead, the entertainer surprised him: "That little son-of-a-bitch (referring to Sinatra), he's needed this for years. I've been working with him for sixteen years, and nobody's had the guts to stand up to him."[291]

Then there was the matter of President John F. Kennedy's aborted intervention on Sinatra's behalf. Kennedy visited Las Vegas in 1963 and Governor Sawyer rode in a automobile caravan with him from McCar-

288 Olsen, 402-403.
289 Claiborne interview,107.
290 Olsen, 403-405.
291 Olsen, 405-407.

ran Airport to the hotel. During the ride, Kennedy asked Sawyer, "What are you guys doing to my friend, Frank Sinatra?" Sawyer replied, "Well, Mr. President, I'll try to take care of things here in Nevada, and I wish you luck on the national level." Olsen surmised that lobbying by the President of the United States was the highest level of political pressure that could be applied to anyone.[292] But it failed to sway the Democratic governor who recognized that any hint of mob connections to casinos would hurt Nevada nationally. Ironically, President Kennedy's brother, Attorney General Robert Kennedy, had set his sights on Las Vegas when he began investigating loans made by Jimmy Hoffa Las Vegas resorts using funds from the Teamsters Central States Pension Fund. In fact, the Kennedys' crusade against the mob eventually drove Sinatra to the Republican Party. The singer supported Richard Nixon in the 1968 election and forged a close relationship with Vice President Spiro Agnew. With regard to gaming and Las Vegas resorts, Sinatra continued to appear in Las Vegas, and occasionally in Reno and at Harrahs-Tahoe, but he would again seek a gaming license in 1980-81, when a new Gaming Control Board approved his application.

Since the 1940s, Las Vegas has attracted the rich and famous - even the infamous - for a variety of reasons, depending on the individual. Potential resort profits lured some like "Bugsy" Siegel and Horace Heidt, while the gambling itself appealed to others such as Nick "The Greek" Dondolas. For some, like Joseph "Doc" Stacher, Nevada represented a safe haven from legal problems elsewhere. As Las Vegas developed its "star" status as the entertainment capital of the world, established celebrities increasingly flocked to the city seeking the limelight it offered. Frank Sinatra and the "Rat Pack" fit that category. All brought their legal problems with them, and many retained Claiborne as their local attorney.

As Claiborne's reputation and trial skills grew, so did his client list of famous people. Nick "The Greek" Dondolas was arguably the most famous gambler in Nevada, if not the world, in the 1950s and 1960s. At one time, he was a major high stakes player. Because Benny Binion's Horseshoe Club was the first casino with "no-limit betting" in Las Vegas,

292 Sawyer, 94; Olsen, 407.

Dondolas started gambling there and eventually met Binion. The two became good friends. At one point, Dondolas was listed as an officer of the
Horseshoe Club, which Binion owned until his conviction for tax evasion
in 1953 sent him to Leavenworth Prison and forced him to relinquish
his gaming license for the rest of his life.[293] When Dondolas finally went
broke, as most gamblers do if they play the game long enough, Binion
staked him for the last five years of Dondolas' life. Because of Claiborne's
friendship with Binion, he represented Dondolas on various legal matters
over the years.[294]

Horace Heidt was a popular band leader in the 1940s and 1950s. As
a youth, he attended the University of California where he was a star
guard on the football team, but after a fractured back during a scrim-
mage ended his potential career in professional football, Heidt turned to
music. A sophisticated investor, he owned several hotels and restaurants
in Southern California which provided him with a $2 million annual
income by 1946.[295] Heidt performed so much on the road that he wanted
to spend more time in one place, so he settled in Las Vegas. He bought
several undeveloped parcels of land on the corner of Main and Bonanza
Street in Las Vegas from Clem Malone, who was a county commissioner.
Malone immediately sold the same three lots to someone else and then
claimed the Heidt sale was an error. That, along with a conflict concerning the number of bar licenses allowed in the area, kept Claiborne busy
for a long time representing Heidt, whom he got to know quite well.[296]

After Claiborne favorably resolved these cases, Heidt built what was a
major hotel at that time in Las Vegas, the Biltmore. It included a number of cottages similar to the design of the El Rancho Hotel on the Strip.
Claiborne recalled the hotel was furnished better than any place in Las
Vegas. The Biltmore employed an age-old ploy to enhance its importance
in the minds of customers: using the public paging system to attract attention. Practically all of the major movie stars were paged by the hotel
at one time or another during the evening. Indeed, the minute a patron

293 Review-Journal, May 13, 1951.
294 Claiborne interview, 103.
295 Review Journal, September 7, 1950.
296 Claiborne interview, 195-196.

came in, they would hear major stars being paged. "Paging Clark Gable, paging all the top stars," recalled one patron. It "completely flabbergasted" the people from rural areas who came into Heidt's hotel and believed the movie stars were actually in the same hotel with them. Some described it as a "breathtaking experience."[297]

Claiborne represented actor Dick Haymes in his divorce from Nora Eddington, the widow of Errol Flynn. Rita Hayworth came to Claiborne's office and explained that they were just waiting for his divorce so the two of them could get married. She wanted to know if she and Haymes could do that immediately, or if there was a waiting period, as was common in many states. They were married the day after the divorce, with Claiborne in attendance. In this case, he made an exception to his rule against taking divorce cases.[298]

Linda Lovelace was the most famous porn star in the mid-1970s in America for her performance in the film "Deep Throat." While she was staying at the Dunes Hotel, a maid saw heroin in Lovelace's room and reported it to the authorities. Because she was registered in the room, the District Attorney's office charged Lovelace with two counts of possession of drugs, cocaine and pills. Los Angeles attorney Robert Shapiro, who later helped defend O. J. Simpson in his famous murder trial, referred her to Claiborne for representation. When he initially saw her in jail, Claiborne "was shocked. I was expecting to see a crude individual. She was the sweetest person. I couldn't believe it." Claiborne got the charges dismissed. Over the years, she called Claiborne four or five times. "She was so dumb. I really felt sorry for her. If there ever was a human being that was taken advantage of, it was Linda Lovelace. As I remember, she only got $200.00 out of 'Deep Throat.'" The most memorable moment of this case was the Sun's screaming headline: "Claiborne to be Linda's Mouthpiece." Claiborne later joked that he took a lot of ribbing for that from the town's legal community.[299]

For years, Claiborne had a mostly undeserved reputation for being a "mob lawyer," a predecessor to future Las Vegas Mayor Oscar Goodman,

297 Review-Journal, February 10, 1955; Claiborne interview, 195-196; Cahill, 740-741.
298 Claiborne interview, 176.
299 Claiborne interview, 298-299; Sun, March 14, 1974.

who made his reputation defending such notorious clients as Anthony Spilotro and Frank Rosenthal. But this was not the case. Claiborne himself claimed he represented only one member of the "mob" in his whole career, "Doc" Stacher. "I have all my life steered away from the mob guys in my practice and I have had numerous opportunities. I simply always had a feeling that there was no way you could represent one of those guys without pretty soon learning too much, and when you learned too much about their activities you were expendable, in my opinion. And I wanted to live a long time. That was my sole reason."[300] One of those opportunities involved "Lucky" Luciano. Claiborne was attending a Yankees game in the 1950s when a person came up and introduced himself and invited him to have dinner with Luciano. Claiborne had no idea how they knew he was in New York. The mob had recently shot a lawyer who represented them in Los Angeles and dumped his body on the side of a highway. But Claiborne went to dinner anyway. When Luciano proposed that Claiborne be their lawyer in Las Vegas, Claiborne told him he had all the clients he could handle. Luciano told him that "we'll pay you good." Claiborne answered, "It's not a matter of money. From what I read in the LA newspapers, your lawyers don't live very long. I'd like to live to at least 90." Luciano "just laughed."[301]

While not in the mob, Joseph "Joe" Conforte, the owner of the Mustang Ranch brothel near Reno, was one of Claiborne's more controversial clients. He had many brushes with the law, and some included Claiborne, either as his attorney or as the object of his bribery accusations in 1980. Claiborne first represented Conforte in 1968 when he was indicted and tried for a violation of the Mann Act, which prohibited the transportation of women across state lines for purposes of prostitution. Claiborne recalled the case involved a minor whom Conforte hired to work at the Mustang Ranch. Despite Conforte's criminal background and reputation in the community, Claiborne won his acquittal on the Mann Act charges. But prosecutors remained interested in the brothel operator. In 1977, a ten-count indictment charged Conforte and his wife, Sally, with

300 John L. Smith, *Of Rats and Men: Oscar Goodman's Life from Mob Mouthpiece to Mayor of Las Vegas* (Las Vegas: Huntington Press, 2003), 60.
301 Claiborne interview, 163.

the willful attempt to evade federal employee withholding taxes. The
Confortes retained Claiborne, who claimed the prostitutes were independent contractors, not employees, and not subject to the assessment of
payroll taxes. The jury rejected that argument and convicted the Confortes on four counts. Claiborne later learned there was strong animosity
between Conforte and the federal trial court judge, Bruce Thompson,
which stemmed from Conforte's attempt to join a Reno bridge club where
Thompson was a member. After Conforte was admitted to the club,
Thompson tried to have him removed because of his reputation and the
type of business he conducted. After giving Sally probation, Thompson
sentenced Joe to five years in prison on each count, the terms to run con-
secutively for a total of twenty years. Conforte was also fined $10,000.00
on each count, for a total of $40,000.00. The Court of Appeals upheld
the convictions, but vacated the sentence and returned the case to the
trial court for further sentencing. Thompson then scheduled a sentencing
hearing for December 23, 1980. The night before the hearing, Conforte
fled the country.[302] This case is significant because it served as the basis
for Conforte's later claim to federal prosecutors that he bribed Claiborne,
after becoming a judge.

Not all of Claiborne's cases were in Nevada. In 1973, he tried a case in
Kansas City where he represented a man accused of blowing up a com-
petitor's LP gas company plant on behalf of the Empire Gas Company.
F. Lee Bailey, the famous criminal lawyer, represented the co-defendant,
Empire. At trial, all defendants were acquitted. Claiborne understood
why Bailey enjoyed "such a good reputation. I saw enough of him to
know that he was a very, very good lawyer, but he was not good in that
case." He was newly married, had his bride in the courtroom every day,
and was "showboating for her effect." Bailey used part of the trial in
a book he wrote entitled For The Defense. Bailey printed Claiborne's
cross-examination of Alfred Earl Hartflinger, the key witness, as an example of an effective cross. Although Bailey did not credit himself for the
examination, he left the impression that it was his own. The next time

---

302 Claiborne interview, 316-319; John L. Smith, Of Rats and Men, 164; Conforte v. United States, 457 F
 Supp. 646 (1978); Conforte v. United States, 624 F. 2d 869 (1980); State Bar of Nevada, at 144.

Claiborne saw Bailey, he asked, "You print my cross-examination of Harf-linger, but you didn't give me credit for it. The implication is, that it was your cross-examination." Bailey responded, "It didn't say that." "Oh, I know it didn't say that," Claiborne admitted. Bailey just laughed and told Claiborne, "Well. I tell you what you do Harry, sue me." To be fair, Bailey did write, "Harry Claiborne, who should be even more famous than he is, gave a marvelous final argument on behalf of Harold Jones. He was very emotional, almost righteously indignant, and when he finished there was very little meat left on the bones of Hartflinger's testimony."[303] In trial lawyer slang, this was the highest of compliments.

303 Claiborne interview, 119-121; F. Lee Bailey with John Greenya, For The Defense (New York: Atheneum Publishers Inc., 1976), 212-246.

CHAPTER EIGHT

BUILDING A FORMIDABLE REPUTATION: THE 1950s THROUGH THE EARLY 1970s

Horace Tucker may have been Claiborne's most memorable criminal client. Tucker came to Las Vegas during the construction of Hoover Dam, and settled in North Las Vegas in the early 1940s. He owned the most popular bar in North Las Vegas, the Tower Club on Main Street (that portion of Main Street was later re-named Las Vegas Boulevard North), at the site of present-day Jerry's Nugget. Claiborne frequented the bar when stationed at the Army Gunnery School during the war and became friends with Tucker. Appointed the first Mayor of North Las Vegas following its incorporation in 1946, Tucker retired after one term to become the "king maker" in North Las Vegas politics. The most influential political figure in that city, he ran an efficient political machine that usually controlled local elections. According to Claiborne, he was the classic "big fish in a small pond."[304]

On May 7, 1957, the morning of an election day, Tucker and one of his friends, Earl Clayton Kaylor, started drinking Coors beer and both got drunk. Tucker excused himself and went to bed. Kaylor stayed in the front room to "take a nap." Tucker awoke at 3:30 p.m. and found Kaylor stretched out dead on the floor, shot five times with a .38 caliber handgun that belonged to Tucker. The autopsy indicated that the shooting occurred while Kaylor was in a sitting position. Tucker denied any knowledge of the shooting to authorities. "All I can tell you is that I didn't shoot him," Tucker claimed. The police arrested Tucker and took him to

---

304 Claiborne interview, 113-114; Review-Journal, May 8, 1957.

jail. Convinced that Tucker was innocent, Claiborne approached District Attorney George Dickerson, who agreed to conduct a lie detector test. Dickerson hired an examiner from the Pasadena Police Department, Art Farley, considered one of the best on the West Coast. Dickerson agreed to the polygraph for two reasons: to test if Tucker was telling the truth, and to determine his degree of drunkenness. A person not aware of his actions while drunk is not responsible for them, explained the District Attorney. The preliminary reports of the test indicated that Tucker "had no guilt feelings" himself and was apparently unconscious of his actions at the time of death. Police released Tucker after three days in custody and did not charge him with a crime.[305]

Six years later, on October 8, 1963, another friend of Tucker's visited his house just before another election. Both of them got drunk on Coors beer and Tucker went to bed. Tucker awoke and found that his friend, Omer Jack Evans, was shot with Tucker's pistol through the heart while sitting on a couch. Although neighbors reported hearing gun shots at 11:45 p.m., two hours elapsed before Tucker notified the police. When the police arrived, they found Tucker in pajamas and slippers, and numerous beer cans in the kitchen and living room. When Tucker finally called the police he reported finding "an old man on his couch and I think he had a heart attack." He told the officers that he was asleep and awoke to discover Evans' body on a front room couch. The police found the gun in a chair where Tucker admitted sitting before going to bed. They arrested Tucker again and took him to jail.[306] The newspaper headlines said it all: "Another Victim Found in Ex-Mayor's House: NLV Mystery Murder." The murder appeared to be a "re-creation" of the prior killing, the newspaper reported. North Las Vegas Police Chief Nick Janise conducted the investigation and eventually called the polygraph examiner from the 1957 killing. Farley told Janis that the prior results were inconclusive, an opinion that directly contradicted the earlier reports that had cleared Tucker.[307]

While released on bail and awaiting trial, Tucker invited Claiborne

305 Review-Journal, May 8-10, 1957; Claiborne interview, 113-114.
306 Claiborne interview, 113-114; Review-Journal, October 8-9, 1963.
307 Review-Journal, October 9-10, 1963.

to his home to discuss the case. Claiborne quipped that he would visit Tucker only if he had no Coors beer in the house. Claiborne was taking no chances, even kidding to friends that he has not had a Coors beer since that time.[308] Claiborne again took Tucker's case. The District Attorney charged Tucker with murder and a jury convicted him of second degree murder on March 21, 1965. Four days later, District Court Judge John Mowbray sentenced Tucker to 10 years to life in prison. Claiborne appealed to the Nevada Supreme Court, which reversed the conviction and returned the case to District Court for retrial. The court ruled that Mowbray committed an error when he allowed the state to introduce evidence of the 1957 Kaylor homicide. Since no evidence connected Tucker to the Kaylor killing and anonymous crimes had no relevance to the Evans case, prejudicial error occurred when the court permitted the jury to hear and consider it.[309]

There was a second trial and this time the jury convicted Tucker of only involuntary manslaughter. The judge sentenced him to one year in jail, the maximum allowed by law. Two months later, Claiborne saw Dr. John B. Demman, the jail doctor, who said that Tucker was "a very sick man. He's not going to last very long. He has a heart condition, he's really on his way out." Claiborne petitioned the court to release him, which it did. Claiborne had once again served his client well. The former club owner and political kingpin spent only sixty days in jail for arguably killing two people. Paul Price, a popular Las Vegas Sun columnist for many years, turned it into a public joke because Tucker lived for many more years. Every year, on the anniversary of Tucker's release, Price's column read: "Good morning, Harry, it appears your old client Horace Tucker had an anniversary today. So many years ago, you told the Court that he was dying of cancer (Claiborne denied saying that Tucker was dying of cancer; rather, it was a heart condition) and the Court released him from jail. I saw Horace yesterday and I know you would be pleased on his anniversary of his release to know that he is doing well."[310]

Claiborne recalled the worst thing he ever said about a case occurred

308 Wiener interview, 55; Claiborne interview, 113-114.
309 Tucker v. State of Nevada, 82 Nev. 127, 129 (1966); Review-Journal, March 25, 1965.
310 Claiborne interview, 113-114.

when he came down from visiting Tucker right after they jailed him for the second time. In response to a reporter's question, Claiborne quipped, "This is the biggest indictment of law enforcement in the whole community. They were charged with the responsibility of keeping the citizens safe. This is the second time somebody's gone into Horace Tucker's house and killed somebody." Years later, Claiborne told an interviewer: "Oh, God, I lived to regret that."[311]

Claiborne believed Tucker had a mental condition that caused him to black out and truthfully did not remember anything. Before the second trial, Claiborne decided to consult with Dr. William Joseph Bryan, who claimed that he could revive the memory of witnesses through hypnosis. Several years earlier, Claiborne defended Bryan himself in Reno for furnishing liquor to a minor, a gross misdemeanor.[312] Bryan later moved to Los Angeles, where he began a hypnosis practice. He became a well-known consultant on jury selection and eventually wrote a book on the subject - and even sent Claiborne an autographed copy.[313]

Claiborne asked Bryan to see Tucker. Claiborne waited outside while Bryan examined his client. After about 20 minutes, the door flew open and Tucker ran at full speed down the hall into the cabana area and ran around and around the swimming pool. Claiborne started chasing him. A room waitress appeared with a tray full of plates in front of Tucker. He knocked her down and the dishes went everywhere. Claiborne eventually caught him. Weighing nearly 400 pounds, Bryan ambled over, walked up to Tucker and snapped his finger. Tucker was hypnotized. Bryan said, "Well, Mr. Tucker, let's go back and pick up where we left off." Tucker made a vulgar statement and then said, "Come on, Harry, I'm going home." Tucker refused to go back. Bryan later confided to Claiborne that Tucker was at the point in the story where the victim came to his house, but that is when Tucker "snapped" and bolted out the door toward the pool.[314]

Some criminal prosecutors have a theory concerning "guilty" defen-

311 Claiborne interview, 113-114.
312 Bryan v. State of Nevada, 78 Nev. 38 (1962).
313 Claiborne interview, 274-275.
314 Claiborne interview, 248-249.

dants who escape conviction either through the legal maneuvering of a good defense attorney, or via an acquittal by a bad jury. The person habitually disposed to committing crimes will be arrested and convicted for the next crime he commits. But, the criminal process frequently scares a criminal to go straight - thus the phrase "scared straight"- and the person will not commit another crime. When that happens, they believe the system worked and provided an even more effective rehabilitation than a prison term.

At least one of Claiborne's cases fits this theory. "Tea Bags" Thompson was a "burglar, a thief and an excellent crook. He would have gotten, at least, honorable mention in the association of crooks," Claiborne later noted. Thompson, named Tea Bags for the big heavy bags under his eyes, worked with another burglar who was a key member of a gang that operated across the West. On one occasion, Thompson received $5,000, probably his cut for a burglary. A friend invited him to Lake Tahoe for dinner. The friend arrived with his girlfriend. Thompson sat in the back seat. Suddenly, the girl turned around, pointed a gun at Thompson and demanded his money. Thompson grabbed for the gun and during the struggle, it fired, killing the driver and causing two superficial wounds to the top of the girl's head. That was Thompson's story.

Herbert Ahlswede, Washoe County deputy district attorney, embraced a different theory. The deceased driver was a drug addict. The gang believed that if the police arrested the driver, he would implicate the others. So, the gang decided to kill him. Thompson drew the short straw as the one to commit the murder. While driving to Lake Tahoe, Thompson pulled his gun and shot the driver. The car ran off the road and hit a rock. When the girl jumped out and started running, Thompson chased her, grabbed her hair and shot her in the head. Afraid she was playing possum, he grabbed her by the hair, and shot her again in the head. This accounted for the two wounds. The girl wore a red wig so all he was doing was lifting her wig up, not her head, and the shots just grazed her. The police found her and treated her wounds, and were waiting for Thompson when he arrived at his apartment. At the station, two detectives walked in with the girl who identified Thompson and they arrested him.

At trial, the girl testified that Thompson shot the man, then jumped over the seat and continued to struggle with him, eventually shooting him three times. This all occurred while the driver was steering the car. Ahlswede brought the car seat into the court room to show that the blood stains were clearly on the driver's side of the seat, not the passenger side. Because no blood stains appeared in the passenger seat where the girl sat, the evidence seemed to support Ahlswede's theory.

Claiborne noticed that one of the jurors leaned forward, stared at the seat, and shook his head. At the recess, Claiborne looked at the seat again but saw nothing wrong with it. But he kept staring at the juror, who would look at Claiborne and then look at the seat again. Claiborne's instincts told him that something was wrong. At the next recess Claiborne examined the seat and discovered what was wrong. The "outer" portion of the seat was a darker color brown than the rest of the seat. It hit him. Ahlswede placed the seat backwards. The darker colored portion was not the "outer" part of the seat, but rather the back part of the seat that fit underneath the back rest portion of the total seat. The darker color was the original color of the seat and was protected from the sun. The lighter portion of the seat was faded by the sun. Ahlswede based his entire case on the wrong positioning of the seat. Claiborne said nothing at the time of his discovery.

During his closing argument, Ahlswede told the jury: "Now in this case, ordinarily you would have to make a choice between the defendant and the woman as to which is telling the truth. I'm going to relieve you of that burden. You do not have to make that choice. The defendant says that the struggle for the gun took place with the victim underneath the steering wheel on that side of the car." Then the prosecutor pressed his point, "You have to convict him because he lied when he said the shots were fired in the struggle over the gun on the girl's side of the seat. See, the blood is on the driver's side." Claiborne remembered Ahlswede looking at him as if to say, "I got you this time." But the prosecutor's overconfidence got the better of him.

In Claiborne's closing he argued, "If Mr. Ahlswede is right, then you should convict him. If he is not right, you should acquit him. Well, he is not right." Claiborne turned the seat around facing correctly and a big smile broke out on the face of the juror who had been staring at the seat earlier. Claiborne went on: "See here, this portion, the outer portion was underneath the seat, where the sun and the weather could not hit it and bleach it out. You see, here is the bleached area." He turned the seat around, pushed it in the frame and proclaimed to the jury: "See, it fits." He then turned to Ahlswede and said, "Now, Mr. Ahlswede, since you put all your eggs in one basket, here's the truth, and you lose. Because you already told the jury it was one way or the other, you lose." The jury acquitted Thompson.

Later, Thompson embraced Claiborne and promised him, "I'll clean myself up and do something with my life and I'll never be in the court-room for any crime after this one. Never, from this day forward, will I commit any kind of crime." He moved to Los Angeles, got a job and eventually worked his way up to become superintendent of his company. He married a respectable woman, had three kids, and became involved in community service, including the Boys Scouts, Little League, and other groups. In time, he became a pillar of the community. Thompson was "scared straight."[315]

Claiborne took cases in various counties throughout Nevada, as did other prominent attorneys. And he often defended unpopular clients. One was Beverly Hooper, a renegade rancher from Pleasant Valley in Eu-reka County. Everybody in the county knew and hated him. Once, while playing poker with some men, Hooper left the game, donned a mask, and returned to rob them. During his escape, he ran out the door and into a post, knocking himself out. He confessed to Claiborne that he had previ-ously hanged some men he caught stealing his cattle. Many also believed that he killed his wife. On another occasion, Hooper burglarized a busi-ness in Eureka during the summer time. He took off his hat during the caper because it was so hot. In his hurry to leave, he left his hat lying on

315 Claiborne interview, 143-146.

the table. On the inside of the hat band was written "Beverly Hooper."[316]

Claiborne, however, represented him on a different matter. An elderly lady ran the only hotel in town. A young man, 15 or 16 years old, lived on-site and worked for her. Since he had no home, she took him in while he attended school. Early one morning, someone came to the hotel, tied up the young man with a rope, then went upstairs and bound and gagged the lady. He robbed the safe and left both of them tied. The lady suffocated. The young man eventually got loose and called the sheriff. A witness saw a truck leave which was the same color as Hooper's. Hooper was tall, six foot ten inches, and because he was in and out of the hotel all the time, the young man knew him. The District Attorney charged Hooper with murder.[317]

Judge John Sexton presided over the trial. Sexton, yet another McCarran boy, was a real character and a drunk. He would not drink during a trial, except sometimes at lunch. Nevertheless, he frequently came to court drunk. "You had to love John Sexton because John Sexton loved everybody else," according to Claiborne. He was the happiest drunk Claiborne ever encountered and yet was a fine judicial scholar. Saxton traveled all over Nevada trying cases because the court in his district in Battle Mountain had few cases. He was the visiting judge in Las Vegas every summer when the local judges went on vacation. Claiborne believed that, except for Frank McNamee, there was no Nevada judge more knowledgeable than Sexton. When in Las Vegas, Sexton always stayed at the Thunderbird Hotel. He always got drunk and urinated in the potted plant in the lobby. He was so likable that management never threw him out. But his drinking detracted from his image. Now, when Sexton's name is mentioned, people laugh because of his alcohol abuse. It destroyed not just his ability, but his reputation as well, Claiborne believed.[318]

Because Hooper was so well known, and disliked, twelve jurors could not be found in Eureka County who could be impartial toward him in a criminal trial. Every potential juror, except one, publicly declared that they "not only had an opinion of the case, but they were all of the opinion

316 Wiener interview, 14.
317 Wiener interview, 14.
318 Claiborne interview, 245; Wiener interview, 17.

that he was guilty." The one unbiased potential juror had just moved into the area and knew no one.[319] Sexton moved the case to Reno in an effort to get an unbiased jury. Claiborne's investigation revealed that the main witness, the young man, worked for the lady for nearly two years. She paid him little money beyond his board and room. After the robbery-murder, he bought a new motorcycle with cash, an act that raised Claiborne's suspicions.

At trial, the young man could not explain how he got that much money. On the night of the murder, he also managed to untie himself very soon after he supposedly heard Hooper drive away. Because Hooper was a rancher and experienced in securely tying the legs of cattle, the young man's quick escape from the rope seemed unlikely. In front of the jury, Claiborne had the young man tie up Claiborne's assistant in exactly the same manner the assailant tied him that night. Then Claiborne tied up the young man in the same way the young man tied the assistant. Claiborne then told the jury, "Now, you see, I've tied him up just exactly like he tied him up." He untied the assistant. He then told the young man to untie himself and Claiborne would time him to determine how long it took. He could not untie himself. That convinced the jury and they found Hooper not guilty. Although Claiborne never asked a client if he was guilty, he could always tell from the defendant's demeanor and responses. Hooper, however, was smart and devious. Claiborne conceded that he never could decide if he was guilty or not. After the trial, Claiborne lost track of Hooper, so whether or not he was "scared straight" is anyone's guess.[320]

Some cases just seem to have a classic Las Vegas flair to them. The circumstances of the event, evidence concerning the dollar value of the grievance, and the jury's acceptance of the way things were done in Las Vegas all came together at times to help Claiborne and his clients. Charley King, an owner of the Golden Nugget, took his secretary to the El Rancho Vegas Hotel on six different occasions to have sex. Her husband eventually learned about it. The often-used claim of "alienation of affec-

319   Wiener interview, 14.
320   Claiborne interview, 243-244; Wiener interview, 15.

tions" was no longer the law in Nevada, so the husband sued King under an old civil remedy called "criminal conversion," which used invasion of the sanctity of a husband's home as grounds for suit.[321]

From the beginning, Claiborne believed the husband and his wife conspired to shake King down for money. Claiborne kept telling King that she would testify against him but he refused to believe it. Claiborne was right. She testified to the circumstance of all six occasions, including the times and dates. During closing argument, the husband's lawyer, John Mendoza (later a Clark County District Court Judge), emphasized how King's conduct impugned his client's honor, and demanded $100,000 as just compensation. Claiborne argued in his closing:

> The plaintiff talked about being dishonored. He wants to put a dollar and cent value on his dishonor. I am going to admit, Mr. King and his secretary went out and they had sexual intercourse at the El Rancho on six different occasions. His secretary was truthful about this. Now, she is a nice person. She went willingly. She wasn't forced. She wasn't threatened by loss of job if she didn't go. And apparently, she enjoyed it or she wouldn't have willingly gone the second time. Now, she's not a professional. Everybody in town knows there are fifty prostitutes working the streets of the strip every night. I understand, and I don't think the plaintiff's lawyer is going to dispute me, but the going price for sexual intercourse with a prostitute is a hundred dollars. That price is fixed among the prostitutes. His wife is definitely not a prostitute. She's not a professional. So, I'm going to be generous. Even though she is not a professional, I figure Mr. King does owe the Plaintiff $600.

The jury returned a verdict for $600, $100 for each occasion. [322] Claiborne was skeptical of eye witness identification of defendants. This

321 Richard Wightman Fox, *Trials of Intimacy* (Chicago: Chicago University Press, 1999)
322 Claiborne interview, 291-292; Sun, September 23, 1973.

natural suspicion, supported by his experience as a policeman, proved to be of an inestimable value in one of his more bizarre cases where mis-identification almost sent an innocent man to prison. Claiborne insisted one of the best legal representations of his career was for a man named Morris McGaughey. He owned a motel on the Boulder Highway and had never been in trouble before. A successful businessman, he was the vice president of the Nevada Motel Association. On one Friday afternoon in a local bank, as one woman conducted her business with a bank teller and another woman stood at the counter in the middle of the lobby making out a deposit slip, a man walked behind the woman who was with the teller. When she left, the man put a nickel-plated pistol in the teller's face and robbed her. He ran past the other woman, then past a third woman who was in front of him in line. While going out the door he knocked down a fourth woman before jumping in his beige Lincoln sedan and driving away.

McGaughey had a second job. He operated advertising sky lights for business openings. One night he had a lighting job at the El Cortez Hotel. He took a break with his assistant and went inside to have a drink. He sat next to the women who had been in front of the bank robber on the teller's line, and she whispered to her husband: "The guy sitting next to me is the guy who robbed the bank." Her husband called the police ,who then called the FBI. An FBI agent came down and met a detective at the front door, and they sat next to the husband. McGaughey went back outside to work. The woman identified him again. The FBI agent returned to his office and got the names and addresses of the other two witnesses, who came down and identified him. The police followed McGaughey home to his motel, got a search warrant, and searched his place. They found a silver plated .32 caliber pistol. Sitting in front of the motel was a beige Lincoln. They arrested him on the spot. While in jail, he was also identified as the robber of three local supermarkets. In all, 13 witnesses identified him.

Claiborne believed McGaughey was innocent from the start, but could not explain the eye witness identification. McGaughey passed a lie detector test, but the results were inadmissible into evidence at trial. Since Claiborne had no evidence to support a defense, he tried the case with "sincerity," that is, using character witnesses who emphasized McGaughey's reputation as a law-abiding citizen. Claiborne managed to get a hung jury in federal court on the bank robbery case. The supermarket cases were tried in state court, where he got acquittals in two of the supermarket robberies and a hung jury on the third.

While waiting for McGaughey's retrial in federal court, Claiborne visited Eureka County on another case and stopped to talk with the county sheriff, who was an old friend. While waiting for the sheriff to join him, Claiborne read the wanted posters on the wall. He saw an artist's rendition of McGaughey for a bank robbery in Reno on a certain date. Shocked by this coincidence, he took the poster with him. Claiborne called McGaughey and his wife into his office and asked where they were on the date indicated on the poster. They determined he was not only at a Motel Association convention at the Thunderbird Hotel in Las Vegas, but was presiding as Vice President. Claiborne obtained affidavits from twelve people in attendance, all swearing that McGaughey was in fact present at that time. He then got a photograph of McGaughey and went to the Reno bank that was robbed and talked to the manager. They located the teller who was robbed, handed her the photo and asked if she knew that man. She responded: "Why I should, he robbed me." Claiborne corrected her, "This is the man who robbed you," and showed her the poster. She instantly replied: "Well, it's the same man." Claiborne retorted, "No, it's not. That's what the FBI thinks too. But it's not." He obtained her affidavit as well.

Claiborne disclosed all this to the prosecutor, Assistant United States Attorney Robert Linnel, who agreed to dismiss the charges but needed authorization from the Justice Department. His superiors in Washington refused. Claiborne suggested they show his information to the judge presiding over the federal case pending retrial, Roger D. Foley. Foley said, "I knew in my heart this man was innocent but I couldn't establish any evidence of it in my mind. By God, this man came within three votes

of losing his freedom. Bob, dismiss it! You know he's innocent." Linnel
showed Foley the letter from the Justice Department refusing to dismiss
the charges. Foley immediately dictated an order dismissing the charges.
Justice Department officials were so angry with Linnel's support of Claiborne's argument that they later banished him to a small town in eastern
Washington. When Claiborne met him several years later, he said, "It's
ironical. You were sentenced and McGaughey went free." Justice was
served several months later when the police captured the man depicted
on the wanted poster while he was robbing a bank in St. Cloud, Minne-
sota. They looked like identical twins. The real culprit carried a nickel-
plated pistol and drove a beige Lincoln sedan. He later confessed to 67
different bank robberies, including the one in Las Vegas.[323]

In another bizarre, but far more high-level case, Claiborne teamed up
with future Las Vegas Mayor Oscar Goodman to defend the builder of
Caesars Palace and Circus Circus from federal prosecution. Jay Sarno
was a major contributor to the Strip's success in the 1960s. He envisioned and built two of the most original casinos on the Strip: Caesars
Palace in 1966 and Circus Circus in 1968. Sarno met his future best
friend and business partner, Stanley Mallin, in a fraternity house at the
University of Missouri in 1946. "Jay had more chutzpah than anyone
I've ever met," Mallin claimed. Thanks to their contacts with Jimmy
Hoffa, Sarno and Mallin tapped Teamsters Central States Pension Fund
monies to realize their vision of building unique hotels in Las Vegas, but
the same connections made them targets for federal investigators. After
months of examining the books of the Circus Circus, the Justice Department accused Sarno of several tax code violations. On September 27,
1973, Sarno and Mallin met an IRS agent, Robert Smith, in the steam
room at Circus Circus and offered him $75,000 to drop the investiga-
tion and another $50,000 if the agent could secure a $400,000 refund
on taxes previously paid. The meeting was arranged by Leo Crutchfield,
who had his own issues with the IRS. On March 7, 1974, the grand jury
indicted Sarno, Mallin, and Crutchfield on 11 counts of bribery and conspiracy. The court later separated Crutchfield's trial from the other two

323 Wiener interview, 12-13; Claiborne interview, 240-243; Review-Journal, August 16, 1978.

defendants for procedural reasons.[324]

It was a measure of the respect that Claiborne then enjoyed that both Sarno and Mallin wanted to retain him as their lawyer for the trial. As Claiborne later observed, "Jay Sarno was a very interesting man. He was a genius, there's no question about it. Like nearly all geniuses, he had kind of a screw loose." Although Sarno and Mallin wanted to retain Claiborne, he explained to them that he could not represent them both because a conflict of interest could arise. They understood that problem but still wanted him and whatever associate he preferred. So they told him, "Get somebody, we want you to try it." Claiborne called Oscar Goodman. It was understood that Claiborne would be lead lawyer in the trial. When Goodman arrived, Claiborne asked him which defendant he wanted to represent. Goodman did not know Mallin - few people did - but he was half-owner of everything Sarno owned, except, he "was worth ten times as much as Sarno," Claiborne believed. Goodman replied, "I'll take Mr. Sarno if that's all right with him," and Sarno nodded his agreement. Claiborne remembered that he "almost busted out laughing. I figured ol' Oscar knew which one of the guys had the most money. He never heard of Mallin. I went to laughing. Mallin looked at me and he was laughing, too. He got the same message." The trial started on February 18, 1975, and ended on March 13 when the jury failed to agree upon a verdict. They were deadlocked eight to four for conviction. Judge Foley then entered a not guilty verdict because, as a matter of law, the government failed to prove that Crutchfield was not an "unwitting" agent used by the IRS to entrap the defendants.[325]

Undaunted, the government filed perjury charges against Sarno, but not Mallin, for lying about his conversations with the IRS agent during the trial. Sarno again came to Claiborne for representation on the new charges. Claiborne told him that Goodman was his attorney and to go see him, but Sarno insisted. "He wasn't very complimentary about Oscar." So, Claiborne represented Sarno and won an acquittal on those charges as well.[326]

324 Smith, Of Rats and Men, 64-66; Earley, Super Casino, 50-51, 66-69.
325 Claiborne interview, 314-316; Review-Journal, February 25, 27-28, 1975, March 4-6, 14, 1975.

Clearly, Sarno was frustrated with Goodman's defense of him, but Goodman recognized that Sarno was no Boy Scout. During the first trial, Claiborne started calling character witnesses on behalf of Mallin. "I called the first one. 'Do you know Mr. Mallin?' 'Yes, I know him.' 'How long have you known him?' 'Ten years.' 'Do you know his reputation in the community for truthfulness and veracity?' 'Yes, I do.' 'Tell the ladies and gentlemen of the jury what it is.' 'It's good.' Sarno eventually punched Oscar and said, 'Ask him about me.' Oscar didn't do it. Second witness, same thing. Oscar just sat there. Sarno said, 'Ask him about me.' Oscar didn't do it. As the third witness was leaving the witness stand, Sarno said, 'Goddamn it, ask him about me.' Loud enough that you could hear him, everybody could. Oscar was trapped. He said, 'Just a minute, do you know Mr. Sarno?' 'Yes.' "Do you know his reputation for truthfulness and veracity?' 'Yes.' Oscar then asked, 'What is it?' The witness said, 'Fair.'" Goodman did not ask the fourth character witness any questions about Sarno. While reflecting on this trial, Goodman marveled at Claiborne's ability to light up a courtroom. When he criticized the government's conduct, the jury sat up and listened, according to Goodman.[327]

Aside from prominent hotel owners and celebrities, Claiborne also defended elected officials. The criminal prosecution of an elected public official guarantees newspaper headline coverage. Nate Adler, Clark County Public Administrator, was indicted on July 31, 1975, for attempting to obtain money under false pretenses. The Public Administrator takes charge of estates in which the deceased has no will. Often, the Public Administrator is the first person to visit the death scene. It is his duty to seal off the premises, take an inventory of the deceased's property as soon as possible, and safeguard it until it can be properly probated. Usually that required the rental of storage space during the probate period. Adler stored the belongings of the estate of James Gillespie for nearly seven months and charged the estate $11,340.00, based on 1400 square feet at the rate of 10 cents per square foot per day. The heirs of the estate

326 Claiborne interview, 316; Sarno v. United States, 593 F.2d 404 (1979).
327 Claiborne interview, 315-316; Smith, Of Rats and Men, 65-66.

became enraged when they learned of the charges. Later investigation showed that Gillespie lived in a furnished, two-bedroom apartment approximately 880 square feet in size, and his belongings consisted of clothing, furniture no larger than a chest of drawers, and perhaps a living room chair. Adler admitted that the rental rate was incorrect, due to an error by his secretary. It should have been 10 cents per month, not per day, and the corrected billing was $368.00. Also, he did not determine the amount of space needed; he did not even inspect the warehouse or Gillespie's belongings. His assistant, Charles Lecker, made that decision. After his indictment, the 68-year-old Adler retained Claiborne to represent him. The week-long trial, which provided front page coverage, concluded on March 2, 1977, when the eight-man, four-woman jury found Adler guilty on all counts. As a convicted felon, he was removed from public office, given a suspended sentence, and placed on probation for five years.[328]

Adler's appearance and demeanor likely contributed to not only the newsworthiness of the case, but also his conviction. Claiborne laughingly recalled, "He weighed about 300 pounds. God, he was a mess. His office was a mess. He was filthy, sloppy. During the trial, I smell something terrible. I thought, 'Goddamn, something's dead around here.' I looked and he was sitting at counsel's table with his shoes off. Both shoes off. Goddamn, did his feet stink." During closing argument, Claiborne actually told the jury, "Adler is fat, he is ugly, but he is innocent." The jury clearly disagreed with at least the last comment. Claiborne even had trouble getting witnesses to testify for Adler. Repeatedly, Adler would suggest that Claiborne talk to a certain prospective witness, but the witness would not support the public administrator's version of the story. "Every witness we talked about, backfired. None of them supported him. Hell, I would've called them if I was a prosecutor. Not one of them supported him. I'd tell him that and he said, 'That surprises me, Harry.' Time after time. I almost said, 'That doesn't surprise me.' But it would always surprise him. I don't think he was really surprised."

328 Review-Journal, February 23-26, 1977, March 2-3, 1977; Adler v. State of Nevada, 95 Nev. 339 (1979).

Adler came to Claiborne as a referral from Louis Wiener, who did
his friend and colleague no favor. Adler came to Claiborne's office and
with righteous indignation, asked, "Have you been seeing in the paper
what's happening to me? What do you think about it? It's all politics,
Harry." Adler continued, "Louie Wiener is my lawyer. I just wondered
what you thought about this thing and what you'd do if you were in my
shoes." Claiborne asked, "Why aren't you talking to Louie about it?"
Adler admitted, "I'm a little tight for money." That should have been the
tip off to Claiborne, but he took the case anyway. Although this did not
qualify as one of Claiborne's many pro bono cases, Adler "never paid me
a quarter. He kept putting me off." Claiborne represented him on several
related matters, and Adler would tell him after each one, "You know I'm
good for it." The first time, Claiborne told Adler, "Oh sure. I know that!"
The second time, Claiborne observed, "I don't know, your record's not
very good." The third time, Claiborne responded, "Goddamn it. This is
the last time, Adler." He must have been saving his money for surgery
because not long after the trial, Adler had approximately 100 pounds sur-
gically removed, but he died shortly afterward, and Claiborne was never
paid.[329]

Fortunately for Claiborne, he had enough affluent clients to offset
deadbeats like Adler. Indeed, Claiborne represented the Dunes Hotel
(now the site of the Bellagio) for many years. The Dunes was the recipient
of Teamsters pension money from Jimmy Hoffa to finance its high rise
and other additions. The disclosure that a prominent Las Vegas casino
owner was allegedly a confidential government informant made headlines in an otherwise routine case. Sid Wyman, one of the resort's major
executives, was indicted in 1977 with four other defendants for running
an illegal bookmaking business. Due to health reasons, he was granted a
separate trial that was indefinitely postponed. Claiborne represented one
of the other defendants, and Gary Logan represented another. The prosecutor was Kevin O'Malley from Washington, D.C. In May 1977, a federal
court jury convicted the remaining four defendants.

In July, the defendants' lawyers moved the court for an acquittal, new

329 Claiborne interview, 302-304.

trial, or dismissal of charges because one of their co-counsels, Logan, had a conflict of interest that came to light during the trial. Jackie Gaughan, owner of the El Cortez, Union Plaza, and other casinos, was the expert witness for the defendants. Logan was close to Gaughan. The day before Gaughan was to testify, Logan met with the prosecutor, O'Malley, who told Logan that he had an FBI affidavit identifying Gaughan as a confidential FBI informant. Gaughan denied it. But, unless they could reach an agreement, O'Malley threatened to use this information in his cross examination of Gaughan, which, of course, would make it public. O'Malley agreed not to use this information if Logan would tell him the substance of Gaughan's testimony. Logan agreed, but never told Claiborne and the other defense counsel.

Claiborne became suspicious during the trial. Claiborne remembered that after trial one day, "In getting my books together, I saw O'Malley doing the same thing. He looked at Logan and gave him a nod. That made me suspicious." The next day, Claiborne asked Logan point blank, "You went upstairs yesterday with the prosecutor. I think you have an obligation to tell us what you were talking about." He said, "We weren't talking about this case." "Okay, good enough," Claiborne replied. But Claiborne started having his doubts, and again confronted Logan, who admitted, "(O'Malley) asked me if I could come up and talk to him. I did. He told me that Jackie Gaughan was an informant for the FBI. It would ruin him in this town. He wouldn't voluntarily advise the court that he was an informant and would keep it quiet. If it got out, he'd be ruined in this town, particularly among the gamblers. If I would tell him what he was going to testify to, he would withhold that information." Claiborne recognized that Logan "was trying to save Gaughan because he was a friend of Logan's mother, sent Logan and his brother to college and law school. He was trying to save Jackie," but Claiborne's obligation to his client came first. At the post-trial motion hearing, Judge Roger D. Foley found neither prosecutorial misconduct by O'Malley nor unethical conduct on the part of Logan, but he did grant the defendants a new trial. However, the information concerning Gaughan was widely reported in the newspapers.

The defendants were later acquitted.[330]

One big case led to another. The Lawrence Arvey affair had all the elements of a front-page criminal trial. A candy and ice cream magnate, Arvey, a.k.a. "The Candyman," was indicted for infamous crimes against nature, lewdness with a minor and lewdness, open and gross. Nancy Pipkin, a prostitute who Arvey used periodically, testified that Arvey went swimming with her and her two daughters, ages six and nine, while they were all nude. Further, he took nude photographs of the nine-year-old girl and even tried to induce the girl to perform an "abnormal sex act" with him, but the mother stopped him. Arvey retained both Goodman and Claiborne to defend him. During pretrial proceedings, Arvey wore a dreadful wig and beard to the courthouse to avoid public scrutiny, but it had the effect of exaggerating his already poor image. The trial began on January 26, 1978, and before long Arvey began trying to ingrati- ate himself with the jury by looking at them and smirking, sometimes shaking his head, and rolling his eyes during the testimony. Judge Paul Goldman put an immediate stop to his antics. Despite Claiborne's claim that Arvey was framed by a child's imagination, the jury found him guilty of all charges on February 3. Bail was immediately revoked, Arvey taken into custody and sentencing scheduled. Claiborne filed a motion to reset bail, but Goldman denied it. They filed a motion in the Supreme Court to set bail pending appeal, which it did in the amount of $100,000.00. In June, Pipkin was found beaten and near death in San Diego. Three days later, Arvey skipped bail and has not been seen since. Claiborne admit- ted, "We were responsible, I guess, for nobody else being granted bail by the Supreme Court." He remembered Arvey as a well-known person in the community, a big political contributor to both parties and prominent in many civic organizations. Like Adler, Arvey was physically unattract- ive, "big and fat. Heavy-set doesn't express his size. Fat, fat."[331]

The Supreme Court of any jurisdiction conjures images of dignity, solemnity and proper decorum. Certainly, the Nevada Supreme Court is no exception, but sometimes humor creeps between the pillars of justice

330 Claiborne interview, 309-310; Review-Journal, July 12-14, 1977.
331 Smith, Of Rats and Men, 83-84; Claiborne interview, 312-313; Review-Journal, January 27-31, 1978, February 1-3,1978.

to provide some comic relief. Not surprisingly, Claiborne occasionally contributed to this tradition. He particularly enjoyed the oral arguments before the Nevada Supreme Court when he represented the owner of the Playhouse Lounge. The Clark County Liquor and Gaming Licensing Board had revoked his liquor license after detectives walked into the lounge and spotted five prostitutes sitting at the bar. The detectives testified in District Court that there "were no fewer than five acts of solicitation" in the bar on the evening of May 23, 1973. Claiborne challenged the constitutionality of the Clark County Code the Lounge supposedly violated. When he arrived at the Supreme Court for arguments, Claiborne learned that the Supreme Court had invited the senior class of McGeorge Law School to attend and listen. Claiborne decided to give them an experience "they'll never forget." He began his argument. "These five whores were walking down the street..." Justice Al Gunderson began to smile. He knew it was going to be an enjoyable morning. Claiborne continued, "...as was customary. Minding their own business. Walking down the street to establish themselves at their place of employment, which was a street corner." Then the trouble began, he declared, "Here comes the Sheriff's prostitute squad in two cars. Two carloads of cops. They pull alongside the five whores. They recognized that the police was alongside them and they all began to run. The five whores ran into my client's bar. They figured that once they ran in there, the safest place to be was the men's room. They would never look for a whore in a men's room." But there was a complication: "There was a farmer from Iowa visiting here. He was at the urinal relieving himself when five whores come running in on him. He turned around and the police come flying into the room behind the five whores and they arrested him, evidently for indecent exposure. Eventually, he was found not guilty in Justice Court." The farmer got on the first bus he could find out of town, and the last thing he said was, "I'll never return to Las Vegas." Claiborne won the case. His client flashed on the Lounge's large electric sign: "Harry Claiborne for President!" And he kept it up for a week.[332]

Claiborne witnessed another interesting performance in the Supreme

332 Claiborne interview, 299-300; Cline v. Clark County Liquor & Gaming, 91 Nev. 303 (1975).

Court. Charley Garner, appellate lawyer for the Clark County District Attorney's office, and Claiborne appeared in the court for an oral argument. Immediately after Garner began his argument, Justice Milton Badt began firing questions at him. Garner stood silently, then turned around and walked out of the courtroom. The justices just sat there stunned. Eventually, they began looking at each other. They finally leaned together and began talking. Justice Badt said to the bailiff, "Go find Mr. Garner, right now." The bailiff returned with Garner, explaining that he found him walking down the street. Badt scolded Garner, "We expect an explanation for you walking out on the Court." Garner looked straight at him and in all seriousness said, "Your Honor, you asked me so many questions, so fast, that I got to where I just couldn't think. I went outside for some fresh air." Garner's response was so absurd, but honest, that Justice McNamee put his head down on the bench and began laughing, Claiborne remembered. Badt said, "All right, ten minutes after we conclude here, we're going to determine whether or not we are going to cite you for contempt." Claiborne later saw Garner in a restaurant and laughingly observed, "Well, you're not in jail, Charlie." Garner replied, "No, they just reprimanded me." Claiborne offered, "That was a stupid thing to do." Garner conceded, "I just didn't know what I was doing." Then he blamed Badt for causing it.[333]

During his career, Garner provided more than his share of courtroom entertainment. During one trial with Claiborne, "I saw this gaping hole on the seat of his pants. He had no underwear on." When he turned his back on the jury, the women would "look at the ceiling, rather than at him." When Claiborne told him of the problem, Garner simply nodded and continued with his case. At noon, Claiborne assumed that he would go home and change clothes. He mentioned that to the judge who responded, "Hell, I fully expect him to come back without changing clothes." "By God, he was right," Claiborne later recalled, "He never changed during the lunch hour."[334]

333 Claiborne interview, 228.
334 Claiborne interview, 228.

Photo Courtesy of Las Vegas News Bureau

Photo Courtesy of the Claiborne Family

CHAPTER NINE

PRO BONO CASES

While Claiborne certainly charged Benny Binion, Jay Sarno, and other wealthy clients top dollar for his services, he estimated that 25 percent of the clients he represented was free of charge and notably tried 50 pro bono cases over the years.[335] He once had five in one year. Not until 1963 did the government provide and pay for legal representation for indigent criminal defendants.[336] Previously, most state Bar associations offered representation through a volunteer system. Either attorneys volunteered on a case-by-case basis or the trial judge would appoint counsel. Either way, the attorney was neither paid for his time nor reimbursed for costs. Accepting an indigent case, or pro bono, was an expensive undertaking, but attorneys recognized their obligation to the Bar and community to provide this representation.

Often, a judge would press Claiborne to take such a case. On one occasion, Judge Roger T. Foley approached Claiborne and said, "I was impressed with this defendant. This defendant just damn well may be innocent. I made up my mind that I'm going to get him the best lawyer in America, and that's you." Claiborne stared at him and said, "Boy, are you the biggest bull shitter in the State of Nevada. What the hell can a guy say to that? You know I can't say, 'Well, of course I'm not.' I'll take the case."[337]

Claiborne's largest and most difficult pro bono case began with scream-

---

335 Review-Journal, August 16, 1978.
336 Gideon v. Wainwright, 372 U. S. 335 (1963).
337 Claiborne interview, 76.

ing newspaper headlines in Reno: "Lawyer slain in Reno court room! Two men wounded." The tragedy worsened five days later when one of the wounded men, also a lawyer, died. The victims, popular Reno attorneys Eli Liverato and Ed Mulcahy, were both active in Bar and community activities. At the time, both men represented clients who were involved in a contentious dispute relating to a divorce. White Pine County District Court Judge Jon Collins (later Nevada Supreme Court Justice and founding member of the law firm Lionel Sawyer & Collins) presided over the case involving Robert "Sandman" Williams, his estranged wife, and mother-in-law. Although Williams and his wife had a divorce action pending, this court hearing was an ownership dispute between Williams and his wife over their sand and gravel business (thus the nickname "Sandman"). Attorney Samuel Francovich represented Williams and the two deceased attorneys represented his wife.[338]

Judge Collins had just begun to announce his decision when Williams pulled a .38 automatic pistol from beneath his shirt and started shooting. He shot Liverato first, and then a trial witness. He then tried to kill his wife, but she jumped under the table. He then turned his gun on his mother-in-law, but missed, and instead hit her brother as well as attorney Mulcahy. Police found eight empty cartridges in the courtroom. Francovich, a decorated World War II Navy pilot, grabbed Williams and scuffled with him until the court reporter wrestled the gun away. As he left the court room, Williams asked the arresting deputies, "What happened?"[339]

Two days after the shooting, eight Reno law firms, representing twenty-three attorneys, filed a civil lawsuit against Williams, which immediately disqualified them from a court-appointed representation of Williams in the criminal case. Supreme Court Justice Milton Badt was upset and believed that the Reno lawyers deliberately removed themselves from being appointed to represent Williams. But many Reno attorneys agreed that while Williams had the right to legal representation, it was almost impossible for him to engage local counsel. At Badt's request,

338 Reno Evening Gazette, November 25, 1960.
339 Reno Evening Gazette, November 25, 1960.

Claiborne agreed to represent Williams on a pro bono basis. Later, the
court also appointed Reno attorney Les Fry. Claiborne believed that Fry,
a highly principled lawyer, felt guilty because of the way the Reno Bar
had reacted.[340]

Jury selection began on June 28, 1961 and took three days. According
to court observers, the last jury selection that took this long was a murder
case 13 years earlier. Due to the publicity and potential juror bias, over
72 potential jurors were questioned. District Court Judge Merwyn Brown
from Winnemucca presided and Washoe County District Attorney William Raggio and Eric Richards represented the State.[341]

Raggio since has gone on to a long career as a legislative power bro-
ker, but in the 1950s and 1960s, he was, in Claiborne's opinion, the best
prosecutor in Nevada. Raggio served as Washoe County District Attorney from 1959 until 1971. Elected to the Nevada State Senate in 1972, he
soon rose to become Republican leader and perhaps the most renowned
legislative leader in the body's history.[342]

Because Claiborne argued that Williams was not guilty by reason of
insanity, the trial became a contest between opposing psychiatrists.
The defense claimed that Williams suffered from delusions of persecu-
tion, which included the confiscation of his sand and gravel business.
Williams also believed that Judge Collins tried to aggravate his heart
condition. In fact, Williams had a heart attack prior to the trial and still
experienced palpitations during the trial. Williams' lawyers asked for a
continuance, but Collins refused. So in Williams' delusional mind, he
believed that Judge Collins had tried to kill him.

Witness testimony demonstrated that Williams was a very angry and
potentially dangerous man, who often warned people that he would shoot
anyone who interfered with his family affairs. Testimony revealed that
Williams had threatened that if anyone took any of his property there
would be three shots fired - one at his wife, one at his mother-in-law, and

---

340 Reno Evening Gazette, November 26, 1960, December 10, 1960; Claiborne interview, 200.

341 Reno Evening Gazette, June 30, 1961; Nevada State Journal, June 30, 1961, July 1, 1961.

342 Wiener interview, 21; Robert E. Dickens, "William Raggio: Personality, Power, and Politics," in
     Richard O. Davies, ed., The Maverick Spirit: Building the New Nevada (Reno: University of Nevada
     Press, 1999), 212-33.

one at any witness. A neighbor told of Williams target practicing with a
human shaped cardboard target.[343]

Claiborne called Williams as his first witness. Described as a nervous,
pain racked old man at 57 years of age, he sobbed dramatically and
claimed he had "no guilty feeling and I can not even visualize shooting them." Nonetheless, he believed he was justified in shooting them
because they were trying to rob him of everything he owned. The judge
and the attorneys went into the back room and decided against him,
he claimed. Judge Collins tried to kill him by running overtime court
sessions knowing that he had heart problems. He then concluded his
testimony by complaining that he had no chance for acquittal because
the jury had already decided against him. He also contended that he did
not think that Claiborne was working hard enough, claiming, "I feel you
could win the case if you try."[344]

During the trial, Williams wrote notes constantly and handed them to
Fry, who read them before putting them in his pocket. One day at lunch,
Claiborne asked about the notes. He told Fry that he needed to know
what Williams was thinking and maybe the notes contained good ideas.
At least they should pay attention to what their client was telling them.
Fry reached into his pocket and pulled out a note at random that read,
"Claiborne has sold me out." Claiborne later recalled with frustration,
"I've never taken such a beating in my life and he claimed I was selling
him out."[345]

Both sides called many witnesses and presented psychiatric testimony
by eminently qualified physicians. The conflicting testimony was whether Williams knew right from wrong and whether he realized the nature
and quality of his actions. To prove legal insanity, the Reno Evening Gazette explained to its readers, the defendant must not be cognizant of the
facts. Heated, and sometimes uncontrollable, arguments and shouting
matches between the attorneys contributed to the tension. The case went
to the jury on July 12, 1961 at 4:52 p.m.[346]

343 Nevada State Journal, July 7, 1961.
344 Nevada State Journal, July 8, 1961; Reno Evening Gazette, July 7, 1961
345 Wiener interview, 7.
346 Reno Evening Gazette, July 10-12, 1961; Nevada State Journal, July 11-12, 1961.

The jurors had six possible verdicts. Three required a first degree conviction with the only difference being the penalty. It could be the gas chamber, prison for life, or life in prison with the possibility of parole. The other three verdicts were second degree murder and two acquittal choices, either not guilty by reason of insanity or simply not guilty.[347] On July 14, after 11 hours of deliberation, the jury found Williams guilty of first degree murder and sentenced him to life in prison without the possibility of parole. Jury members reached a verdict of first degree murder after only a few hours of deliberation. The initial vote was 7 to 5 for the death penalty. They ruled out insanity "first thing" during their deliberations, but eventually decided against the death penalty because they believed Williams, in his own mind, felt he had been provoked into shooting the men. As one juror later described their view of Williams, he was a broken, old man who helplessly watched his sand and gravel "empire" crumble before him, his wife turned against him, and seemingly even the judge and his own attorneys did not understand him. Williams ultimately died in prison.[348]

The trial took its toll on Claiborne, but it also tested his mettle and demonstrated his devotion to giving every defendant the best possible defense. Afterward, Judge Merwyn Brown claimed he took the Williams trial because "the Judges in Reno were too close to the slain attorneys." He believed it was his most difficult case during his 16 years on the bench. In chambers, Brown commented that the verdict demonstrated the fallacy of the defense in claiming insanity, but he also credited Claiborne and Fry for giving the defendant the best defense possible. According to some observers, Brown at times seemed on the verge of holding Claiborne in contempt of court for his "disrespectful attitude," but failed to do so for fear of jeopardizing the trial.[349] Claiborne recalled it as probably the hardest case he ever tried. Because he received so many threatening and harassing telephone calls at his hotel, Claiborne stayed at the home of Reno attorney John Squire Drendel. But he was still vulnerable in

347 Reno Evening Gazette, July 13, 1961.
348 Claiborne interview, 200-208; Nevada State Journal, July 14, 1961; Reno Evening Gazette, July 14, 1961.
349 Nevada State Journal, July 14, 1961.

public. Indeed, one woman who was attending the trial actually attacked Claiborne in a restaurant.[350]

But this was definitely one of the high points in Claiborne's career. Indeed, Reno attorneys generally commended Claiborne for his skillful and courageous representation of Williams. Some jury members even credited Claiborne for "putting on quite an act that we will never see again in the court room." Other jurors praised Raggio for "standing up to Claiborne and giving one of the most brilliant summations we have ever heard." In recognition of his efforts, the Nevada State Bar Association later passed a resolution commending Claiborne for his "defense of an unpopular cause, at his personal expense and under criticism, (which) exemplifies adherence to the highest ideals of our profession." Robert Herz, executive secretary of the State Bar, praised Claiborne's conduct "as an example to the entire Bar of the State of Nevada." Past President of the Washoe County Bar Association Robert Taylor Adams introduced a resolution that declared, "As a lawyer from Washoe County, I wish to commend on behalf of the entire Bar of the State of Nevada as an outstanding example of such action by a Las Vegas lawyer. I refer to Harry Claiborne. I suggest to you that his recent defense of an unpopular cause, at his personal expense and under criticism, exemplifies adherence to the highest ideals of our profession. It is easy to live up to an ideal when it is popular. It is difficult when such adherence to principle means sacrifice."[351]

Claiborne's problems during the trial involved not just his ungrateful and unstable client, but Judge Brown. According to Claiborne, the selection of Brown created its own problems. Years earlier, Claiborne had filed an affidavit against Brown for judicial misconduct based on a conflict of interest in a civil lawsuit. Brown was a part-owner of the insurance company involved in the case but never disclosed his stake in the company. When Claiborne learned of it by accident from an insurance adjuster, he felt he had no choice but to settle the lawsuit for whatever money he could get under the circumstances. After the settle-

350 Claiborne interview, 202-203, 205.
351 Review-Journal, January 5, 1962, 2; Nevada State Journal, July 14, 1961.

ment, he started to drive home, but turned around and went back to confront Brown in his chambers. Brown said, "I'm glad you settled that." Claiborne responded, "Well, I didn't have much choice. Under the circumstances, why didn't you disclose to us that you had an interest in the insurance company that wrote the insurance policy?" Brown angrily replied, "That had nothing to do with this case. Are you telling me that you think I would have been prejudiced?" "That's exactly that I'm telling you." Brown retorted, "Well, get out of here."[352] Claiborne later filed a judicial complaint against Brown. Ralph Denton had a similar problem with Brown. After settling a case assigned to Brown's courtroom, he received a settlement check which was countersigned by Brown as the insurance agent for the company that Denton was suing. Brown was going to try the case without telling Denton of the obvious conflict of interest.[353]

Years later, Brown made Claiborne's life miserable during the Williams trial. Claiborne surmised that Brown got revenge for filing the judicial complaint. Claiborne and Fry ate lunch every day at the Holiday Hotel during the trial and saw Brown come in and "drink his lunch." Claiborne counted the judge's drinks before returning to the afternoon session of court. "There were always 4 or 5, and I never saw him go to the dining room to eat while I was there," Claiborne recalled. One day Claiborne tipped off Fry that they were going to have some fun when they got back to court after lunch. After about 5 minutes in court, Claiborne asked to approach the bench. He then went to the bench, sniffed the air and said, "Are you drunk?" He sniffed 4 or 5 more times and said, "Are you?" Brown leaned way back away from Claiborne. He again asked, "Are you drunk? Are you drinking, Judge?" Brown ordered him to "Keep your voice down!" Claiborne blithely replied, "God, you smell like you fell in a beer barrel. I want you to know, right now, that I have a man's life at stake, and I can't risk his freedom to a drunk judge. I'm not going to do it." Claiborne knew the first 2 or 3 jurors heard this conversation. An angry Brown then said, "We're going into chambers." In chambers, and in

352 Claiborne interview, 240.
353 Ralph Denton, 183-84.

front of the court reporter, Brown shouted at him: "Now you have done it, you son-of-a-bitch!" Claiborne turned and said to the court reporter, "Take that down! Let the record show that he called me a son-of-a-bitch! The Judge called me a son-of-a-bitch!" Raggio stood in the hallway with his arms folded and grinning from ear-to-ear. He could not have had it any better. Claiborne said, "I demand that you go out to the hospital and take a blood alcohol test." Brown told the court reporter, "Don't take that down." Claiborne yelled, "Take it down." This went back and forth several times. Finally, Brown declared: "I'm not going to do any such a damn thing. Get out of here! Get out of here! All of you, get out of here. Go back to court." Brown was smarter than Claiborne thought because he told the jury, "Ladies and gentlemen of the jury, the court is going to be occupied with other matters this afternoon. You're excused and free to go home and be back tomorrow morning at 8:30." He glared at Claiborne and went, "Ha!"[354]

Claiborne was tenacious as a lawyer. On one occasion, he tried to help the Tomiyasu family save their land and produce business. Yonema "Bill" Tomiyasu and his family moved to Las Vegas in 1916, settled on 85 acres of land, dug a well by hand, and started growing produce. Claiborne estimated that they had the finest artesian well in the Las Vegas Valley. Their business flourished, and they eventually expanded into the nursery business with their son, Nanyu. In 1961, they visited Japan and turned the business over to their son to manage while they were gone. However, Nanyu failed to make the mortgage payments on the property. The bank sent notice after notice, and finally, a notice of foreclosure. The Tomiyasus never responded. Claiborne maintained that the father did not know of the delinquency, but the court records indicate that he was aware of the problem but was short of funds. The bank finally foreclosed on the land. The 80 acres involved, worth $200,000, were sold for $18,025.73, one dollar more than the mortgage balance. Bill Tomiyasu, age 82 and a Clark County resident for 43 years, and his wife lost everything. Feeling compassion for the old couple, Claiborne agreed to represent them for free. He filed suit to return the property, and won at the

354 Claiborne interview, 238-239.

trial court level. But the Supreme Court reversed the decision, holding that the bank complied with all statutory requirements for a foreclosure proceeding and that the inadequacy of the price alone was not sufficient to set aside the trustee's sale. Claiborne eventually appealed through the federal system and to the U. S. Supreme Court, but to no avail. The Tomiyasus lost their land, and Claiborne was out $70,000 to $80,000 of his own money trying to help the family. Years later, a frustrated Claiborne still wondered about it: "I cannot understand why a guy (Nanyu) with a year's time would not even remember that he had this small chore to do (make the mortgage payment). I don't know to this day whatever excuse he gave his dad."[355]

Claiborne also maintained a close working friendship with the Las Vegas police department after he started practicing law. Claiborne took his personal association with fellow policemen seriously. Indeed, he knew everyone on the police force. Knowing that their profession often placed officers in situations that exposed them to personal liability without adequate funds to defend themselves, Claiborne often represented them for free. This reflects relationships generally found only in small town environments. In the post-war era, there still existed a close relationship between the legal community and residents in a town where many people still knew one another.

Claiborne defended Floyd "Tex" Young, who was accused of molesting a young girl. Because Claiborne had worked with Young as a cop, he defended him at no charge. "I had to; he was a comrade." Young and his wife took the 13-year-old girl into their home to adopt, but she claimed that Young molested her. The prosecutors, deputy district attorneys George Dickerson and John Mowbray, considered child molestation the worst crime imaginable and "went wild" whenever Claiborne tried to talk about settling the case prior to trial. Preparing for the case, Claiborne learned that the girl had earlier claimed that her father molested her and reported him to the Boulder City Police Department several years later. Her mother claimed the girl was a habitual liar. When Claiborne

355 Claiborne interview, 217-218; Golden v. Tomiyasu, 79 Nev. 503 (1963); Tomiyasu v. Golden, 81 Nev. 140 (1965).

interviewed the Boulder City policeman involved in the earlier claim, he learned of still another incident. She was in school, climbed on top of her desk and brought out a bottle which had a skull and crossbones on it with 'POISON' written on the label. She swallowed the contents and fell faint into the aisle. The school rushed her to the hospital and pumped her stomach. It was grapefruit juice. Dr. James French verified the story, as did the teacher.

Despite this evidence, Mowbray refused to budge and declared, "I believe the girl. That rotten bastard needs putting away and I'm going to put him away." But Claiborne uncovered more information about the girl. A girlfriend who attended "sleep overs" at the girl's house reported that the girl had pornographic books which she showed her. At trial, Claiborne charged that the state's three major witnesses were motivated by spite and bias. He argued further that the so-called victim, in accusing Young, was merely repeating her past conduct. Every time she got in trouble, Claiborne observed, she would claim she was molested as a way of making herself the center of attention. Mowbray, in a powerful closing argument, admitted the girl was perhaps not a "little saint," but that Young was in part responsible for the girl's conduct. "He made her what she is," said Mowbray.

But Claiborne's evidence and persuasive arguments were convincing. After nearly four hours of deliberation, the jury found Young innocent. The Review-Journal described it as a complete and, to many courtroom observers, an astounding victory for Claiborne. As Claiborne and Young left the courtroom after the verdict, a furious Mowbray shook his finger in Young's face and said, "God will exact vengeance on you. Wait and see." Claiborne replied, "You stupid son-of-a-bitch."[356]

In another case involving former police "comrades," Claiborne defended four veteran detectives fired for making disparaging statements about their supervisor. When Police Chief Robert Malburg resigned his office, booking sergeant Archie Wells became acting chief of police until the City Council appointed a permanent chief. Stanley Halstead, a newcomer to the department, applied for the job. Halstead asked Chief of Detectives

356 Claiborne interview, 129-130; Review-Journal, May 11, 1952.

B. J. Hanlon, Detective Pete Reid, Sergeant Eddie Davis, and Captain George Thompson to meet with him. Without their knowledge, Halstead bugged the meeting room. He told them that he would soon be appointed chief of police and wanted to talk with them to get a lay of the land. He wanted to know which officers he could trust, as well as the good and the bad cops on the force. He also advised them he intended to completely reorganize the department, but that they had been recommended as officers who should be retained. Halstead then asked each man for his opinion of Acting Chief Wells and how he was running the department. He assured them that their responses would be kept confidential. Claiborne recalled, "They said a lot of derogatory things about everybody. They just didn't stop at just Wells, they went after everybody. They had more grievances than he ever thought." Someone sent the tape recording to Wells. Although he denied any association with Halstead or any involvement with the recordings, Wells fired all four of them for "causing dissension in the department." Claiborne defended them pro bono. The Police Department had a weak case, and after a month of hearings, the men returned to work with back pay.[357]

In later years, some of Claiborne's respect for certain police officers waned. He represented Richard Charles Roy, a 22-year-old busboy pro bono. Roy lived down the street from a drug dealer who was being staked out by a couple of undercover detectives. Roy could neither read nor write, and the cops could easily see that he was mentally retarded. They befriended him and asked if he would help them. They gave him $20 to buy some marijuana from the dealer, which he did, and brought it back to them. The officers then charged him with the crime of selling marijuana. Although Roy was convicted by a jury and sentenced to four years in prison, Claiborne won a reversal from the Supreme Court justices who reasoned that the defendant could not be a seller when he was acting on behalf of the police. Disgusted by their actions, Claiborne referred to the undercover policemen as "those rotten bastards," a far cry from the high esteem in which he held his earlier "comrades."[358]

---

357 Claiborne interview, 154-155; Review-Journal, April 26, 1950; Griffin, Policing Las Vegas, 12-16.
358 Claiborne interview, 283; Roy v State of Nevada, 87 Nev. 517 (1971).

Not all of Claiborne's pro bono work was satisfying. Bill Villa was "blind" and used a seeing eye dog. Over the years, Claiborne handled many cases for him - all free of charge. One day, while walking to lunch, Claiborne saw Villa standing on the corner with his dog. The dog started to cross the street and Villa jerked him back because the traffic light suddenly changed to red. Claiborne "started to think of all the work I've done for the guy and if he was a phony, I'd die." When he returned to his office, he announced to his two secretaries, who were very fond of Villa, that "Your friend Bill Villa is no more blind than I am." To prove his point, the next time Villa came to the office, Claiborne put a wastebasket right in the middle of the hallway where Villa had to walk. Ruby, his secretary, said, "Oh, he'll fall over it and hurt himself. My God, you're just plain mean." When Villa arrived, he began walking down the hallway. "He's got the white cane and he doesn't even put it in front of him. He walked right around the basket." After Villa left, Ruby, who was crying, said, "I wish I hadn't seen it." Although Claiborne never said anything to Villa, he stopped representing him.[359]

---

[359] Claiborne interview, 281.

CHAPTER TEN

FEDERAL JUDGESHIP

The roots of Claiborne's appointment as a federal judge lie in his developing friendship with Senator Howard Cannon. The 1964 Senate race in Nevada created a personal and professional relationship between Claiborne and Howard Cannon, Nevada's U. S. Senator from 1959 until 1983. This relationship extended to Claiborne's near involvement in President Richard Nixon's potential impeachment proceedings and the background investigation of Nelson Rockefeller prior to his nomination as Vice President, before culminating in 1978 with Cannon's nomination of Claiborne for a federal judgeship. The senator benefitted from Claiborne's legal and tactical skills in turning back a serious challenge to his United States Senate seat by Paul Laxalt in 1964. A very powerful figure in Washington during the 1960s and 1970s when Democrats controlled Congress, Cannon was chair of the Senate Rules Committee and of the Commerce Committee and a high-ranking member of the Armed Services Committee. Prior to the election, Cannon and Claiborne were "friendly, but casual." But in 1964, they became friends and their relationship was a long and mutually beneficial one.[360] As Claiborne remembered, Cannon "was a good lawyer and he was a good man, no question about it. I had a very good relationship with him. I was always impressed with his ability. He had the personality of a cold mashed potato sandwich. But he was good to Nevada. One thing, he never politically voted in a way that might damage the State of Nevada. I liked Howard Cannon. He was a

360 Claiborne interview, 115.

workhorse."[361] During Senate Rules Committee hearings in 1974 regarding Rockefeller's Vice Presidential confirmation, Claiborne worked with
Cannon every day and regretted his departure from Congress. "I think it
was so sad that he got defeated (by Chic Hecht in 1982). I left (Washington) with the feeling that he was the best United States senator that this
state ever had. He worked so hard. He wasn't spending 80% of his time
creating building blocks for his future. He was taking care of business
every day, into the night. A lot of nights, I had been with him in there.
We'd leave his office and go have dinner at 9:00 at night. Marvelous man.
I didn't think too much of him when I ran against him (in 1964). My
respect for him grew, the longer I was around him."[362]

Claiborne and Cannon knew each other for years. The latter served as
Las Vegas city attorney in the early 1950s and they interacted frequently.
In 1958, Cannon ran for the Senate and won. Ironically, Claiborne challenged Cannon in the 1964 Democratic Party primary for the Senate seat.
Claiborne claimed there was a "groundswell" of opposition to Cannon
among Democrats and believed Nevada voters preferred a man of courage, conviction, and good character to represent them in Washington.
Although Claiborne had a "man-on-the-street" appeal that Cannon could
not match, according to some, his campaign soon deteriorated into a
piecemeal, uncoordinated exercise. Review-Journal reporter Jude Wann-
iski described the differences between the two campaigns: "Cannon has a
solid voting record and a lengthy list of accomplishments, but somehow it
sounds rather flat on television. It's all too polished and mechanical and
far-removed from the voters, who still like to feel close to their elected
representatives." Claiborne, on the other hand, "seems forceful, animated
and determined - even if less organized. He bills himself as a fighter and
he sounds that way. He mispronounces words here and there, and, for a
lawyer, mangles the English language to an unbelievable extent. But it's
all masculine and vigorous." For Claiborne, the main issue was integrity,
and he hammered Cannon for his involvement with the Bobby Baker
scandal brewing in Washington. Robert Gene "Bobby" Baker, Wash-

361 Claiborne interview, 116.
362 Claiborne interview, 261.

ington insider and right-hand man for Senate Majority Leader Lyndon Johnson, resigned his job as Secretary to the Majority in 1963 under a cloud of conflict of interest, corruption, and influence peddling. Cannon was a member of the Senate Rules Committee that investigated Baker's wheeling and dealing over a sixteen-month period consisting of forty-five days of closed hearings and resulted in a 1967 conviction on eight counts of tax evasion and conspiracy. Opponents claimed that the Democratic member lead investigation was so inadequate that it subverted the purpose of the inquiry in order to protect fellow Democrats.[363] The Nevada media, however, barely covered the scandal because Cannon was popular, had the ears of President Lyndon Johnson , and was therefore good at securing federal money for Nevada. Cannon "trounced me pretty good," Claiborne later confessed.[364]

Much like its predecessors, the 1964 Democratic primary campaign still required a lot of face-to-face meetings with voters in small towns, unlike today's contests where heavy media advertising dominates the process. The relatively rural nature of campaigning in the early 1960s allowed a more spontaneous interaction with voters and other campaigners on the political trail. Claiborne campaigned in Elko during the Fourth of July celebration where Peter Echeverria, Reno attorney and good friend, was master of ceremonies. Echeverria introduced Claiborne with "tremendous flourish," but all in the Basque language. Claiborne had no idea what he was saying, but in the end, the crowd just roared with laughter and clapped. Echeverria ended with, "Harry!" They shook hands and Echeverria sat down. Claiborne made his speech, they shook hands again, and he left to attend another Fourth of July celebration in another town. Later, Claiborne learned what Echeverria told the crowd: "This is a wonderful friend of mine and I love him. He's the best damn lawyer I have ever seen! I'm not for him. I'm gonna vote for Cannon. He's gonna lose, but despite that, be nice to him."[365]

Claiborne recalled the political prediction he received from an old man

363 Michael Vernetti, Senator Howard Cannon of Nevada (Reno: University of Nevada Press, 2008), 97-102.
364 Claiborne interview, 115; Review-Journal, July 11, 1964, July 15, 1964, August 19, 1964.
365 Claiborne interview, 279.

in Fallon. After handing the man his card, Claiborne said, "I'm Harry Claiborne and I'm running for the United States Senate and I'd appreciate your vote. More than that, your help, if you feel so inclined." The old man looked at Claiborne, smiled, and said, "God, I feel sorry for you, young man. You're really gonna get whooped." He patted Claiborne on the head and said, "But, I'll pray for ya." Off he walked. Claiborne didn't know how to reply, but did a lot of thinking about what the man said. Surely, he knew something, Claiborne surmised.[366] Hank Greenspun later wrote that Claiborne did accomplish one thing with his campaign. "He finally got all the newspapers to agree on the same thing ... that he did not belong in the U. S. Senate as long as the people had Howard Cannon as the alternative."[367] Maybe that is what the man in Fallon thought as well.

The night Cannon won the Democratic primary election, Claiborne went to Cannon's headquarters, congratulated him, and promised to do whatever he could to help him win the general election against Paul Laxalt, a popular Basque who had strong support in rural Nevada. Claiborne even agreed to work on Cannon's campaign. He delivered many speeches for Cannon in the following months. In the general election on November 3, 1964, despite Barry Goldwater's drag on all Republican candidates, Cannon defeated Paul Laxalt by only 48 votes. Laxalt demanded a recount.

Cannon convinced Claiborne to head his recount election team. Claiborne wrote a twenty-six page legal brief on Nevada election law which he recalled forty years later as "brilliant." He focused on the issue of illegal ballots and attached samples of illegal ballots for illustration purposes. The legal brief formed the procedural basis for Cannon's recount team to follow when examining questionable ballots. Claiborne conducted educational sessions with lawyers recruited to help the senator. They reviewed all possible ways ballots could be voided. Their strategy was that if a precinct heavily favored Cannon, they would make no objections to the ballots. If it heavily favored Laxalt, then they were to go "gung

366 Claiborne interview, 335.
367 Sun, September 3, 1964.

ho" to contest it. Matching key lawyers with key precincts, Claiborne, who now declared himself a recount expert, went to Laxalt's home base, Ormsby County, where Laxalt was represented by his brother Peter. In analyzing ballots, they assumed that if Cannon got more votes in a precinct than Laxalt, there likely would be more people marking void ballots in Cannon's favor. It was a simple matter of statistics. It worked. Completed on December 2, 1964, the recount showed Cannon won the election by a slightly greater margin than the original count, 84 votes out of 134,624 cast. To Claiborne, the recount proved that his method and group of lawyers were better at establishing a basis to reject Laxalt ballots and support Cannon ballots than Laxalt's team. Laxalt filed a contest of the election with the Nevada Supreme Court on December 3, 1964.[368]

In response, Cannon filed a motion to dismiss Laxalt's Supreme Court petition on the grounds that the United States Senate, not the Nevada Supreme Court, had exclusive jurisdiction over United States Senate election results; that is, the United States Constitution prevented a state court from considering the merits of a federal senatorial election. The attorneys representing each side reflected a Who's Who of prominent, politically influential Nevada lawyers: future Nevada Supreme Court Justice Cameron M. Batjer; brother of the candidate Peter Laxalt; John Tom Ross, Laxalt's brother-in-law and son of former U. S. District Court Judge John R. Ross; John W. Diehl of Fallon, prominent Reno lawyer, twice president of the Washoe County Bar Association, Chairman and member of the Board of Directors of Southwest Gas Corporation, and member of the Board of Regents of the University of Nevada Clark J. Guild, Jr.; and H. Russell Thayer of Carson City represented Laxalt, while Claiborne; the Foley Brothers firm; George Rudiak; and the Woodburn firm in Reno represented Cannon. On December 22, 1964, the Nevada Supreme Court granted Cannon's motion to dismiss Laxalt's election contest and certified Cannon as the winner.[369]

Cannon's friendship exposed Claiborne to national politics and policy for the first time in his career. During the 1970s, Cannon chaired the

368 Claiborne interview, 115; Political History, 304; Vernetti, Senator Howard Cannon, 112-13.
369 Laxalt v Cannon, 80 Nev. 397 (1964).

Senate Rules Committee. So, when it appeared that President Richard Nixon might be impeached, Cannon called his trusted and legally talented attorney, and told Claiborne: "I want you to come back here and confer with me in a few days. I'm not going to tell you what it's about over the phone. It's a sensitive matter. I'd rather talk to you in person." It could be done in one day. When he arrived in Washington, Cannon told him, "Nixon is going to be impeached. Historically, the Rules Committee has conducted impeachments. I'd like you to serve as general counsel if you would. I'd like to ship the books on impeachment to you." Claiborne returned to Las Vegas to prepare for the senate trial based on the impeachment he thought would be conducted under the Rules Committee's jurisdiction, but Nixon resigned shortly afterward on August 8, 1974.[370]

Earlier, the vice presidency had also become vacant due to the resignation of Spiro Agnew over corruption charges stemming from his days as Baltimore County's Chief Executive and Governor of Maryland. Once again, Cannon called Claiborne and asked him to be special assistant to the United States Senate Committee on Rules and Administration in the Vice Presidential confirmation hearings of Nelson Rockefeller, who was nominated by now-President Gerald Ford. Claiborne was in charge of the investigation process. Senator Henry "Scoop" Jackson of Washington hired six investigators and Claiborne supervised them as part of his responsibilities as committee counsel. The divorced New York governor, who ran a spirited campaign against Barry Goldwater for the Republican Presidential nomination in 1964, was an unpopular choice with conservative Republicans, many of whom viewed him as too liberal and an adulterer. A heavy contingent of Republican Senators, led by Senator Jesse Helms of North Carolina, despised him and were always sending derogatory material to the committee, which it investigated. During the investigation, Claiborne got to know Helms, whom he described as the "most delightful old gentleman you ever saw in your life. I enjoyed him tremendously. He started calling me 'Brother Claiborne.' I said to Cannon, 'I don't understand why people say he's hard to deal with, I find him just absolutely enjoyable.' Cannon looked at me and said, 'I

370 Claiborne interview, 259.

think I'll send you home." The Attica Prison riot that Rockefeller brutally
repressed in 1971, resulting in the deaths of 39 men, was a major issue.
People objected to hundreds of his administrative acts while in office that
contributed to the mounting opposition to his selection. Conservatives,
many tied to religious constituents, made Rockefeller's divorce an issue,
while at the same time ignoring the divorce of California Governor Ron-
ald Reagan, whom many of them would support for president in his 1976
campaign. But Ford wanted Rockefeller, and the committee eventually
approved the nomination.[371]

Although Claiborne never personally interviewed Rockefeller, Cannon
did in his presence. Claiborne described Rockefeller as "friendly, border-
ing on being an extrovert. You could see from his very presence that he
was a kind and caring man. But he had some steel in him. His friendly
nature may have been somewhat of a shield. That's the way he came off
to me and I think that's the way he came off to all the other senators."[372]

Cannon advised Claiborne that the investigation would not be partisan
in nature. In fact, the senator assured him: "I want you to know that. We
don't, and will not, color anything. You're going to get some pressure,
and you're going to get a lot of it. And your investigators are going to get
a lot of it. You make damn certain to them that we'll call it like we see it.
He may be a good man and qualified to be Vice President, or he may not
be. But whatever it is, that's the way I want it presented."[373]

Traditionally, the nomination of an individual for a federal judgeship
is the perk of the highest elected official in the state who is of the same
political party as the President. The selection of the individual can be
for any number of reasons; political, based on a personal relationship, or
anything important to the politician. Nevada follows that tradition. Since
Cannon was the senior Democratic official in Nevada, he had the privilege of the nomination to the Democrat president, which turned out to be
Jimmy Carter. While working on the Rockefeller confirmation hearings,
Claiborne and Cannon spent many nights together. One night Cannon
asked him: "If a judgeship opens up, would you take it?" Claiborne

371 Sun, November 14, 1974; Claiborne interview, 260-261, 116; State Bar of Nevada, at 207.
372 Claiborne interview, 259-261.
373 Claiborne interview, 261-262.

thought about it and replied, "Probably not, but I would sure like to be asked. I would expect that to be a long time down the road. By then, I might want it." About two years later, Cannon informed him that federal Judge Bruce Thompson was taking senior status, making a judgeship available. Claiborne was not interested in a judgeship earlier because he was too young and loved being in the courtroom as an advocate. But now, at 60 years of age, he was ready to go on the bench. "Do you want it?" Cannon asked. Claiborne said he did and Cannon promised, "You got it."[374]

Benny Binion reportedly bragged that Cannon recommended Claiborne to the judgeship as repayment of a favor to Binion. He also boasted that he delivered Cannon's vote to President Carter on the Panama Canal Zone Treaty. Cannon's former administrative aide, Chet Sobsey, commented on the relationship between Cannon, Binion, and Claiborne, "There was no special connection between Binion and Cannon. Binion wasn't a big (campaign contribution) giver." While Cannon tried on numerous occasions to obtain a pardon for Binion's criminal conviction, Sobsey felt the reason was Cannon's commitment to Binion's lawyer, Claiborne, not to Binion. Cannon's loyalty to Claiborne stemmed from the 1964 senate election and recount, and endured for the remainder of Cannon's Senate service.[375]

Claiborne's age was a consideration in the confirmation process. Some members of Congress and the judiciary preferred younger men who would be long-term judges. "They passed the word to all senators to please not nominate people who are 60 and over. I think I barely got under the wire. Wouldn't have made any difference because Cannon said he had the juice to do it anyway. So, I didn't worry about it and he didn't worry about it either." Cannon made it appear that others were under consideration, such as U. S. Magistrate Joseph Ward and federal Bankruptcy Judge Lloyd George, but Claiborne was the only nominee.[376]

374 Claiborne interview, 323-325.
375 Sally Denton and Roger Morris, The Money and the Power: The Making of Las Vegas and its Hold on America, 1947-2000, (New York: Alfred A. Knopf, 2001), 35; Vernetti, Senator Howard Cannon, 130.
376 Claiborne interview, 323-324; Sun, May 18, 1978.

Once Claiborne's nomination went from Cannon to President Jimmy
Carter, the investigation began. One roadblock quickly appeared that
almost damaged Claiborne's chances for confirmation. During this time,
a lawyer friend of Claiborne informed him, "I went into (State District
Court Judge Paul) Goldman's chambers and his secretary was not there.
The door was closed. I could not clearly hear the conversation. I did
hear enough of it that I got the hell out of there. Thought I would come
over and talk to you. He's talking to some investigator and he's calling
him by his first name, Bill. He's telling him that you lied in a case with
him in open court. That you denied that you had seen a psychiatrist report, when actually you had." This pertained to the Lawrence Arvey case.
Claiborne knew that "Bill" was Bill Jansen, the FBI agent conducting
Claiborne's investigation. Previously, Jansen interviewed him for nearly
20 hours. Goldman was wrong and Claiborne needed to correct it.

Claiborne called Jansen and asked to meet with him. When Jansen
arrived, Claiborne said, "I'm informed that Judge Goldman has reported
to you that I lied in his court about a psychiatric report." Jansen said, "I
can't answer that. I can't verify or refute it. I'm not allowed to." Claiborne replied, "If he did, and I think he did, you will report it and it will
affect whether or not I'm confirmed. So, I'm going to write the Attorney
General of the United States and put him on record that I demand the
right to be advised as to what Judge Goldman said and the right to refute
it." Jansen said, "Okay. I'll tell you what, Harry. What I'll do, and this
is the best I can do, is call my supervisor and ask advice about what to
do." The next day Jansen contacted his supervisor, who said that Jansen could relay to Claiborne what Goldman had said and give Claiborne
the opportunity to refute it. Jansen confirmed what Claiborne's friend
told him. Claiborne obtained a transcript of the court hearing in question that supported Claiborne's position. He showed it to Jansen and
it resolved the issue. Claiborne immediately confronted Goldman and
demanded: "Why did you tell Bill Jansen that I lied in your courtroom?"
Goldman declared; "I didn't tell him that." Claiborne angrily replied,
"You're Goddamn lying. If you didn't tell him that, I want a letter from
you stating that you did not tell him that." Goldman refused to give him

such a letter. By then, he really did not need the letter. Claiborne never really understood Goldman's motive for his comments to Jansen.[377]

President Jimmy Carter nominated Claiborne to fill the vacancy on the federal bench in July, 1978. The United States Senate scheduled his confirmation hearing for August 8, 1978. The hearings opened by announcing that a "substantial majority" of the Standing Committee on the Federal Judiciary of the American Bar Association agreed that Mr. Claiborne was "well qualified" for appointment to the federal bench. A minority of the Bar Association's committee, however, found him not qualified on the sole ground that Claiborne was sixty-one years of age. Nevada Senators Cannon and Laxalt testified on Claiborne's behalf and recounted his numerous professional accomplishments. Cannon praised his reputation as "one of the foremost criminal attorneys in the West." The print media throughout Nevada echoed the testimony of the Nevada senators.[378]

Otherwise, Claiborne's nomination process went smoothly. No one protested his appointment except one female attorney, Eugenia Ohrenschall, who later served in the state Assembly. She did not question his qualifications, but believed a woman should receive the appointment. She wrote a letter to that effect but appeared late for the confirmation hearing and missed it. Unlike many of the judicial confirmation hearings today, Claiborne's was not confrontational. The hearing was before the entire Senate Judiciary Committee. Rather than ask Claiborne how he would rule on various hypothetical questions concerning the issues of the day, the Senators simply asked personal questions raised during the investigation. The hearing was short and the Senate confirmed him by a unanimous vote on August 11, 1978, just three days after the hearings began.[379] Senator Cannon later called Claiborne on the telephone to congratulate him. When Claiborne said, "Hello," Cannon responded, "Your Honor." Claiborne knew by his comment that he was approved.[380] He was sworn in on September 1, 1978.[381]

377 Claiborne interview, 311-312; Review-Journal, June 17, 1978.
378 State Bar of Nevada, at 205-206.
379 Claiborne interview, 324-326.
380 Review-Journal, August 16, 1978.
381 Sun, September 2, 1978.

Claiborne filled the position vacated in Reno by Judge Thompson. Of course, a Las Vegas lawyer appointed to a Reno judicial position did not sit well with some Reno residents, but they knew another federal judgeship would be created within a year by pending federal legislation. Cannon passed the word that a Reno lawyer would get it. A year later, Renoite Edward Reed was appointed to a newly created Nevada federal judgeship. He stayed in northern Nevada and Claiborne transferred to Las Vegas.[382]

382 Claiborne interview, 326; Sun, July 25, 1978, 1.

Photo Courtesy of the Claiborne Family

CHAPTER ELEVEN

THE FALL FROM GRACE

Claiborne's tenure as a federal judge had more than its share of controversy. Tensions were already running high between the federal court and the Federal Strike Force, a special division of the Justice Department, when Claiborne returned to Las Vegas in the fall of 1979. The Justice Department created the Strike Force to investigate and prosecute organized crime. Although authorized to begin investigating one specific issue at a time, members of the group could, and did, extend their inquiry into different areas of criminal activity. The Strike Force unit in Las Vegas consisted of three attorneys, headed by Geoffrey Anderson. Claiborne recalled that he had no issues with the Strike Force, Anderson, or, to his knowledge, any of the FBI agents at the time. Judge Roger D. Foley, on the other hand, was "up to his neck with problems with them. He was fighting with the Strike Force all the time."[383] Foley suspected that Anderson leaked information to a newspaper from sealed affidavits in a case pending in his court. In retaliation for Foley's criticism, Anderson sought Foley's disqualification from at least one case prosecuted by his section. Federal Judge Thompson denied the disqualification motion and indicated that Anderson was "schizophrenic" and his attitude toward the issue of judicial disqualification was unbecoming a federal attorney.[384]

The tension continued. Foley learned in April of 1980 that the Strike Force attorneys prominently displayed insulting materials and caricatures of him on a bulletin board in their office. Defense attorney Oscar

383 Claiborne interview, 335.
384 State Bar of Nevada, at 132-133; Sun, April 10, 1980.

Goodman claimed the bulletin board was in full view of, and had an intimidating and prejudicial effect upon grand jury members and grand jury witnesses. The material consisted of a mock man-on-the-street interview with numerous individuals including former Clark County Sheriff John McCarthy, Claiborne, Foley, Goodman, and other individuals, some of whom were reputedly connected with organized crime in Nevada. Sardonic responses to the question, "(d)oes organized crime really run the casinos and the State of Nevada??" appeared beneath the photographs of those depicted. In the space reserved for Claiborne's photograph appeared the notation "no pictures please." The material included a depiction of Foley as a clown dressed in circus regalia. The Nevada Supreme Court later wrote, "We observe, however, that although the unknown author of the sarcasm ostensibly compiled it in jest, the fact that it was displayed within the confines of the United States Department of Justice and apparently within the purview of members and witnesses of the grand jury, demonstrated an appalling arrogance, contemptuousness, and lack of decorum." The United States Marshals removed the items upon the order of Foley on April, 4 1980. Foley wanted Claiborne to accompany him to look at the material, but he declined. Claiborne was not interested "in playing a kid's game with them." Although Claiborne believed he had no problems with them, Foley told him that some FBI agent complained about his actions. That information was passed to Foley because of his position as Chief Judge. "I was shocked they considered that I was prejudiced against them. I learned later on, maybe, that I granted more acquittals than other federal judges."[385]

Claiborne assumed Foley's administrative duties as Chief Judge for the District of Nevada in May 1980. Claiborne believed that Foley resigned because he had some run-ins with the Chief Judge of the Ninth Circuit, and was "kind of disgruntled." At about the same time, Foley announced that he would no longer preside over Strike Force cases due to the ongoing tensions. Claiborne was now on the hot seat with both the high profile cases and the Strike Force.[386]

---

385 State Bar of Nevada, at 133; Claiborne interview, 333.
386 State Bar of Nevada, at 134; Claiborne interview, 136.

In later years, Claiborne analyzed the circumstances that eventually led to his problems. Foley believed that Anderson came to Las Vegas with the preconceived idea that the gaming community owned Foley. For his part, Claiborne thought Foley was correct. Strike Force members did not trust Foley from the day they arrived in town. Had it not been for their antagonism toward Foley, and the resulting tensions, Foley would not have refused to hear their cases and Claiborne would not have been the only judge hearing Strike Force prosecutions. He would have just been handling his own cases. "Of course, I would've not been in a position to shoot my mouth off about how I felt about what they were doing and that corruption thing," he admitted.[387]

Joseph Yablonsky's arrival in Las Vegas as Special-Agent-in-Charge of the local FBI office in January of 1980 set in motion events that eventually lead to Claiborne's prosecution. Yablonsky had a proven track record of developing cases against organized-crime figures and was handpicked for the Las Vegas assignment by FBI Director William Webster. During his four-year term, Yablonsky oversaw an operation consisting of 140 employees, 82 of whom were special agents and five were supervisors, and a $5 million annual budget. Described as a tough street cop in hard towns - Miami, Boston, New York - he earned the nickname of "King of Sting" for the cases he made against the Lansky network as an undercover cop. Not the prototype FBI agent in dress or demeanor, the 51 year old veteran with 29 years in the Bureau chomped cigars, wore gold chains and dressed as flashy as the hoods he impersonated for years, while talking in the crude profanity of the underworld. And bragged. Yablonsky's years as head of Las Vegas' FBI headquarters were marked by a vigorous campaign against organized crime as well as local corruption.[388]

Organized crime had a strong foothold in Las Vegas by the late 1970s. According to Yablonsky, when he arrived in the Las Vegas office, at least five major casinos were being skimmed by the New York, Chicago, and Kansas City branches of the Syndicate. Convicted felon, Frank "Lefty" Rosenthal directed the mob's operation out of the Stardust Hotel under

387 Claiborne interview, 347.
388 Denton, The Money and the Power, 332; Dennis Griffin, The FBI, August 31, 2009, http://www.examiner.com.

the guise of being its food and beverage manager. Further, fencing of
stolen art and jewelry, drug money laundering, and other illegal activities
were rampant. Mobster Anthony "Tony the Ant" Spilotro was operating
his own burglary, arson, and assassination-for-hire operation known as
the "Hole in the Wall Gang", so named for their habit of simply cutting
a hole in the wall of a business for entry and avoid the standard alarm
systems. Worse, Spilotro had infiltrated the police department with his
own "moles" to provide him with information as to their investigation
to such an extent that the federal agents refused to cooperate with local
authorities for fear of leaks. "A lack of confidence in Metro (police department) kept us from having an institutional association with them at the
time. But we (Department of Justice lawyers) and the FBI were later
able to develop several relationships with Metro personnel on a personal
level," former Strike Force lawyer Stanley Hunterton recalled. For years,
Rosenthal and Spilotro, boyhood best friends from Chicago, virtually ran
Las Vegas.[389]

Political corruption was also rampant. Yablonsky's political investigations soon attracted considerable coverage by the local media. Targets
reportedly included Benny Binion, Stardust Hotel executive Herb Tob-
man and his partner Herb Sachs, Dunes Hotel lawyer and manager
Morris Shenker, Caesars Palace's former owner and current owner of
Circus Circus Jay Sarno, casino owner Frank Fertitta, entertainer Wayne
Newton, banker Parry Thomas, and a number of other Strip figures.
To Yablonsky's credit, numerous indictments and convictions resulted
from an 18 month sting operation code-named "Yobo", a misspelling of
his name. Despite the communities conflicting feelings about the use
of sting operations, Yobo did uncover extensive corruption in Las Vegas
which resulted in the conviction of several high placed politicians, most
notably state senators Floyd Lamb and Gene Echols, Clark County Commissioners Woodrow Wilson and Jack Petitti, and Reno City Councilman
Joe McClelland, all for accepting bribes from undercover FBI Agent Steve
Rybar. McClelland's conviction was later reversed. The dollar amounts

---

389 Denton, The Money and the Power, 333; Griffin, The FBI, August 31, 2009; See Nicholas Pileggi's
     book Casino: Love and Honor in Las Vegas for an accurate description of this chapter in Las Vegas
     history.

involved in exchange for favors were surprisingly small. Lamb, one of the most powerful senators in Nevada's history, accepted $20,000 and a one percent "finders fee" for allowing a loan from the state retirement system for a casino development. Wilson, the first black Nevadan to be elected to the Nevada legislature, was convicted for taking a $5,000 bribe while a county commissioner. Petitti and Echols were convicted for taking $5,000 and $1,000, respectively.

On just his second day in Las Vegas, Yablonsky met with Sun editor Hank Greenspun, and during the visit bragged about the adornments on his office walls, which were newspaper articles and photographs of his previous FBI criminal investigations. According to Greenspun, Yablonsky boasted that he was "going to hang Claiborne up" on a large vacant spot on his office wall that was specifically reserved for him. Corroborating Yablonsky's bold prediction was former IRS District Director for Nevada Gerald Swanson, who later revealed that Yablonsky made similar comments to him during a meeting between the two in December 1981.[390]

Claiborne recalled that Greenspun called him the day he met Yablonsky and asked the judge to stop by his office on the way home from the courthouse, which he did. "Hank thought there was something mentally wrong with (Yablonsky)." According to the conversation as related to Claiborne by Greenspun, Yablonsky said, "I'm going to plant an American flag in Las Vegas. The Mormons run Las Vegas with the help of the gamblers. You know, Mr. Greenspun, the Mormons are a bunch of crooks. I'm gonna clean it up. I'm gonna start with a federal judge." Claiborne did not believe Yablonsky even knew his first name because he referred to him as "this Claiborne." Claiborne thought it was just some cop popping off. "Well, he wasn't popping off," he conceded. Years later, he received the same information from one of Yablonsky's contemporary staff members who confided to Claiborne that he would be Yablonsky's

---

390 During Swanson's visit with Yablonsky at the FBI office in early December 1981, Yablonsky pointed to copies of news articles publicizing his earlier exploits and bragged to the effect: "I'm going to hang Claiborne's picture up there, too, before I retire." United States v. Harry Eugene Claiborne, CR-R-83-57 WEH, Defense's Motion in Limine to Exclude the Testimony of Joseph Conforte filed February 15, 1984, Exhibit B, Before the US Grand Jury for the District of Nevada, Memorandum of Interview of Gerald F. Swanson on February 2, 1983, page 10.

target once the new FBI boss arrived.[391]

As Yablonsky bragged about his intentions and even hinted as to his intended targets, the town kingpins reportedly called on "their champion, Paul Laxalt, close friend of President Reagan" to stop the investigations. Laxalt allegedly told Attorney General William French Smith that if the investigation was not curtailed, he would call for Senate hearings on the Justice Department abuses in Las Vegas. Further, "In October 1982, Laxalt brought in the formidable Hank Greenspun to remonstrate with Justice officials to stop the investigation of their mutually close friend Judge Harry Claiborne," according to one source. Claiborne claimed that "Hank Greenspun was no friend of mine. In fact, he used to criticize the hell out of me a lot. He never wrote one favorable column about me other than Jack Entratter's trial," one of the owners of the Sands Hotel, who was a friend of Greenspun and Claiborne got him acquitted from a manslaughter case. Yablonsky not only pressed on, but began to look at Laxalt as well. "I guess none of us knew very much about Paul Laxalt except that he was Reagan's buddy and you sure couldn't read anything critical about him in the Nevada papers, but we had to wonder why this guy put so much on the line to protect a bunch of sleaze in Vegas," said a Justice prosecutor who worked in Las Vegas. Yablonsky claimed, "Greenspun always wanted a piece of the action and he was an extortionist, fashioned himself a lord of a fiefdom. He saw me as a threat to all the finagling deals he had made to make himself a rich man." Although he came up empty in his investigation of Laxalt and suspicion of Greenspun, ultimately, as he predicted, Joe Yablonsky's prize trophy turned out to be Claiborne who, as one author sarcastically described, was "a senior farcical figurehead of the state's confederacy of gamblers, gangsters, and government."[392]

For many local observers, Yablonsky's behavior raised serious doubts about his character, veracity, and judgment. During the 1982 political campaign for Nevada Attorney General, for instance, Yablonsky secretly

391 Claiborne interview, 356-357.
392 Denton, *The Money and the Power*, 336-347. Note: the authors acknowledge "Joe Yablonsky, for his indomitable honesty about the city that touched and scarred him so deeply," 459; Claiborne interview, 356.

solicited Air Force help to check into the military career of candidate Brian McKay, hoping to obtain derogatory information about him. McKay was running against Yablonsky's friend Mahlon Brown, then the United States Attorney for Nevada. Yablonsky initially denied contacting the Air Force, but a week later admitted that he made the request. Years after his election as Attorney General, McKay observed that "Joe had a long-standing, good reputation that became severely tarnished. I would say that at the end of his tenure here, he had come close to losing touch with reality."[393] Clark County District Attorney at the time and future governor Bob Miller expressed "serious concerns" about Yablonsky's credibility.[394] Lamond Mills, the U. S. Attorney for Nevada from 1981 to 1985, even called Yablonsky "an embarrassment."[395] Gerald Swanson, former IRS District Director in Nevada, called Yablonsky a "rogue" agent and observed that "I've dealt with federal agencies for more than 20 years, and Yablonsky was the most unethical federal agent I've ever seen. He was a headhunter. To him, the end justified the means."[396]

As a result of the subsequent FBI investigation, FBI Director William H. Webster announced that Yablonsky's actions were "inappropriate and made at a time and under circumstances likely to bring into question the integrity of the FBI inquiries." He also characterized Yablonsky's actions as involving "extremely bad judgment in utilizing the files of another agency to inquire about Mr. McKay for a reason I did not consider adequate or sufficient." Webster censured Yablonsky and placed him on probation. Although Webster did not remove him from his position, the Sun reported that the 54-year-old Yablonsky faced mandatory retirement in six months. A top Justice Department investigator later admitted that the FBI had not adequately examined the allegations.[397] But it did not end there. After his retirement, Yablonsky engaged in another questionable action. His bank mistakenly credited his account with $40,000 as a result of a computer error. Yablonsky not only failed to notify the bank of its error, but kept the balance in his cash management account for three

393 Cincinnati Magazine, April 1988
394 Sun, March 27, 1983.
395 Sun, March 26, 2004.
396 Sun, March 30, 2001.
397 Sun, July 2, 1983, March 30, 2001; Review-Journal, July 2, 1983; State Bar of Nevada, at 146.

years. It was ultimately discovered during a bank audit. A grand jury
investigated the matter, under the direction of the Justice Department's
Public Integrity Section, but did not return a criminal indictment against
Yablonsky. He was quietly allowed to repay the $40,000 without interest.
He faced no sanctions. There was talk that the Justice Department did
not want to compromise the high-profile Claiborne case by tainting the
integrity of Yablonsky any further.[398] Yablonsky retired in 1983, but unlike other retiring FBI Agents in Las Vegas, no cushy jobs were awaiting
him at the Strip, or anyplace in Nevada.[399]

Claiborne believed these government operations were "not only mor-
ally, but legally wrong." Having defended the Thunderbird Hotel's owners in the 1950s in the wake of a sting operation in which state and local
officials participated, he reasoned that the government "had no right to
create a crime, involve an individual in criminality when he may have
never even thought of such things and was not involved in that activity
before hand or any other illegal activity," and, rightly or wrongly, Claiborne publicly said as much. He even threatened, on one occasion, to
dismiss these cases and release all the Yobo defendants. Because Foley
refused to hear Strike Force cases, including Yobo cases, Claiborne was
the sole federal judge before whom the cases could be prosecuted. After
Claiborne's public statement, the lines were drawn between him and
the government. Strike Force attorney Geoffrey Anderson, who took his
orders directly from Yablonsky in the Yobo cases, according to Claiborne,
asked Claiborne to disqualify himself from all the Yobo cases, but Claiborne stubbornly refused.[400]

In April 1980, the news media reported that Claiborne was the target
of a grand jury investigation by the Strike Force and the FBI. Claiborne
heard of the investigation when a reporter told him about it, but knew
none of the specifics at the time.[401] He later learned that the jurors were
hearing evidence into allegations that Claiborne had hired private detective Eddie LaRue to conduct illegal wire taps on the home of one of his

398 State Bar of Nevada, at 146; Sun, March 30, 2001.
399 Denton, The Money and the Power, 337, 349; Review-Journal, November 7, 2003
400 Claiborne interview, 336-337, 348.
401 Claiborne interview, 338.

girlfriends in 1977 and 1978.[402]

In response, Claiborne publicly stated on April 10, 1980 that the allegations were old and were investigated without any evidence of wrongdoing by the police and the FBI prior to his conformation by the United States Senate for his judicial position. He accused Anderson of deliberately initiating the grand jury investigation with the intent to force him to disqualify himself in other Strike Force cases. Similar to what Anderson did to try and disqualify Foley. "Its their way of getting the hell out of my court." Claiborne claimed that "I'm concerned now they're intent upon destroying this town. I think they think everybody in this town is a crook. They have no respect for the law. Anderson has no respect for decency and he has no respect for people's civil liberties and they don't care who they destroy." He also referred to the Strike Force attorneys as a "bunch of crooks," and claimed that "I'm not going to let them ride roughshod over this community. I'm going to stop them." Claiborne further called for the disbandment of the grand jury, suggesting that it was tainted by the improper tactics of some Strike Force agents and attorneys. One month later, however, Claiborne voluntarily removed himself from handling any further Strike Force cases.[403]

Although Claiborne did not recall having any problems with Anderson, he believed that Anderson took his orders from Yablonsky in the Yobo cases. According to Claiborne, "Anderson was a smart lawyer. He was gung-ho. That's how he did his job. That's how he dealt with people. He was perfect for the role that he occupied. I don't think there was anybody that he could have prosecuted that he wouldn't have gotten a lot of glee out of their conviction, personally. He was that way. Otherwise, he wasn't a bad guy. I had no trouble with him at all." The same would not be true of later Strike Force attorneys.[404]

Eddie LaRue was a colorful Las Vegas detective who conducted investigations for Claiborne, as well as other Las Vegas attorneys. In 1977, the police arrested LaRue for an unrelated act and found a report in his car addressed to Claiborne concerning a surveillance. An investigation began

402 Sun, April 10, 1980.
403 Sun, April 19, 1980; State Bar of Nevada, at 134-135.
404 Claiborne interview, 348.

as to whether an illegal electronic surveillance was made at Claiborne's request while he was still in private law practice. The police investigated the matter prior to Claiborne's appointment to the federal bench. Although they cleared Claiborne of wrong doing, the FBI reopened the case three years later.

Claiborne recalled that Sheriff Ralph Lamb called him in 1977 and told him of the allegations against La Rue and the possible implications against Claiborne. Claiborne told Lamb that he wanted to submit to a lie detector test. Lamb arranged for it to be administered by Charles Lee, a Metro homicide investigator and polygraph operator. Claiborne claimed that it was the first time he ever met Lee. Claiborne took the test. Lee rendered his opinion that Claiborne testified truthfully and the police dropped the matter against Claiborne.[405]

In April of 1980, the Las Vegas federal grand jury subpoenaed Lee to answer questions concerning the 1977 polygraph. Lee testified that in his opinion Claiborne truthfully denied any participation in LaRue's alleged illegal activities. Then Clark County Sheriff John McCarthy called Lee into his office and informed him that he "had been visited by two Federal Strike Force agents sent by Yablonsky." According to Lee, McCarthy told him that as a result of Lee's grand jury testimony, Yablonsky considered Lee to be an "uncooperative witness" and that Yablonsky was going to "come down on Lee like a ton of bricks."[406]

Lee was later demoted and reassigned to a desk job answering telephones. He was also subjected to an intensive three year investigation by the FBI, including extensive covert and electronic surveillance. Lee and his attorney claim, based in part on information subsequently obtained under the Freedom of Information Act and the Privacy Act, that Yablonsky targeted Lee for investigation and was instrumental in Lee's demotion.[407]

After Lee's grand jury testimony, the government sent a copy of Lee's polygraph chart to an FBI agent in Washington for re-examination. The government examiner determined that Lee was wrong and that Claiborne

405 Claiborne interview, 352.
406 State Bar of Nevada, at 136.
407 State Bar of Nevada, at 136.

had, in fact, lied. He so testified before the grand jury. When Claiborne learned of the turn of events, he called Lee's supervisor at the police department, Captain Bill Conger. Claiborne said he was going to write a letter to Conger asking him to chose three respected members from the appropriate polygraph association, send them Lee's chart and obtain their opinions in a written report as to Claiborne's truthfulness. Conger selected five examiners, and all five, according to Claiborne, determined that he was truthful.[408]

The federal government later indicted Eddie La Rue on six counts of installing illegal listening devices, entirely unrelated to the incident concerning Claiborne. Nonetheless, an FBI agent advised LaRue to "give up" Claiborne and the charges would be dropped. He refused. The government moved La Rue's case to federal court in Reno, where he was acquitted after a one week jury trial. This criminal trial cost him $35,000 in attorney fees alone, plus expenses. LaRue swore in an affidavit that he was wrongfully indicted for the sole purpose of giving the FBI leverage to make a deal with him to "get" Claiborne. "He was their target, not me," La Rue maintained. In the end, the Las Vegas grand jury did not issue an indictment against Claiborne.[409]

Other pre-indictment investigation activities raised questions of the propriety of the governments actions. On March 19,1981, Claiborne opened his monthly American Express bill and found that it contained an American Express statement addressed to Clark County District Court Judge Thomas O'Donnell, along with his own statement. Claiborne requested an explanation from the credit card company and observed: "It would not be surprising that someone's bill was also included with mine but our curiosity is more than aroused in view of the fact that Judge O"Donnell is my closest and best friend. If I were of a suspicious nature, I might suspect that someone is monitoring our accounts and replaced both of them in the same envelope by mistake." American Express could not explain the mix-up.[410]

The Strike Force changed strategies when it looked to Portland,

408 Claiborne interview, 353.
409 State Bar of Nevada, at 137.
410 State Bar of Nevada, at 137-138.

Oregon, and for the first time, claimed that brothel owner Joseph Conforte bribed Claiborne, in the Portland federal building while Claiborne was sitting on an unrelated case. The first Portland grand jury convened on May 11, 1982, but its mandate expired without returning an indictment. The second grand jury convened on March 16, 1983, but it never indicted Claiborne either.[411]

Completely lacking in scruples, Conforte was well acquainted with legal proceedings, having been in and out of court on a variety of charges for more than two decades. The owner of the notorious Mustang Ranch outside Reno, Conforte was one of the more controversial people in Nevada during this time. His first significant brush with the law involved a 1960 conviction for an extortion plot against Washoe County District Attorney William Raggio for which the brothel owner was sentenced to the Nevada state prison.[412] Then, in June 1963, he pleaded guilty to federal income tax violations and was sentenced to federal prison. He was released in 1965. By 1968, he was in trouble again, this time accused of violating the Mann Act which prohibited the transportation of women across state lines for purposes of prostitution, but was acquitted while being represented by Claiborne. In 1970, the IRS filed a civil complaint for condemnation and forfeiture of certain trailer houses used by Conforte in his prostitution business. This case was also decided in Conforte's favor.[413] In 1976, an employee of Conforte's shot and killed Argentine heavyweight boxing contender Oscar Bonavena outside the Mustang Ranch. This event only worsened Conforte's negative image and the local newspaper editorials began assailing Conforte's "web of influence" in local affairs. Bonavena's family filed a civil wrongful death suit in 1977 alleging that Conforte was negligent in the supervision of his employee which resulted in Bonavena's death.[414] Also in 1977, a ten-count indictment charged Conforte with the willful attempt to evade federal employee withholding taxes and he was convicted.[415] The Court of Appeals upheld the

411 State Bar of Nevada, at 139; Claiborne v. United States, 765 F. 2d 784, 788 (1985).
412 Reno Evening Gazette, June 29, 1984.
413 Conforte v. United States, 457 F. Supp., at 645-646 (1978).
414 State Bar of Nevada, at 143.
415 Conforte v. United States, 457 F. Supp, at 646; Conforte v. United States, 624 F.2d 869 (1980).

convictions, but vacated the sentence and returned the case to the trial judge for further sentencing. In the meantime, in July 1979, the Washoe County grand jury indicted Conforte and charged him with bribing the Lyon County District Attorney for help in obtaining a license to operate a brothel. Washoe County District Attorney Cal Dunlap publicly announced on September 15, 1980, that if Conforte were convicted, Dunlap would seek habitual criminal enhancement of the sentencing to impose a life sentence, based on Conforte's prior felony convictions. Indeed, on February 26, 1982, a supplemental information alleging habitual criminal enhancement was filed in court against him.[416]

Gerald Swanson, former director of the IRS for the District of Nevada, testified before the federal grand jury on April 13, 1982 that since 1956 the IRS had been working to get Conforte in conformance with the tax laws. Conforte arranged his tax matters in a fashion which made it "virtually impossible to determine his proper income. Beginning in February of 1978, the IRS instituted jeopardy assessment proceedings against Conforte's assets because of the likelihood that Conforte might flee the jurisdiction or place "his assets outside of the collection reach of the Internal Revenue Service."[417]

The night before the December 23, 1980 re-sentencing hearing in federal court on the conviction for evading employee withholding taxes, Conforte fled to Mexico and later to Brazil with a substantial amount of cash. He admitted fleeing the jurisdiction to avoid his inevitable prison sentence. On March 10,1981, he was indicted in federal court for failing to appear in court. Nevada filed similar charges for his failure to appear for the Lyon County bribery case. Before fleeing in 1980, however, Conforte began paving the way for his return. Conforte telephoned Geoffrey Anderson suggesting that in exchange for "some help" from Anderson, he could supply incriminating information about Claiborne. "If you want him, I will give him to you in (sic) a platter," Conforte told Anderson. Yablonsky seemed to confirm both the time frame and the essence of the conversation.[418]

416 State Bar of Nevada, at 142; Reno Evening Gazette, September 15, 1980.
417 State Bar of Nevada, at 142-143.
418 State Bar of Nevada, at 144.

It is unclear if this conversation was the first contact between Conforte and federal agents investigating Claiborne. Conforte testified that when he talked to Anderson in December 1980, he did not know of the investigation of Claiborne, nor did he know an FBI agent named Dan Camillo. Yablonsky testified in a related case that he assigned an agent to contact Conforte only after Anderson had talked to him in December 1980. Claiborne claimed that Yablonsky assigned Camillo to contact Conforte in the early summer of 1980, and Conforte told the agent that "he had nothing on the judge." It was after Conforte's tax conviction was affirmed on April 29, 1980, that Yablonsky instructed Camillo to take "one last shot" due to Conforte's "frame of mind." Conforte again refused to implicate Claiborne. If true, this was approximately eight months before Conforte fled the country and told Anderson that he could deliver Claiborne. Something, or someone, changed his mind.[419]

In June or July of 1981, Camillo and another FBI agent made contact with Conforte through his former bodyguard. Conforte retained Reno lawyer Peter Perry to assist him in negotiations with the government. Numerous meetings occurred between Conforte, Perry and agents of the FBI, the Public Integrity Section and the IRS in Brazil, Costa Rica, and Mexico. According to Swanson, Yablonsky contacted Archie Banbury, an agent in the Criminal Investigation Division of the IRS, on the issue of Conforte's tax demands and Banbury suggested that the IRS interview Conforte and convene a grand jury to look into the Claiborne matter. Although skeptical based on his prior dealings and knowledge of Conforte, Swanson gave permission for the IRS interview in Brazil. Swanson "wanted Banbury to get corroborative evidence before allowing the IRS to get involved in a grand jury proceeding as part of the 'deal' being proposed." After Banbury's return, Swanson was still skeptical because no corroborating "smoking gun" evidence was found.[420]

In February 1982, the IRS received a complaint from Peter Perry alleging that Swanson may have been involved in soliciting a bribe from Conforte, according to FBI Director Webster. The FBI and the Public

419 State Bar of Nevada, at 144-145.
420 State Bar of Nevada, at 147.

Integrity Section, assisted by agents of the IRS and Perry initiated a "sting" operation targeting Swanson. Swanson later claimed that federal agents targeted him in the "Confortescam" sting in order to remove him as "an obstacle to the 'deal' that would help them 'hang a federal judge.'" Although the grand jury failed to indict Swanson, he was placed on administrative leave on April 7, 1982 and later transferred to Dallas. A Treasury Department investigator later submitted a report condemning "the FBI-IRS sting operation as 'very dangerous, misleading and poor work.'" Still having very bitter feelings toward Yablonsky, Swanson complained that "He was never called to task in this. He totally abused his power." The Nevada Supreme Court later concluded that "(A)gain, as in the cases of Eddie LaRue and Charles Lee, it would appear that there is indeed factual support for (Claiborne's) assertion that in the pursuit of Judge Claiborne's removal from office, some federal agents may have overreached and abused their authority by dealing harshly, unjustifiably and apparently retributively with those who stood in the way of Judge Claiborne's prosecution.[421]

Conforte returned to Nevada on December 4, 1983.[422] At that time, Conforte's legal status included approximately $26 million in IRS liens against his property (although the exact amount was uncertain due to Conforte's accounting practices), pending criminal sentencing in both the federal employee withholding tax case and the Nevada bribery case, potential monetary fines in each case, and two civil lawsuits.[423] Conforte had everything to gain and nothing to lose in cooperating with the government.

Conforte improved his status considerably by agreeing to testify before the federal grand jury and at Claiborne's later trial. The Department of Justice recommended: 1) that Conforte be re-sentenced in his federal tax conviction case to concurrent, rather than the original sentence of

421 On April 15, 1982, Swanson reported to the US Attorney General's office in Reno for a voluntary polygraph exam. According to Swanson, a secret service agent, Riley Skeeling, afterwards told Swanson that he should commit suicide based upon the results of the exam. Swanson later learned he had passed the exam. United States v. Claiborne, CR-R-83-57 WEH, Defense's Motion in Limine, Exhibit B, p 9-13; State Bar of Nevada, at 148-149; Sun, March 30, 2001.
422 Claiborne v. United States, 781 F. 2d 1327,1329 (1986); State Bar of Nevada, at 142.
423 State Bar of Nevada, at 143.

consecutive, five-year terms on each of the four counts on which he was convicted, 2) that all but 15 months of each five-year sentence be suspended, 3) that any sentence imposed should be served concurrent with any sentence imposed by Nevada on any pending charges, 4) that the federal charges for fleeing the jurisdiction be dismissed, and 5) that the Department of Justice would assist Conforte in negotiating plea agreements with regard to the pending Nevada charges. Obviously, this was a very good deal for Conforte. On December 15, 1983 (eight days after Conforte's Reno grand jury testimony), federal Judge John Lewis Smith of the District of Columbia re-sentenced Conforte in conformity with the terms of the above recommendation.[424] He served a total of five months in prison.[425] Although the agreement did not address the pending tax liens, Conforte testified that although the IRS claimed his tax liability was about $19 or $20 million, he eventually settled his entire tax liability for $7.3 million.[426] Clearly, if they were willing to accommodate Conforte so much, federal prosecutors desperately wanted to get Claiborne.

The Justice Department convened a fourth grand jury in June 1983. Although the two prior grand juries considered charges of bribery involving Conforte, the Reno grand jury heard the live testimony of Conforte and returned a seven-count indictment against Claiborne on December 8, 1983, one day after Conforte's testimony and only four days after he returned to Nevada.[427] Four counts, the "Conforte counts," involved the claim that Claiborne solicited and received bribes from Conforte; two other counts involved tax evasion (unrelated to the alleged bribes) concerning the under reporting of income on his 1979 and 1980 federal income tax returns; and the final count alleged that he filed a false financial disclosure statement with the Judicial Ethics Committee for the year 1978.[428]

Claiborne's trial began in Reno on March 12, 1984. Conforte testified for three days and claimed that he paid Claiborne $85,000 in bribes

---

424 Claiborne v. United States, 781 F. 2d, at 1329; State Bar of Nevada, at 150.
425 Claiborne interview, 345.
426 State Bar of Nevada, at 149-150, 152.
427 State Bar of Nevada, at 139.
428 State Bar of Nevada, at 154.

in 1978 and 1979. Specifically, Conforte said he bribed Claiborne in exchange for favorable rulings in a pending criminal case against him. However, Claiborne's lawyers proved that Claiborne had never presided over or ruled on any aspect of Conforte's case. That case was handled by another judge. Conforte also testified that he paid another bribe to Claiborne for his favorable treatment of certain subpoenas issued to Conforte's employees in a voting fraud investigation. Federal prosecutors offered no evidence besides Conforte's unsupported testimony to support this claim. Claiborne supposedly took another bribe to secure a favorable result in Conforte's appeal of his federal conviction regarding employee payroll taxes, although the case was pending before the appellate court at the time of the claimed bribe and was beyond Claiborne's jurisdiction or alleged influence.[429]

After twenty-two days of testimony and eight days of deliberation (over 52 hours), the jury announced that it was "hopelessly deadlocked." Jurors later reported they were 10 to 2 for acquittal on the bribery charges and 9 to 3 on the income tax counts.[430] Judge Walter Hoffman of Virginia, appointed by U.S. Chief Justice Warren Burger to preside over the case, declared a mistrial and scheduled a new trial.[431]

Due to the brothel owner's lack of credibility, no one was surprised when the prosecutors announced on June 27, 1984, that they were dropping the "Conforte counts" against Claiborne. They claimed the evidence relating to those counts "may have distracted the jury in its consideration of (the remaining counts) and contributed to its inability to reach a verdict on those counts."[432] Observers said Conforte made a poor witness and the prosecution presented little evidence to corroborate his testimony. There was even talk about demanding that the Justice Department indict Conforte for perjury.[433] The prosecutor, Steven Shaw, reportedly conceded to a special panel of the Circuit Court that Conforte had lied both to the grand jury and at the federal court trial, although he claimed

429 Claiborne v. United States, 781 F.2d, at 1328-1329.
430 Claiborne interview, 345.
431 Sun, April 14, 1984.
432 Claiborne v. United States, 765 F 2d, 784, 789 (1985).
433 Sun, July 29, 1984.

to have had no knowledge of Conforte's fabrications at the time he presented Conforte's testimony. Yet Shaw took no steps to charge Conforte
with perjury or to revoke his probation.[434]

The re-trial began on July 31 and proceeded on only the two federal
income tax counts of tax evasion for the years 1979 and 1980 and the
judicial financial disclosure report for 1978. The government claimed that
Claiborne intentionally under-reported taxable income in the amounts
of $19,000 and $88,000 for the years 1979 and 1980, respectively. The
income represented legal fees earned before becoming a judge, but he received the money after taking the bench. Payment to Claiborne was made
in the form of checks. Both parties agreed that Claiborne did not deposit
all the checks in his bank account, but cashed several at a local casino,
Binion's Horseshoe. The government conceded that Claiborne properly
reported the income represented by money deposited in his bank, but he
failed to report the checks he cashed.[435]

The issues surrounding the two tax years were straight forward. The
1979 Income Tax Return did not include $19,000 in income, the only
question was - why? Claiborne produced a copy of a letter to his accountant dated April 11, 1980 which included the following: "Enclosed
check in the amount of $8,000 and W-2 form from the U. S. Courts as
requested. Fees received during 1979 for practice before I become a judge
are $41,073.93." The legal fees of $41,073.93 plus the amount on the W-2
was a correct disclosure of his income for that year. Claiborne testified
that he instructed his secretary to deliver the letter and its enclosures to
his accountant on the morning of April 11, and his secretary testified that
she did just that. Neither the accountant nor his wife could remember
receiving the letter. However, the $8,000 check made payable to the IRS
was received and cashed by the IRS, and the accompanying application
for an extension of time to file his tax return was received and approved
by the IRS, both suggesting that the accountant did receive the letter,
processed the check, and mailed the application for an extension to the
IRS. "The only real issue in 1979 is whether Wright (the accountant) got

---

434 Sun, January 27, 2004.
435 Claiborne v. United States, 765 F. 2d, at 796-797.

the letter dated April 11," argued the government attorney during closing argument. In short, if the jury believed that the secretary delivered the letter, he had properly disclosed his income and Claiborne was innocent. But, as the government successfully argued, Claiborne had signed the tax return, under oath, which did not reflect the proper amount of income.[436]

The 1980 Income Tax Return took a different twist. After 30 years with the same accountant, Claiborne decided it was time for a change and hired Tax Planning, owned by Jerry Watson. Claiborne supplied Watson with a handwritten list of his tax information which included his salary as a federal judge and $88,500 income received that year "from private practice before appointment" to the bench. This handwritten list, written on several yellow sheets of paper, fully disclosed his income for the year. As above, but argued by the defense attorney this time, the only real issue as to 1980 is whether Claiborne gave Watson the "yellow sheets." Watson, however, contrived a plan to reduce Claiborne's tax liability by somehow writing off losses he supposedly suffered from quitting his law practice. He combined the $88,500 fee with proceeds from the sale of his library, creating a capital gain which was then offset against a $250,000 "loss" from his practice. This was incorrect because there was never a sale of the law practice to generate a "loss", and the fees were ordinary income, not capital gains. The concept was absurd, yet he assured Claiborne that it was proper. To compound the problem, when Claiborne went to Watson's office to sign the return, he was told that it was not ready. A secretary brought him a number of loose papers. The signature page had a paper clip on it and he essentially signed the tax return "in blank", that is, he signed the "return" without knowing what information it would eventually contain. When filed, it presented a red flag for an audit because it was written in pencil, and Schedule D, containing capital gains information, had an arrow drawn on it with the words "type here." The "creative" tax calculation essentially removed the $88,500 in legal fees from taxable income, and the physical nature of the return guaranteed an audit. But Claiborne had signed it. At the later impeach-

---

ment hearing, Senator John W. Warner, R-Va., derided the two people who prepared the 1980 tax return as "Tweedle-Dum and Tweedle-Dee", and noted that one of them invoked the Fifth Amendment as protection against self-incrimination.[437]

On August 10, 1984, the jury returned guilty verdicts on the two income tax charges, but an acquittal on the judicial financial disclosure report. The jury deliberated only four and one half hours. The newspaper reported that a "trace of a smile" crossed Judge Hoffman's face as, hands shaking, he read the verdict.[438] Judge Hoffman sentenced Claiborne to serve two years in federal prison on each count, the terms to be served concurrently, imposed a $10,000 fine, and assessed him costs of prosecution in the amount of $14,384. Claiborne began serving his sentence in May 1986. He eventually served the entire sentence and was denied parole twice.[439]

Claiborne's conviction triggered his impeachment hearings. In September 1986, proceedings were instituted in the United States Senate on four counts of impeachment. Aired live on C-SPAN and covered by all the major networks and newspapers, the trial was conducted before a twelve-member special committee of the Senate, rather than the Senate as a whole. A vote by the full Senate was scheduled for October 9, 1986. Before the full Senate voted, transcripts from the committee hearings were placed on each of the senators' desks. They contained the evidence which the full Senate was to consider in rendering its decision on Claiborne's impeachment trial. Senator Cannon fully supported his friend during these proceedings. Before the vote, Cannon said, "Look at the desks. You will find a copy of the transcript on their desk just like the Senate pages put it. Unopened. Not read." Claiborne believed that none of the transcripts were opened or read before the Senators voted on his impeachment. Claiborne attributed this to "indifference" by the Senators.[440] On that date, and without further hearings, the full Senate voted that Clai-

---

437 United States v. Claiborne, CR-R-83-57 WEH, Closing Arguments, 60-61; United States v. Claiborne, 765 F.2d at 796; State Bar of Nevada, at 183-188; Houston Chronicle, September 20, 1986.
438 Sun, August 11, 1984.
439 Claiborne interview, 358; State Bar of Nevada, at 169-170.
440 Claiborne interview, 357.

borne was guilty of three of the four counts of impeachment based upon the evidence contained within the unopened and unread transcripts.[441]

Consequently, Claiborne became the first sitting United States federal judge removed from the bench in 50 years, and the 13th federal official impeached by the House. He was also the first federal official convicted by the Senate without the benefit of the full Senate hearing the evidence. As only the second sitting federal judge to be imprisoned, Claiborne lost not only his position on the bench, but spent 13 months in a federal prison in Alabama and five months in a North Las Vegas halfway house.[442]

On May 27, 1986, the Nevada Bar Counsel requested that the Nevada Supreme Court temporarily suspend Claiborne from the practice of law and refer the matter to the Southern Nevada Disciplinary Board to assess the extent of the discipline resulting from his conviction. The Supreme Court asserted its inherent authority to discipline the Bar, and recognized its obligation to conduct an independent and de novo review of the record to determine whether discipline in any particular instance was warranted. On May 18, 1988, the Supreme Court issued a 131-page written opinion entitled State Bar of Nevada v. Harry Eugene Claiborne. It declined to impose punishment upon Claiborne by way of professional discipline, and dismissed the State Bar Disciplinary proceedings.[443] In effect, Claiborne could continue to practice law in Nevada.

The decision was very controversial. It was by far the lengthiest decision the Nevada Supreme Court issued during that term, and included a laundry list of Claiborne's defenses against the accusations of federal prosecutors and critics of his right to return to practicing law. The government's prosecution of Claiborne sharply divided Nevadans, especially members of the tight-knit legal community. Some argued that the decision indicated that the Supreme Court was second-guessing the impeachment process itself. Others believed that the hypocritical high and mighty federal prosecutors from Washington were determined to get somebody who did not fit their mold. Hank Greenspun fiercely defended Claiborne in numerous articles in his newspaper, some of the key infor-

441 State Bar of Nevada, at 171; Sun, January 20-21, 2004.
442 Sun, January 21, 25, 2004.
443 State Bar of Nevada, at 233.

mation reportedly came from federal agents unhappy with the FBI chief's overreaching. In contrast, the rival Review-Journal, also reportedly the long-time recipient of information fed to it through contacts inside the FBI and Justice Department, wrote editorials criticizing the justices for their decision.[444] The community simply split over the issue.

The federal courts disbarred Claiborne the day he entered prison. It was automatic. Eventually, he petitioned the federal courts for reinstatement, but it was initially denied. The court stated that he could re-open his petition in one year, which he did. In April 1990, it granted his petition and his right to practice law before the federal courts was reinstated.[445] Claiborne continued practicing in state and federal courts until the day he died.

Ten years later, Claiborne admitted that the way he handled his income taxes "was downright stupid. I should have been cautious. I should have known they would have gone after me for tax offenses. If I had been more careful with my return, none of this would have happened." He acknowledged that no one accepted his explanation that he was just too busy on the bench to pay close attention to his tax return.[446]

---

444 Sun, March 30, 2001; Review-Journal, January 21, 2004; Smith, Of Rats and Men, 400.
445 Claiborne interview, 358.
446 Sun, October 5,1996.

EPILOGUE

In 1993, fifty years after he came to Nevada, Claiborne argued his last jury trial at the age of 76. It involved a dispute over a timeshare. The day before trial, outside Claiborne's presence, Clark County District Judge Jack Lehman - a Las Vegan since the 1950s and a successful trial attorney himself before ascending the bench - told the opposing attorneys that Claiborne was on the other side of the case and "you better come pre-pared." One attorney commented, "Well, I understand he was very good in his day, but he's a has-been, he's old, and he ain't what he was once." When Claiborne learned of the comments, "I went after those bastards with a vengeance. I don't think they think I've lost many steps. I know I have, but they don't know it." The jury was out for a very short time and returned a verdict favoring Claiborne's client. After the judge excused the jury, three jurors came over to the counsel table and asked Claiborne for his business card. His first jury trial was in 1947, and his last was in 1993. Few trial attorneys can boast of a courtroom career lasting 46 years.[447]

Much of Claiborne's reputation was based on his spell-binding closing arguments. Local lawyers adjusted their schedules so they could wit-ness them. He often used a country-boy style, which he admitted was not always genuine, but the juries found it very appealing.[448] However, Claiborne claimed that "my strongest attribute as a lawyer was cross-examination. I don't think there was anybody better."[449] He bragged that "I could break any witness." He would pick out the key witnesses for

447 Claiborne interview, 67-68.
448 Claiborne interview, 72-73, 302.
449 Claiborne interview, 29.

the prosecution, generally no more than two, and concentrate on them in his preparation. His style was to keep constant pressure on the witness. "Don't give the witness time to think what his answer should be. Keep pressing him at the speed that he can't think."[450] When in the District Attorney's office and trying a case with Herb Jones, they had a witness they needed to break, and Claiborne said, "I'll get him, Herb." He began to press the witness, "I took him over about 1:00 o'clock and I went until about 2:30, and then I began to hammer him and hammer him good. About 3:30 the witness stood up in the witness box, stepped down, began to turn around, and fell right in front of me. He had an epileptic fit." Claiborne immediately administered CPR, the witness recovered and they convicted the defendant. Using a similar style in a murder case in Ely, "I had this witness on the stand all Goddamned afternoon. I saw perspiration breaking out on him. I knew right then, I have him now. I began to very gently say, 'Now, you could be wrong, right?' He wanted off the witness stand so bad, he said, 'Yes.' That's all I wanted, reasonable doubt."[451]

Claiborne understood the difference between aggressive witness examination, arguing with a judge on legal issues, and being disrespectful of either the judge or witness. A lawyer must keep in mind that the case may depend on the attorney's demeanor, not that of the witness or anyone else, he cautioned. "You would think ordinarily that if you fight with the judge, that it would turn the jury against you. You can not be disrespectful, but you can challenge him left and right." If it appears to the jury that the judge is not being fair to you, they may hold it against the other side, not yours, he observed.[452]

Claiborne tried many cases outside the friendly confines of the Clark County court system. His reputation for an aggressive and flamboyant style preceded him into other jurisdictions. Judges outside Las Vegas knew him by reputation. They frequently had preconceived notions of his demeanor and his impact upon their courtroom: that is, who was going to be in control, Claiborne or the judge. He recalled one such po-

450 Claiborne interview, 123.
451 Claiborne interview, 121-123.
452 Claiborne interview, 124.

tential confrontation in Reno before Judge Antonio Maestretti, a former Lander County District Attorney. Maestretti said, "I know all about your reputation and I want you to know, right now, you're not going to get away with any of those cunning tricks in my courtroom. You're not going to take charge of this trial." Claiborne looked at him and replied, "Judge, I'm going to make a deal with you. You just forget about all those derogatory things you've heard about me and I'm going to forget about all the derogatory things these lawyers around here have told me about you. We're going to start even." Maestretti's face grew red, but Claiborne recalled him as a good judge and fair to each side.[453]

Claiborne's reputation as a successful criminal defense lawyer sometimes had unexpected, and unwanted, results. Claiborne finished closing arguments in a criminal trial and was awaiting the jury's verdict. An eavesdropper overheard some of the jury's deliberations. The jury was deadlocked at six votes each for acquittal and conviction, when one of the jurors commented that if the defendant was really innocent, why would he have to hire a high-powered defense lawyer like Claiborne? Within minutes, the jury returned a unanimous guilty verdict.[454]

The quality of the judge and opposing counsel greatly affected Claiborne's enjoyment of a trial. "The two worst things for a trial lawyer is to try cases before a stupid judge, and the next worse thing is trying a case against a stupid lawyer. You know exactly what a good lawyer is gonna do. You know exactly where a good lawyer's going. But you take a stupid lawyer, you don't know where the hell he's going. They scare me to death."[455]

Claiborne offered interesting observations about the habits of lawyers in the 1940s compared to today. He felt the "typical old western lawyers and judges sometimes were much more knowledgeable than modern day lawyers for the simple reason that the law was not in the fast lane in those days, like it is now. Lawyers didn't lead a helter-skelter life. They had more time." The nature of the law practice was different. "There was far less litigation in those days. Maybe you would have a trial a year, or

453 Claiborne interview, 124.
454 William Koot, interview by J. Bruce Alverson, April 4, 2007.
455 Claiborne interview, 227-228.

maybe not at all. Your principal service was wills, mortgages, contracts, other business-related transactions. If the old lawyers did not have a client in the office, they would read a law book. That was their habit." Upon reflection, Claiborne made this comparison: "They were, maybe, better lawyers and did their clients a better job than we do for our clients. Really and truly they were better lawyers than we are. Better lawyers, I guess you would say, in viewing the whole picture. They would not be better lawyers now, we would be better lawyers now. But they were better lawyers in their period of time than we are in our period of time."[456]

The increased presence of illegal drugs over the years changed the practice of criminal law. Previously, criminal defendants had no money unless they were "mobbed up." Even if they were successful criminals, they had spent all their money by the time they were indicted and went to court. But drug dealers still maintained their drug business while they were in custody. It was not unusual for them to be operating their business from inside of the jail. "I think it made a lot of lawyers rich. When I was on the bench, I'd say at least one-third of all the criminal cases were those cases. Maybe more, who knows," Claiborne surmised. Consequently, the drug practice not only increased the "client base" for criminal law attorneys by one-third, it created a very solvent defendant as well.[457]

When asked if friends and colleagues started treating him differently once he became a judge, he answered "yes," but could not say why. "But it is the truth. It's kind of like getting and having cancer. Your friends wish you well. They still like you and they still care for you. But, they kind of feel guilty to be around you. I would say there's a very close parallel to that situation of being on the bench, because I have experienced both."[458]

Most lawyers lose themselves when they go on the bench. "You kind of get lost for some reason or another. They don't get out. Especially a federal judge. I guess it's historical. You get appointed as a federal judge, that's the last anybody ever hears from you. They isolate themselves. They think it's expected of them. Seems like they just go in hiding. They

456 Claiborne interview, 250-251.
457 Claiborne interview, 291.
458 Claiborne interview, 327-328.

stop going to community affairs, also," explained Claiborne.[459]

Bill Raggio, who rates Claiborne among the top five trial lawyers he has ever seen,[460] did not believe that Claiborne "fit the mold of an ordinary federal judge. Maybe in that sense, he shouldn't have sought the bench. Today, a federal judge has to be almost impersonal. Harry was outgoing and gregarious. It wasn't his lifestyle . . . . He was a nonconformist - a maverick in judicial robes." During the ceremony for his induction to the bench, Claiborne told reporters, "I plead guilty to being colorful." Even Claiborne acknowledged that his "exuberance" may have created an "imperfect" image for himself. Yet he insisted that he always "kept his feet on the ground."[461]

Claiborne offered another explanation for strained relations between lawyers and judges. "The longer, it seems, that most judges are on the bench, the more disgruntled they get. It is impatience more than anything else. They get impatient with the length of direct examination, with the length of cross-examination. They get impatient with delays, they seem overwhelmed with a desire to get the case over. New judges will let everybody go on and on. In other words, they will let you try your case, and not only the case, but the fringes," Claiborne observed.[462] Every judge has an obligation to make sure that the defendant gets a fair trial. "Lawyers get out of line, especially in criminal cases. Prosecutors get out of line," Claiborne remarked. But, "if a lawyer is guilty of misconduct, the judge must call him on it, and admonish the jury. Otherwise the judge is not doing his job."[463]

Unfortunately, a small minority of judges go too far and become "really terrorists" on the bench. According to Claiborne, the worst was federal judge Jack Ross in Carson City, father-in-law of Paul Laxalt. Before Ross went on the bench, Claiborne participated in many cases with him, and he never went to Carson City without making a social call such as lunch or dinner. Most of the time, Laxalt accompanied them.[464] In court,

459 Claiborne interview, 271.
460 William Raggio, interview by J. Bruce Alverson, January 4, 2007.
461 Sun, October 5, 1996; Review-Journal, January 21, 2004.
462 Claiborne interview, 125-126.
463 Claiborne interview, 301.
464 Claiborne interview, 116-117.

Judge Ross "brutalized me, absolutely brutalized me, and I was shocked, absolutely shocked. I told him afterwards. I told him that I resented it." He looked at me and said, "Listen Harry, you're not getting thin-skinned on me are you?"[465]

At the state court level, Clark County District Court Judge John Mendoza "was another guy that was outrageously abusive to lawyers and that got him defeated (in his re-election bid.) The lawyers almost en masse went out campaigning against him. Good man. Brilliant mind."[466] Clark County District Court Judge Tom O'Donnell was another. "He was a good lawyer and very knowledgeable," Claiborne remembered. But he was a Jekyll and Hyde: "Terrible temperament on the bench and the most wonderful guy to be with you've ever seen in your life. Talk about a transition. I never could understand it." Despite their friendship, he treated Claiborne "as bad as he treated everybody else."[467]

The heavy case load awaiting Claiborne when he took the federal bench shocked him. "If I had known the work load of the court at the time, I would have emphatically said 'no' when Senator Cannon called me" about the appointment. He was working day and night. "I know that my friends in the FBI set out to do three things. They set out to ruin me financially. They accomplished that. They set out to take my freedom. They accomplished that. They set out to really destroy me. They didn't do that. But, what they don't know - they saved my life. I'm sure if they did know, they would not appreciate it. Because at the very end when I was on the bench, it took me all day Saturday and Saturday night to get rested. I know that would have eventually killed me. God, I hate to say it, but I'm living because of the FBI."[468]

While many Justice Department officials disliked Claiborne, colleagues in the legal profession generally admired his trial skills. Indeed, two former district attorneys expressed admiration for Claiborne's trial skills. "Claiborne was without a doubt the greatest criminal defense lawyer in the southwest United States. We always used to call him the 'Arkansas

465 Claiborne interview, 126.
466 Claiborne interview, 134.
467 Claiborne interview, 132-133.
468 Claiborne interview, 329.

preacher.' He just had that knack of captivating a jury," according to
George Dickerson. "I think he's the greatest criminal defense lawyer I
ever saw, head and shoulders above anybody else," George Foley said,
more than 50 years after he first met Claiborne.[469]

How did Claiborne personally deal with his fall from grace - from his
status as a nationally recognized trial lawyer and federal judge to impeachment and prison? "Clearing my name is not a priority anymore,"
he declared years later. "I don't worry about it. They took away a lot of
things I cared for. They took away a lot of things I enjoyed, and they
heaped a lot of pain and suffering on me. But they didn't win because I'm
a better man today than I would have been had I retired and walked away
from the federal bench putting in my full term."[470] He was determined
not to let it eat away at him. "I always figured that bitterness resulted
in continued unhappiness for people. It just isn't worth it. As well as
hatred. I have no hatred toward anybody who brought this on. It takes
a lot of energy to hate. If you've got to pick up the pieces and go forward
with your life, you need all the energy you've got."[471] Claiborne adopted a
pragmatic philosophy about his future. "Go your way. Forget it. It's done.
It's over with. Don't dwell on the past. Go on and have a productive life.
I never thought of it anymore. I never talk about it. I never bring it up. I
never think about it. It's part of my life that's done and gone. I can't res-
urrect my life beforehand. Just go on and do something with what you
have left. As the old saying goes: I never have a thought of what I lost, I
was just grateful for what I had left." He recognized the opportunity that
the Supreme Court decision gave him. "I was so grateful that the Nevada
Supreme Court didn't disbar me. That I was able to be readmitted in
the federal courts. My profession gave me an opportunity to pick up the
pieces and move forward. As a result, I have done well. I went right back
into the practice of law and I've been productive for my clients. I did
well."[472]

To be sure, Harry Claiborne was a character, a maverick molded in

469 Review-Journal, January 21, 2004.
470 Sun, October 5, 1996.
471 Sun, January 20, 2004.
472 Claiborne interview, 225.

the maverick city and state that became his home for more than a half century. But he was also a gifted lawyer and a middle-of-the-road Democrat whose lifetime experiences as the son of an anti-Klan southern father in the Great Depression, as an M.P. in World War II, and as a New Deal rent regulator, gave him a liberal view on many issues. While Claiborne represented big casino moguls such as Jay Sarno and Texas wiseguys such as Benny Binion, he also defended disreputable characters such as Lawrence Arvey and sleazy politicians such as Nate Adler while also taking dozens of pro bono cases in recognition of his responsibilities to the Bar and to his community. True to his commitment, whether his clients were wealthy or destitute, he gave them all the same spirited effort.

In many ways, Claiborne's upward mobility from policeman to high-profile lawyer and eventually to federal judge reflected the opportunities and rewards that mid-century Las Vegas offered talented professionals. While Claiborne's career was in many respects exceptional, other attorneys also prospered in a town racing toward its bright future. Indeed, just as Claiborne was not the same lawyer in the 1940s that he was forty years later, neither was his city, whose dramatic expansion created myriad opportunities for Claiborne and his colleagues. Claiborne's life and career offer a valuable glimpse into the forces that drove the sleepy railroad town of the 1940s to its present-day status as the "Entertainment Capital of the World."

Photo Courtesy of the Claiborne Family

BIBLIOGRAPHY

Newspapers

Ely Record
Houston Chronicle
Las Vegas Mercury
Las Vegas Review-Journal
Las Vegas Sun
Nevada State Journal
Reno Evening Gazette
Reno Gazette-Journal
San Francisco Chronicle

Government Reports

Nevada Senate Concurrent Resolution, Memorializing Former Senator B. Mahlon Brown November 22, 1995.

Political History of Nevada. 10th Edition, issued by Dean Heller, Nevada Secretary of State, 1996.

Collections

Russell McDonald Collection. Reno: Nevada Historical Society.

Legal Publications

Communique: Official Journal of the Clark County Bar Association.
Las Vegas: Clark County Bar Association.

Diamond Jubilee Celebration: 75 Years of Service, 1928-2003.
Las Vegas: State Bar of Nevada, 2003.

Legal Directory for Southern Nevada: Revised to October 1, 1976.
Las Vegas: Nevada Legal News, 1976.

Martindale-Hubbell Inc. Chicago: Reed Reference Publishing Company.

Nevada State Bar Journal. Reno and Las Vegas: State Bar of Nevada.

Nevada Lawyer. Reno and Las Vegas: State Bar of Nevada.

Unpublished Oral Interviews

Transcript:

Claiborne, Harry E., interview by J. Bruce Alverson, 2002-2003.

Thompson, Bruce Rutherford, interview by J. G. Sourwine,
February 10, 1988.

Wiener, Louis, Harry Claiborne, and George Foley, interview by
Cliff Young, 1995-1997.

No Transcript:

Koot, William, interview by J. Bruce Alverson, April 4, 2007.

Raggio, William, interview by J. Bruce Alverson, January 4, 2007.

Seaton, Daniel, interview by J. Bruce Alverson, March 30, 2007.

Young, Cliff, interview by J. Bruce Alverson, January 11, 2006.

Legal Cases

Federal Reporter

Adamson v. California 332 U. S. 46 (1947)

Baker v. Carr, 369 U. S. 189 (1962)

Claiborne v. United States, 765 F.2d 784 (1985)

Claiborne v. United States, 781 F.2d 1327 (1986)

Conforte v. United States, 457 F. Supp. 641 (1978)

Conforte v. United States, 624 F.2d 869 (1980)

Duncan v. Louisiana 391 U. S. 145 (1968)

Formal Dedication of the Foley Federal Building and United States Courthouse, 615. F. Supp. LXVI (1984)

Gideon v. Wainright, 372 U. S. 335 (1963)

Greenspun v. McCarran et al., 105 F. Supp. 662 (1952)

In Memoriam:

Roger D. Foley, 975 F. Supp. LXI (1996)

Roger T. Foley, 384 F. Supp. 1 (1974)

John R. Ross, 221 F. Supp. 4 (1963)

Bruce R. Thompson, 819 F. Supp. II (1992)

Mapp v. Ohio 367 U. S. 643 (1961)

Miranda v. Arizona 384 U. S. 436 (1966)

Reynolds v. Sims 377 U. S. 533 (1964)

Sarno v. United States, 596 F.2d 404 (1979)

Nevada Reporter

A Special Session of the Supreme Court of the State of Nevada, 75 Nev. 533 (1959)

Adler v. State of Nevada, 95 Nev. 339 (1979)

Bryan v. State of Nevada, 78 Nev. 38 (1962)

Cline v. Clark Co. Liquor & Gaming, 91 Nev. 303 (1975)

Colton v. Leypoldt, 72 Nev. 83 (1956)

Golden v. Tomiyasu, 79 Nev. 503 (1963)

Helm v. State of Nevada, 66 Nev. 286 (1949)

In Memoriam:

> Milton B. Badt, 82 Nev. 465 (1966)
>
> Jon R. Collins, 105 Nev. 939 (1989)
>
> Edward A. Ducker, 63 Nev. 477 (1946)
>
> Edgar Eather, 85 Nev. 727 (1970)
>
> Albert (Bert) Scott Henderson, 85 Nev. 731 (1970)
>
> Charles M. Merrill, 117 Nev. 999 (2003)
>
> John Code Mowbray, 117 Nev. 1005 (2003)
>
> Frank H. Norcross, 69 Nev. 357 (1952)
>
> Errol James Livingston Taber, 63 Nev. 497 (1946)

Laxalt v. Cannon, 80 Nev. 397 (1964)

Nevada Tax Commission v. Hicks, 73 Nev. 115 (1957)

Roy v. State of Nevada, 87 Nev. 517 (1971)

State Bar of Nevada v. Claiborne, 104 Nev. 115 (1988)

Teeter v. State of Nevada, 65 Nev. 584 (1948)

Tomiyasu v. Golden, 81 Nev. 140 (1965)

Tucker v. State of Nevada, 82 Nev. 127 (1966)

Not Published

United States v. Harry Eugene Claiborne, CR-R-83-57 WEH.

Books

Bailey, F. Lee with John Greenya. For the Defense. New York: Atheneum Publishers, Inc., 1975.

Bakken, Gordon Morris. The Development of Law on the Rocky Mountain Frontier, 1850-1912. Westport, CT: Greenwood Press, 1983.

Bakken, Gordon Morris. The Mining Law of 1872: Past, Politics, and Prospects. Albuquerque: University of New Mexico Press, 2008.

Bakken, Gordon Morris. Practicing Law in Frontier California. Lincoln: University of Nebraska Press, 1991.

Denton, Sally and Roger Morris. The Money and the Power. New York: Alfred A. Knopf, 2001.

Dickens, Robert E., "William Raggio: Personality, Power, and Politics," in Richard O. Davies, ed., The Maverick Spirit: Building the New Nevada. Reno: University of Nevada Press, 1999.

Earley, Pete. Super Casino: Inside the "New" Las Vegas. New York: Bantam Books, 2000.

Edwards, Jerome. Pat McCarran: Political Boss of Nevada. Reno: University of Nevada Press, 1982.

Fox, Richard Wightman. Trials of Intimacy. Chicago: Chicago University Press, 1999.

Frederick, David. Rugged Justice: The Ninth Circuit Court of Appeals and the American West, 1891-1941. Berkeley: University of California Press, 1994.

Friedman, Lawrence M. Crime and Punishment in American History. New York: Basic Books, 1993.

Friedman, Lawrence M. A History of American Law. New York; Simon and Schuster, 1973.

Glass, Mary Ellen. Nevada's Turbulent '50s: Decade of Political and Economic Change. Reno: University of Nevada Press, 1981.

Greenspun, Hank with Alex Pelle. Where I Stand: The Record of a Reckless Man. New York: David McKay., Inc., 1966.

Griffin, Dennis N. Policing Las Vegas: A History Of Law Enforcement in Southern Nevada. Las Vegas: Huntington Press, 2005.

Hopkins, A. D. and K. J. Evans, eds., The First 100: Portraits of the Men and Women Who Shaped Las Vegas. Las Vegas: Huntington Press, 1999.

Hurst, James Willard. Law and Economic Growth. Cambridge: Harvard University Press, 1950.

Hurst, James Willard. Law and Markets in the United States. Madison: University of Wisconsin Press, 1982.

Hurst, James Willard. The Legitimacy of the Business Corporation in the Law of the United States, 1780-1970. Charlottesville: University of Virginia Press, 1970.

Langum, David J. and Howard P. Waltman. <u>From Maverick to Mainstream: Cumberland School of Law, 1847-1997.</u> Athens: University of Georgia Press, 1997.

Magnesen, Gary. <u>Strawmen: A Former Agent Recounts How the FBI Crushed the Mob in Las Vegas.</u> Minneapolis: Mill City Press, Inc., 2010.

Marschall, John P. <u>Jews in Nevada.</u> Reno: University of Nevada Press, 2008.

Moehring, Eugene P. <u>Resort City in the Southwest: Las Vegas, 1930-1970.</u> Reno and Las Vegas: University of Nevada Press, 1989.

Muncy, Raymond Lee. <u>Searcy, Arkansas: A Frontier Town Grows Up With America.</u> Searcy: Harding Press, 1976.

Pileggi, Nicholas. <u>Casino: Love and Honor in Las Vegas.</u> New York: Simon & Schuster, 1995.

Ralli, Paul. <u>Nevada Lawyer: A Story of Life and Love in Las Vegas.</u> Culver City: Murray and Gee, Inc., 1949.

Ralli, Paul. <u>Viva Las Vegas.</u> Hollywood: House-Warven, Publishers, 1953.

Reid, Ed. and Ovid Demaris. <u>The Green Felt Jungle.</u> New York: Trident Press, 1963.

Riley, Glenda. <u>Divorce: An American Tradition.</u> New York: Oxford University Press, 1991.

Rothman, Hal. <u>Devil's Bargains: Tourism in the Twentieth-Century American West.</u> Lawrence: University Press of Kansas, 1998.

Scrugham, James G., ed. Nevada: A Narrative of the Conquest of a Frontier Land. Chicago and New York: The American Historical Society, Inc., 1935.

Sheehan, Jack. The Players: The Men Who Made Las Vegas. Reno: University of Nevada Press, 1997.

Smith, John L. Of Rats and Men: Oscar Goodman's Life from Mob Mouthpiece to Mayor of Las Vegas. Las Vegas: Huntington Press, 2003.

Stevens, Joseph. Hoover Dam: An American Adventure. Norman: University of Oklahoma Press, 1988.

Vernetti, Michael. Senator Cannon of Nevada. Reno: University of Nevada Press, 2008.

Vernetti, Michael. Lies Within Lies: The Betrayal of Nevada Judge Harry Claiborne. Las Vegas: Stephens Press, 2010.

Ybarra, Michael. Washington Gone Crazy: Senator Pat McCarran and the Great American Communist Hunt. Hanover: Steerforth Press, 2004.

Articles

Alverson, Bruce. "The Limits of Power: Comstock Litigation, 1859-1864," Nevada Historical Society Quarterly, Vol. 43, No. 1 (2000).

Bushnell, Eleanore. "Judge Harry E. Claiborne and the Federal Impeachment Process," Nevada Historical Society Quarterly, XXXII, No. 4 (1989).

Matthews, Burnita Shelton "The Woman Juror," <u>Women Lawyers'</u> <u>Journal</u>, XV, No. 2 (April 1927).

Nickel, Robert V. "Dollars, Defense, and the Desert: Southern Nevada's Military Economy and World War II," <u>Nevada Historical Society</u> <u>Quarterly</u>, Vol. 47, No. 4 (Winter, 2004).

Published Oral Histories

Atkinson, Harry Hunt. <u>Tonopah and Reno Memories of a Nevada Attorney</u>, interview by Barbara C. Thornton. Reno: University of Nevada Oral History Program,1970.

Badt, Milton, interview by Mary Ellen Glass. Reno: University of Nevada Oral History Program, 1965.

Barrett, John, interview by Susan Imswiler. Reno: University of Nevada Oral History Program, 2005.

Bernard, Arthur. <u>Nevada Mine Inspector and Prison Warden</u>, interview by Victoria Ford. Reno: University of Nevada Oral History Program, 2003.

Bible, Alan. <u>Recollections of a Nevada Native Son: The Law, Politics,</u> <u>The Nevada Attorney General's Office, and the United States Senate</u>, interview by Mary Ellen Glass. Reno: University of Nevada oral History Program, 1982.

Biltz, Norman H. <u>Memoirs of "Duke of Nevada":Developments of Lake</u> <u>Tahoe, California and Nevada; Reminiscences of Nevada Political and</u> <u>Financial Life</u>, interview by Mary Ellen Glass. Reno: University of Nevada Oral History Program, 1969.

Binion, Lester Ben "Benny". <u>Some Recollections of a Texas and Las Vegas Gaming Operator</u>, interview by Mary Ellen Glass. Reno: University of Nevada Oral History Program, 1976.

Boyer, Florence M. <u>Las Vegas, Nevada: My Home for Sixty Years</u>, interview by Mary Ellen Glass. Reno: University of Nevada Oral History Program, 1967.

Cahill, Robbins E. <u>Recollections of Work in State Politics Government, Taxation, Gaming Control, Clark County Administration, and the Nevada Resort Association</u>, interview by Mary Ellen Glass. Reno: University of Nevada Oral History Program, 1977.

Denton, Ralph. <u>A Liberal Conscience: Ralph Denton, Nevadan</u>, interview by Michael S. Green. Reno: University of Nevada Oral History Program, 2001.

Farmer, Guy. <u>Gaming Regulator in Nevada</u>, interview by Dwayne Kling. Reno: University of Nevada Oral History Program, 2006

Miller, Thomas W. <u>Memoirs of Thomas Woodnutt Miller: A Public Spirited Citizen of Delaware and Nevada</u>, interview by Mary Ellen Glass. Reno: University of Nevada Oral History Program, 1966.

Olsen, Edward A. <u>My Careers as a Journalist in Oregon, Idaho, and Nevada; in Nevada Gaming Control; and the University of Nevada</u>, interview by Mary Ellen Glass. Reno: University of Nevada Oral History Program, 1972.

Peterson, Peter C. <u>Reminiscences of My Work in Nevada Labor, Politics, Post Office, and Gaming Control</u>, interview by Mary Ellen Glass. Reno: University of Nevada Oral History Program, 1970.

Russell, Charles H. <u>Reminiscences of a Nevada Congressman, Governor, and Legislator,</u> interview by Mary Ellen Glass. Reno: University of Nevada Oral History Program, 1967.

Sawyer, Grant. <u>Hang Tough! Grant Sawyer: An Activist in the Governor's Mansion</u>, interview by Gary Elliott and R. T. King. Reno: University of Nevada Oral History Program, 1993.

Shamberger, Hugh A. <u>Memoirs of a Nevada Engineer and Conservationist</u>, interview by Mary Ellen Glass. Reno: University of Nevada Oral History Program, 1967.

Young, Cliff. <u>Chief Justice, Nevada Supreme Court</u>, interview by Victoria Ford. Reno: University of Nevada Oral History Program, 2002.

Other

Clark County School District, "Louis Wiener, Jr.," http://ccsd.net/schools/wiener/index_ files/Page326.htm. (Accessed April 30, 2007).

Constitution of the State of Nevada.

Insider Viewpoint of Las Vegas. "The Military History of Nellis Air Force Base," www.insidervlv.com/nellisairbase.html. (Accessed April 30, 2007).

INDEX

Sinatra, Frank – 28, 68, 156, 157, 158, 159, 160, 161, 162, 163

Skelton, "Tex" – 59, 60

Soly, Fred – 97

Spilotro, Anthony "Tony the Ant" – 17, 18, 166, 220

Stacher, Joseph "Doc" – 140, 141, 142, 143, 154, 163, 166

Stearns, Dave – 68

Streeter, Jack – 141, 142, 143

Swanson, Gerald – 18, 20, 221, 223, 229, 230, 231

Teeter, Frederick – 71, 252

Thompson, "Tea Bags" – 174, 175, 176

Thompson, Bruce – 94, 104, 167, 212, 217, 249, 251

Thompson, George – 51, 203

Thunderbird Hotel – 28, 67, 97, 98, 141, 143, 144, 146, 147, 149, 150, 151, 152, 154, 161, 177, 181, 224

Tomiyasu, "Bill" – 200, 201, 251, 252

Truman, Harry – 103

Tucker, Horace – 170, 171, 172, 173, 253

Villa, Bill – 204

Wanderer, Emilie – 119

Watson, Harry – 141, 142, 143

Webster, William – 219, 223, 230

Wedge, Virgil – 77

Wells, Archie – 202, 203

Wiener Jr., Louis – 12, 34, 42, 45, 51, 54, 55, 56, 58, 64, 66, 67, 68, 69, 75, 76, 78, 106, 112, 115, 116, 117, 120, 134, 145, 147, 152, 153, 154, 172, 177, 178, 182, 186, 195, 196, 249, 259

Wiley, Roland – 92, 93, 118, 119, 134

Williams, Jimmy "Bad Boy" – 56, 57, 58

Williams, Robert "Sandman" – 194, 195, 196, 197, 198, 199

Wingfield, George – 43, 94, 149

Woodburn, William – 42, 43, 63, 148

Woofter, Billy – 55, 58

Wyman, Sid – 186

Yablonsky, Joseph – 18, 19, 20, 219, 220, 221, 222, 223, 224, 225, 226, 229, 230, 231

Young, Floyd "Tex" – 201, 202